Using the *Sams' Teach Yourself in 24 Hours* Series

Welcome to the *Sams' Teach Yourself in 24 Hours* series! You're probably thinking, "What, they want me to stay up all night and learn this stuff?" Well, no, not exactly. This series introduces a new way to teach you about exciting new products: 24 one-hour lessons, designed to keep your interest and keep you learning. Because the learning process is broken into small units, you will not be overwhelmed by the complexity of some of the new technologies that are emerging in today's market. Each hourly lesson has a number of special items, some old, some new, to help you along.

Minutes

The first 10 minutes of each hour lists the topics and skills that you will learn about by the time you finish the hour. You will know exactly what the hour will bring with no surprises.

Minutes

Twenty minutes into the lesson, you will have been introduced to many of the newest features of the software application. In the constantly evolving computer arena, knowing everything a program can do will aid you enormously now and in the future.

Minutes

Before 30 minutes have passed, you will have learned at least one useful task. Many of these tasks take advantage of the newest features of the application. These tasks use a hands-on approach, telling you exactly which menus and commands you need to use to accomplish the goal. This approach is found in each lesson of the *24 Hours* series.

Minutes

You will see after 40 minutes that many of the tools you have come to expect from the *Sams' Teach Yourself* series are found in the *24 Hours* series as well. Notes and Tips offer special tricks of the trade to make your work faster and more productive. Warnings help you avoid those nasty time-consuming errors.

Minutes

By the time you're 50 minutes in, you'll probably run across terms you haven't seen before. Never before has technology thrown so many new words and acronyms into the language, and the New Terms elements found in this series will carefully explain each and every one of them.

Minutes

At the end of the hour, you may still have questions that need answered. You know the kind—questions on skills or tasks that come up every day for you, but that weren't directly addressed during the lesson. That's where the Q&A section can help. By answering the most frequently asked questions about the topics discussed in the hour, Q&A not only answers your specific question, it provides a succinct review of all that you have learned in the hour.

How to Use This Book

This book offers 24 separate hours devoted to specific topics. You should read them in order in the time frame you prefer—whether it's one hour a day, a few hours a week, or the whole shebang in one long, caffeine-blasting, keyboard-tapping, type-A-personality day.

Special Highlighted Elements

TIME SAVER

When there's a shortcut or other way to do something more quickly and easily, you'll find it under this heading.

JUST A MINUTE

If something needs a little extra attention, it's described here while the 24-hour clock stops for a bit.

CAUTION

When there's something you need to watch out for, you'll be warned about it in these sections.

Quiz and Activities

Each hour ends with one or more suggested activities—called Workshops—for you to undertake related to the hour's subject matter, and a three-question quiz you can take.

Sams'
Teach Yourself
CorelDRAW 8
in 24 Hours

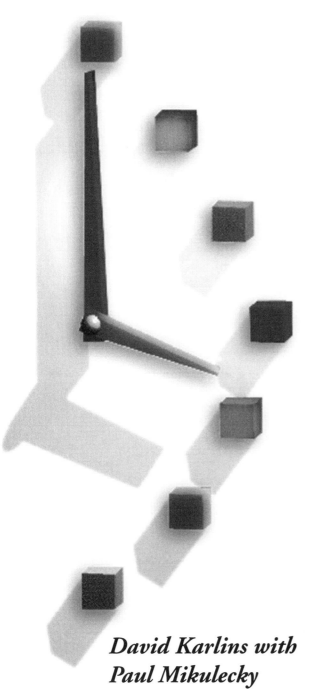

Sams'
Teach Yourself

CorelDRAW 8

in 24 Hours

David Karlins with
Paul Mikulecky

SAMS
PUBLISHING

201 West 103rd Street
Indianapolis, Indiana 46290

Sams' Teach Yourself CorelDRAW 8 in 24 Hours
©1998 SAMS Publishing

Library of Congress Catalog Number: 97-80787
ISBN: 0-672-31253-0

Printed in the United States of America 1 2 3 4 5 6 7 8 9 0

Warning and Disclaimer

Trademark Acknowledgments

Publisher   Jordan Gold
Executive Editor   Beth Millett
Managing Editor   Brice Gosnell

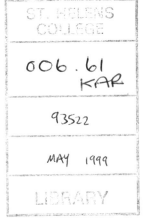

Acquisitions Editor
Todd Pfeffer

Development Editor
Jennifer Eberhardt

Project Editor
Kevin Laseau

Copy Editor
San Dee Phillips

Technical Editor
T. Michael Clark

Cover Designer
Gary Adair

Book Designer
Gary Adair

Production Team
Marcia Deboy
Cynthia Fields
Maureen West

Indexer
Rebecca Salerno

Overview

Contents

Dedication

This book is dedicated to the memory of my old friend, Mark Salzer.

Acknowledgments

In many ways, credit for this book goes to the CorelDRAW community at large. The lessons in this book draw on my experiences with students who I trained in CorelDRAW, as well as suggestions from teachers and readers of my earlier CorelDRAW books. I also got invaluable help from the folks at Corel, including CorelDRAW product manager Joe Donnelly, Michelle Murphy Croteau, Jessica Gould, and Cathy Hanan.

I'm tremendously indebted to my creative and artistic collaborator on this book, Paul Mikulecky. In my humble opinion, Paul is one of the most talented graphic professionals working with CorelDRAW today. I know that readers will find his illustrations illuminating and stimulating.

Todd Pfeffer gave me the opportunity to write this book for Sams. Jennifer Eberhardt provided encouragement, good vibes, and thoughtful editing. A vast crew at Macmillan Computer Publishing made it possible for you to get your hands on this book, including publisher Jordan Gold, brand manager Alan Bower, managing editor Brice Gosnell, executive editor Beth Millett, project editor Kevin Laseau, copy editor San Dee Phillips, technical editor T. Michael Clark, team coordinator Carol Ackerman, and manufacturing coordinator Paul Gilchrist.

Visit our web site at http://www.samspublishing.com.

About the Author

David Karlins is a web site consultant, teacher, and amateur unpublished movie critic. His previous books include *Sams' Teach Yourself FrontPage 98 in a Week* (Sams.net), *Wild Web Graphics with Microsoft Image Composer* (Que), and *Advanced Productivity with CorelDRAW 6* (ACT). Dave enjoys getting email from readers at dkarlins@aol.com.

Hour 1

Dive In! Having Fun with CorelDRAW 8

CorelDRAW 8 is an enormously powerful graphic design package. With that power comes a fairly complex design environment and an almost infinite combination of tools and effects. In this book, you'll meet and work with all these tools and effects.

Not only is CorelDRAW an encyclopedic graphics package, it comes with two additional major programs, as well as many utilities. This book includes hours (20–24) that introduce you to Corel PHOTO-PAINT 8 and CorelDREAM 3-D 8.

With all that said, you can jump into CorelDRAW 8 with a minimum of preparation and create complex illustrations. Don't be intimidated, because it's all easy and you're going to have fun learning. In the first lesson, you'll get acquainted with enough of CorelDRAW's environment to start creating drawings. And you will learn to use lines and line segments to create graphic images.

Welcome to CorelDRAW 8

Before you dive in and start creating your own graphic images, you need to understand a few basic concepts about what CorelDRAW does—both on your screen and behind the scenes. That's what this section is about.

Now you might be asking yourself, "Do I really need to know what's going on behind the scenes in CorelDRAW 8?" Not necessarily, but a basic understanding of the unique way CorelDRAW creates images will help you to design images and transform those images to hard copy or web page output.

CorelDRAW is different from bitmap graphic design packages. CorelDRAW is a vector-based program, which means that it creates and handles images as mathematically defined vectors. *Vectors* are objects with both magnitude (size) and direction (angles, curvature, and so on). The files that store CorelDRAW images consist of lists of lines, with information on their location, direction, length, color, and curves.

JUST A MINUTE

> The majority of graphic design programs are bitmap-based, which means they define images as enormous lists of dots, called *pixels*. Some of the more popular bitmap-based programs include Photoshop, PHOTO-PAINT, and Image Composer.

Defining images as a series of vectors is a more efficient way to work with them than defining images as a huge number of individual pixels. This is because even a simple object might have thousands of pixels, each individually defined, whereas the same image might be defined more rationally as a small number of curve segments. Therefore, CorelDRAW 8 vector image files are smaller than comparable bitmapped image files.

In addition to creating more compact files, CorelDRAW's vector-based images have other important advantages. You can easily resize a CorelDRAW image to a thumbnail sketch or icon or a billboard-sized graphic.

Another advantage to working with vector-based images is that smooth curves are easy to define; they will retain their smoothness and continuity even when enlarged (unlike bitmaps). Figure 1.1 shows a Bézier curve defined in CorelDRAW with text fitted to it. These curves are named after a French engineer who developed the math theory for them in the 1970s. That might be more than enough about the mathematics of curves for some of you, but readers with inquiring minds can find out more about Bézier and his curves by checking out the Bézier Curve web site at `http://www.moshplant.com/direct-or/bezier/index.html`.

The mathematically defined curves generated by CorelDRAW retain their smoothness and continuity even when enlarged. Bitmap images become grainy when enlarged.

1

Figure 1.1.

Text fitted to a Bézier Curve in CorelDRAW.

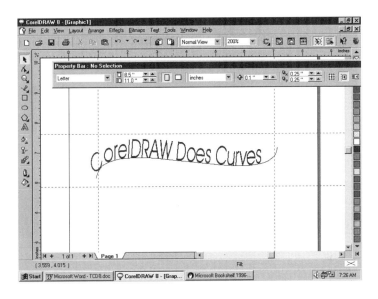

In some ways, however, graphic designers have to live in a bitmap world. This is especially true in the era of the World Wide Web, where much of the target for graphic design is images that appear in, or as, web pages. Popular web browsers cannot interpret images in CorelDRAW's native format. And the relatively grainy resolution of computer monitors (generally 72 dots per inch) tends to negate some of the advantages of creating vector-based images. The relatively small, low-resolution images seen on web sites tend to make curves jagged and grainy regardless of how smooth and high-resolution the original image.

CorelDRAW is a vital and irreplaceable graphic tool capable of creating any graphic image file you will ever need. For one thing, many images are still destined for hard copy, and CorelDRAW's vector-based images are great for printed output. And Corel's vector-based tools provide the most powerful array of features for designing images. CorelDRAW can then easily translate those images into bitmap formats. In fact, CorelDRAW has a powerful capacity to transform objects into both of the widely recognized web-compatible bitmap file formats: GIF and JPEG. So, in that sense, CorelDRAW is the best of both worlds with unparalleled design tools, plus the capability to convert images to bitmap formats as needed.

JUST A MINUTE

When you bought CorelDRAW 8, you also bought one of the most powerful bitmap editors available—Corel PHOTO-PAINT 8. Because more and more CorelDRAW users move back and forth between the vector and bitmap worlds, this book includes three lessons devoted exclusively to PHOTO-PAINT 8. See hourss 20–22 for detailed information about working with bitmap images.

Taking A Quick Look Around

The CorelDRAW environment can be a bit overwhelming, so I'll introduce you to it one piece at a time. In this first section, you'll become familiar with just enough of the CorelDRAW 8 window so you can start to create graphic images.

When you launch CorelDRAW 8 (using the Windows Start button or a shortcut button on your Windows desktop), the Welcome to CorelDRAW window appears, as shown in Figure 1.2.

Figure 1.2.

Starting with the Welcome window.

The Getting Started window provides six options for getting started with CorelDRAW 8, as explained in the following table.

Table 1.1. Starting options.

Icon	Name	What It Does
	New Graphic	Creates a new window in which you can design a graphic
	Open Last Edited	Opens the last graphic image file you worked on
	Open Graphic	Opens the Open Drawing dialog box, enabling you to select from any saved graphic image file
	Template	Enables you to choose from a list of predesigned page templates that you can use as a basis to begin a design

Icon	Name	What It Does
CorelTUTOR	CorelTUTOR	Enables you to select from several categories of online help and instructions
8	What's New?	Lists and explains new features in CorelDRAW version 8

To create a new graphic image from scratch, click the New Graphic icon in the Getting Started dialog box. When you do, you'll see an empty CorelDRAW 8 window, such as the one in Figure 1.3.

Figure 1.3.
A clean CorelDRAW 8 workspace, ready for you to begin drawing.

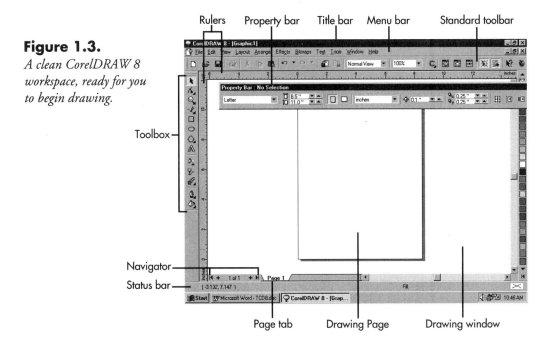

The Drawing window is the whole work area in the middle of your CorelDRAW 8 window, excluding the toolbars, toolbox (on the left), and status bar. This Drawing window is where you have fun creating graphics. The section of the Drawing window bounded by the shaded box is called the Drawing page. This is the part of your composition that prints when you send your file to the printer.

You can store graphic images you don't want to print (but do want to save) in the area of the Drawing window *outside* of the Drawing page.

The Property bar tells you information about any selected object in your Drawing window. In Figure 1.3, because the Drawing window does not have any objects yet, the Property bar indicates "No Selection." The Property bar also displays information about the Drawing page, such as it is Letter page sized, 8 $\frac{1}{2}$- by 11 inches. In Hour 2, "Creating Artistic Text," you'll explore the Property bar in more detail.

JUST A MINUTE

The Property bar can float over your Drawing window, or you can dock it just below the Standard toolbar (or on either side or the bottom of your Drawing window). When the Property bar sits below the Standard toolbar, you can drag on any portion of the Property bar *between* tools and move it onto the Drawing window. If the Property bar is floating over the Drawing window, you can drag the title bar of the Property bar to move it up below the Standard toolbar, as shown in Figure 1.4.

Figure 1.4.

Moving the Property bar off the Drawing window and up beneath the Standard toolbar.

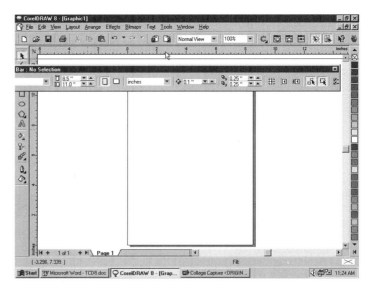

The toolbox is located to the left of the Drawing window. This is where you find all the tools CorelDRAW provides to create and edit graphic objects. When you move your cursor over any of the tools in the toolbox, a ToolTip will appear identifying that tool. In Figure 1.5, the ToolTip identifies the Text tool.

Figure 1.5.

When you move your cursor over a tool without clicking, CorelDRAW displays a helpful hint describing the tool.

You will explore other tools in the toolbox in this hour, and by the time you complete this book, you will have explored them all. Some tools have a small arrow in the lower-left corner. If you hold your cursor down on these tools, *flyouts* appear, and you can transform these tools into other tools. You'll learn about flyout tools as you need them in later chapters.

For your reference, Figure 1.6 shows all the tools in the toolbox. Don't bother to memorize them, please! You can bookmark this page or rely on ToolTips to find the tools you need.

Figure 1.6.

Toolbox tools.

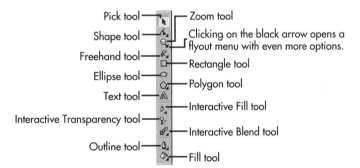

Drawing Lines

Now that you've become acquainted with the CorelDRAW 8 toolbox, it's time to experiment with the most basic tool of the bunch: the Freehand tool. You can use this tool to draw designs or straight lines. First, you'll learn to draw straight lines. You'll experiment with using more complex lines to draw shapes in Hour 8, "Drawing and Editing Freehand Curves," of this book.

1.1: Creating Straight Lines

To create a straight line, complete the following steps:

1. Select the Freehand tool from the toolbox.
2. Click anywhere in the Drawing page to begin your line.

JUST A MINUTE

Remember, the Drawing window is the whole work area in the middle of your CorelDRAW 8 window. The section of the Drawing window bounded by the shaded box is the Drawing page. Only objects on the Drawing page print, but because you are just experimenting now, feel free to draw anywhere in the Drawing window.

3. Click again, somewhere else in the Drawing window to end your line.

When you click a second time, CorelDRAW draws a straight line from the point where you first clicked to the point where you last clicked. That's it. You've just drawn your first line.

Figure 1.7 shows a line selected, with six handles appearing around the line. To deselect the line, click on the Pick tool and then click outside the handles.

Figure 1.7.

Selected lines display handles.

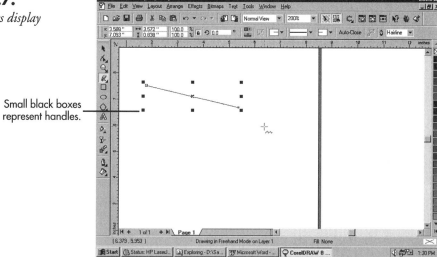

Small black boxes represent handles.

JUST A MINUTE

You can delete a line by clicking on the Pick tool, selecting the line, and pressing the Delete key on your keyboard.

To draw vertical or horizontal lines, hold down the Ctrl key on your keyboard after you click. Your cursor will not act like it is magnetized. It will "stick" to a straight line. Click a second time, and then release the Ctrl key to draw horizontal or vertical lines.

Use the Ctrl key technique to draw *crosshairs*, intersecting horizontal and vertical lines (see Figure 1.8).

Figure 1.8.

Horizontal plus vertical lines.

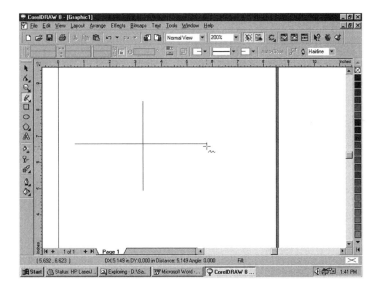

You can also draw lines at 15-degree-angle increments by holding down Ctrl. You'll notice, if you try to draw a slightly off parallel line, CorelDRAW will "resist" your attempts to angle the line. But if you click once, hold down Ctrl, and then draw a diagonal line at an angle of about 15 degrees, CorelDRAW will "snap" your endpoint at exactly 15 degrees. Other snap points with Ctrl pressed down are at 30 degrees, 45 degrees, 60 degrees, and so on.

You can draw many parallel, 15-degree lines, as shown in Figure 1.9.

You can also draw segmented lines, which are bent or zigzag lines. They are one object but consist of more than one line. You create segmented lines by clicking once to start the line, but then double-clicking at each node in the line. Each time you double-click, you create a new, attached line segment. You can end your zigzag line by clicking once.

1.2: Drawing Line Objects

Here's the routine for creating a drawing from lines:

1. Select the Freehand tool in the toolbox.
2. Click in the Drawing area.
3. Double-click on another spot in the Drawing area to create the first node for the object.
4. Double-click at the next node in the object.

5. Keep creating new nodes as needed.

 6. Click once (instead of double-clicking) to create your last node.

Figure 1.9.

Drawing parallel, angled lines.

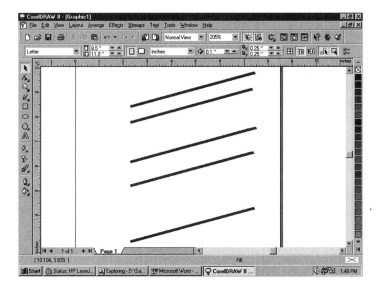

If the final node in your line is on top of another node (such as the point where you started to draw your line), your line will become a *closed* object.

Figure 1.10 shows a couple lines with several nodes. The line on the bottom is a closed object.

When you draw a line, or when you click with the Pick tool to select a line, the lines Property bar appears under the Standard toolbar. If your line is not closed, you'll see an Auto-Close button in the Property bar. Clicking on this button closes any selected line objects.

Selecting Objects

The drawings you made with the Freehand tool are *objects*, or they are made up of many objects. You learned that you can delete any selected object by pressing Delete.

Sometimes, it's hard to tell how many distinct objects make up a drawing, let alone select them. When your Drawing window gets crowded, it can be hard to select an object using the Pick tool.

Selecting Objects with the Tab Key

One easy way to select objects is to select the Pick tool, or any shape tool, and then press the Tab key on your keyboard. Try this quick exercise to select objects using the Tab key.

1

Figure 1.10.

Create closed objects by ending the last line segment on top of another node in the line.

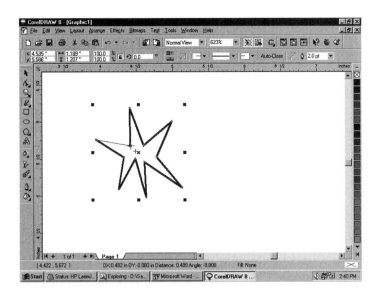

1.3: Selecting Objects with the Tab Key

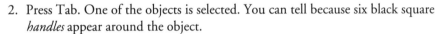

1. Create at least three objects using the Freehand tool.

2. Press Tab. One of the objects is selected. You can tell because six black square *handles* appear around the object.

3. Press Tab again. Another object appears selected.

4. Try holding down Shift while you press Tab (Shift+Tab). This selects the previously selected object.

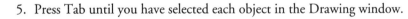

5. Press Tab until you have selected each object in the Drawing window.

Selecting Multiple Objects

With the Pick tool, you can select more than one object at a time. You can select multiple objects with the Pick tool in two easy ways: use the Shift+click technique or draw a marquee.

To use the Shift+click technique, hold down Shift while you click with the Pick tool to select more than one object. You can continue to select as many objects as you have in your Drawing window this way. You can even deselect objects that have been selected by Shift-clicking on them.

You can also select more than one object at a time by using the Pick tool to draw a *marquee* (rectangle) around more than one object (see Figure 1.11). Only those objects *completely* encompassed by the marquee that you draw with the Pick tool will be selected.

Sometimes, when you work with a complex drawing involving many objects, it becomes difficult to tell how many objects are selected. The status bar helps you by telling you exactly how many objects you selected. Figure 1.12 shows three objects selected.

Figure 1.11.

You can select many objects at once by drawing a marquee around them with the Pick tool.

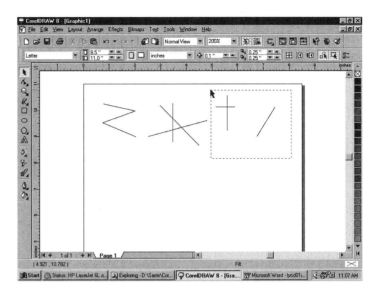

Figure 1.12.

The status bar tells you exactly how many objects you have selected.

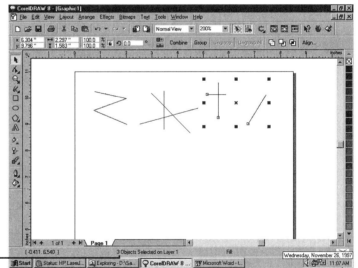

Three objects are selected

Now that you know how to select objects, try this magic trick: Select all the objects on your Drawing window, and delete them by pressing Delete. If you created a masterpiece, select Edit | Undo Delete from the menu bar. If not, you have a nice clear screen and you're ready for Hour 2, "Creating Artistic Text." Selecting objects is helpful when you want to delete them. It will be even more useful when you learn to edit objects in the following lessons.

You now have a good start with CorelDRAW. You created objects and learned your way around a bit. You're ready to start creating more complex shapes and objects.

1

Summary

CorelDRAW 8 is a powerful, yet easy-to-use, vector-based graphics program. Vector-drawing files save objects by calculating lines and curves. (You'll explore the difference between vector and bitmap-based graphic files in Hour 20, "PHOTO-PAINT Basics," where you learn to use CorelDRAW's bitmap cousin, Corel PHOTO-PAINT.)

Vectors are objects with both magnitude (size) and direction (angles, curvature, and so on). The files that store CorelDRAW images consist of lists of lines with information on their location, direction, length, color, and curves. The tools in the toolbox on the left of the Drawing area are used to create drawing objects. You can use the Freehand drawing tool to draw straight or angled lines, or even freehand shapes.

Lines consist of at least two nodes (one at the start, one at the end) and at least one segment. Lines can be drawn with multiple segments and nodes by double-clicking to add nodes and segments as you draw a line.

Workshop

Our resident artist, Paul Mikulecky, has provided a magazine cover illustration that you will learn to create in Hour 2, "Creating Artistic Text" and Hour 3, "Working with Shapes." To start designing the cover, create crosshairs out of a horizontal and vertical line.

1. Start CorelDRAW 8 and open a new document by clicking on the New button in the toolbar or by choosing File | New.

2. Create a set of crosshairs. First, draw a vertical line. Next, draw a horizontal line that crosses the vertical line at its center. (See "Drawing Lines" earlier in this hour for more information.)

3. Somewhere else on your page, practice your skills by drawing some zigzag lines. (Again, see the section "Drawing Lines" if you don't remember how to do this.)

4. Now, move to another place on your page and try re-creating the crude little lizard shown in Figure 1.11. This will help you get up to speed at drawing line objects. Remember to double-click at each nodal point and click once when you are done.

5. Save your file by choosing File | Save. You won't need this file for the workshops in the following lessons, but when you reach the end of this book, you might want to go back and see how your drawings have improved.

After that, practice your skills by drawing zigzag lines. Try drawing a closed shape with lines (connected at a single start and finish node).

Take a stab at drawing a design made up of several lines segments, such as the crude little lizard in Figure 1.13.

Figure 1.13.

The lizard is made mostly from one, many-segmented line.

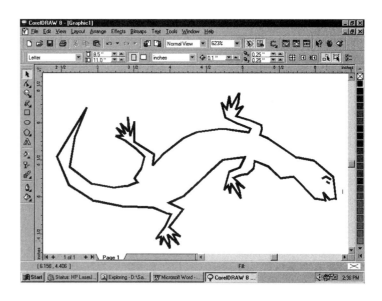

Quiz

1. How do you delete a line?
2. How do you create a 45-degree angle line?
3. How can you tell if an object is closed?
4. How do you create a closed object composed of straight lines?

Quiz Answers

1. You can delete a line by selecting it with the Pick tool and then pressing Delete.
2. By holding down Ctrl after you click to establish the first node in a line, you can constrict the next node to an angle divisible by 15 degrees, including a 45-degree angle.
3. Sometimes, it is difficult to see if an object is closed, or *almost* closed. One way to tell is if you have drawn more than one line segment but not created a closed object, you will see the Auto-Close button in the Line Property bar.
4. You can close an object using the Auto-Close button or by placing the final node of a multiline object on top of an existing node.

1

Hour **2**

Creating Artistic Text

No program provides more control over the look and shape of text than CorelDRAW. You can edit, format, resize, or reshape text in CorelDRAW 8.

CorelDRAW has two kinds of text: paragraph text and artistic text. Paragraph text is better for long blocks of text that need to be edited. Artistic text gives you more freedom to assign artistic effects to letters. Later in this book, you'll learn to stretch text, twist text, fit it to a curve, and do all kinds of other crazy things. All these effects can be applied to artistic text, but most cannot be applied to paragraph text.

In this hour, you explore artistic text. You will create, edit, and format artistic text, and you will learn to stretch, reshape, and resize text objects. And you'll experiment with symbols, images that are available from special sets of fonts.

Working with Artistic Text

When you create artistic text, you create a graphic image that can be edited like any other graphic in CorelDRAW 8. You can easily resize or reshape artistic text; you can easily edit the graphical aspects; and you can easily edit the text content and format.

JUST A MINUTE

CorelDRAW 8 also enables you to work with text as paragraph text. When you lay out an article or a substantial amount of text, you'll find it easier to edit that text if you work with it as paragraph text. See Hour 15, "Designing with Paragraph Text," for more information.

Use artistic text for smaller blocks of text. Icons, web site banners, newsletter mastheads, and other text applications with few characters are ideal for artistic text. You can resize artistic text more easily than paragraph text.

Creating Artistic Text

When you click on the Text tool in the toolbox (see Figure 2.5), you have two options. You can simply click and start typing, or you can drag to draw a text frame and then start typing. For now, all you have to do is click and type. As you do, the Property bar becomes the Editing Text Property bar. Many of the tools in the Editing Text Property bar are more useful for paragraph text than for artistic text, but some are used with artistic text as well.

After you finish typing text, click on the Pick tool, the arrow at the top of the toolbox. When you click on the Pick tool, your new text will be surrounded with eight small, square black handles. These handles activate whenever you select any object with the Pick tool and change the size and shape of a selected object.

JUST A MINUTE

Handles indicate that an object such as artistic text is selected. When a text object is selected, you can change attributes assigned to that object, such as size, color, shape, or location.

The Text Property Bar

One way to change attributes for a selected object is using the Property bar. When you select Artistic Text, the Text Property bar becomes active, as shown in Figure 2.1.

The following table explains the Text Property bar tools and lists.

2

Figure 2.1.

The Text Property bar is active.

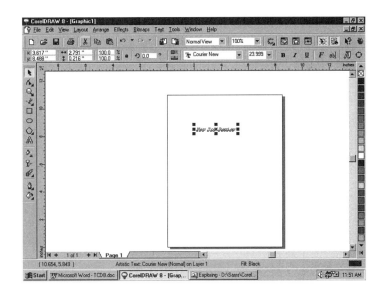

Table 2.1. Text Property bar tools.

Tool	Name	What It Does
x: 3.617 " y: 8.488 "	Position	Identifies (or changes) the position of the object relative to the lower-left corner of the Drawing page, based on the center of the selected object. X is the horizontal location; Y is the vertical location.
2.791 " 0.216 "	Size	Identifies or changes the exact size of the selected object. X represents the width of the object; Y represents the height of the object.
100.0 % 100.0 %	Scale Factor	Enables you to resize the height (Y) or width (X) of the selected object proportional to the current size. For example, changing the X setting to 200 doubles the size of the selected text object.

continues

Table 2.1. continued

Tool	Name	What It Does
🔒	Nonproportional Sizing	When you select this button, size changes made to the x-axis Scale Factor spin box do not affect the y-axis, and vice versa.
↻ 0.0 °	Rotation Angle	Identifies and lets you change the angle to which the text object rotates. Ninety degrees will rotate the text 90 degrees counterclockwise.
⊞	Mirror Buttons	The top Mirror button flips the selected text horizontally; the bottom Mirror button flips the selected text vertically.
Tr Courier New ▾	Font List	This drop-down menu lets you select fonts to apply to the selected text.
23.999 ▾	Font Size List	Assigns font sizes to selected text.
B	Bold	Assigns (or turns off) boldface for the selected text.
I	Italic	Assigns (or turns off) italic style for selected text.
U	Underline	Underlines the text in a selected text object.
F	Format Text	Opens the Format Text dialog box.
ab|	Edit Text	Opens the Edit Text dialog box.

2

Tool	Name	What It Does
	Convert Text	Converts selected text objects to Paragraph Text (or if they are already Paragraph Text, converts them back to Artistic Text).
	Convert to Curves	When you convert text to curves, you can no longer edit it. However, you can edit the individual graphic objects separately.

The Text Property bar enables you to apply all kinds of formatting to selected text objects. If you want to format individual characters (or words) within a text object, use the Format Text dialog box. Let's explore how to do this.

Formatting Text

You can change text font for an entire selected text object, or you can format only certain characters in an artistic text object.

2.1: Formatting Text

1. Select a text object.
2. Click on the Text tool; an insertion point cursor appears. You can drag to select part or all your text to apply new formatting.
3. After you select the text to which you want to apply formatting, pull down the Font List and select a new font. In Figure 2.2, I'm assigning the Desdemona font to my selected text.

You can assign font size in the same way, by choosing a font size from the Font Size List drop-down menu. In Figure 2.3, I'm assigning a font size of 100 points to my selected text.

You can also resize and reshape selected text objects by dragging the handles. When you drag a handle in toward the center of the object, you make it smaller. When you drag out, away from the center, you make the object larger. This technique works with all selected objects in CorelDRAW and works with artistic text as well.

If you drag a corner handle, as in Figure 2.4, you maintain the proportion between height and width as you resize your object.

Figure 2.2.

Assigning the Desdemona font.

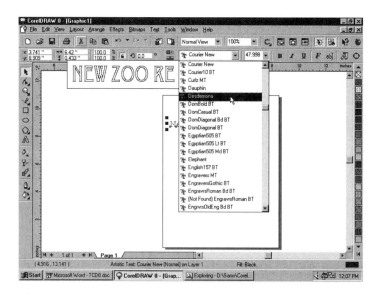

Figure 2.3.

Assigning a font size of 100 points.

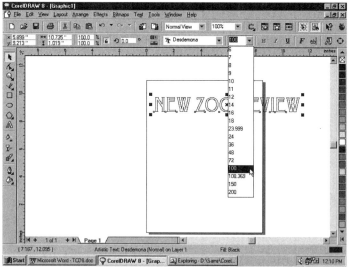

If you drag on a side or top handle, you will change not only the size but also the shape (or proportions) of the text, as shown in Figure 2.5.

You can add (or remove) boldface, italics, or underlining to text using the Bold, Underline, and Italic buttons in the Text Property bar. These attributes are not available for all fonts because some fonts are designed to be specifically boldface or to have a light face.

2

Figure 2.4.

Resizing text using handles, keeping proportions unchanged.

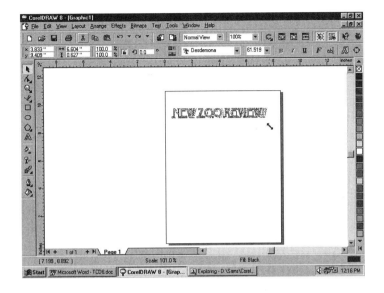

Figure 2.5.

Changing text shape and size. Notice how the letters are getting wider?

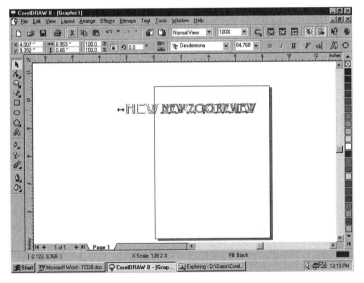

The Format Text dialog box offers more detailed text formatting features. With your text object selected, click on the Format Text tool in the Property bar or choose Text I Format Text from the menu bar. The Format Text dialog box has three tabs. The Font tab allows you to assign fonts and font sizes, as well as other font attributes such as Strikethrough, Overscore, Uppercase (including small caps), and superscript or subscript (available in the Position drop-down list). In Figure 2.6, I'm assigning small caps and a thin line overscore to my selected text.

Figure 2.6.

Adding text formatting in the Format Text dialog box.

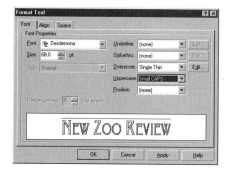

There are two other tabs in the Format Text dialog box. The Align tab provides the same options as the alignment buttons in the dialog box toolbar: None, Left, Center, Right, Full Justify (both margins, if you have enough text to look good stretched margin to margin), and Forced Justify. The Space tab enables you to define spacing between characters (letters), words, and lines in your text. You will often use these tabs to tweak paragraph text where you have many lines of text.

As you experiment with text formatting, you will see the font previewed in the small window at the bottom of the dialog box. When you are satisfied with the appearance of your text, click on the OK button.

Editing and Formatting Text Characters

You can edit text by clicking on the Text tool and then clicking in a text object. The vertical bar cursor represents the insertion point. You can press Delete or Backspace to delete text, or you can type new text at the insertion point. In Figure 2.7, I placed my insertion point before the word "Zoo," pressed Backspace three times to delete the word "New," and am typing the word "The."

For more heavy-duty text editing, you'll find the Edit Text dialog box more helpful. Open this dialog box for a selected text object by clicking on the Edit Text button in the Property bar, or by selecting Text | Edit Text from the CorelDRAW 8 menu bar. Us old-timers still use Ctrl+Shift+T to open this dialog box.

The Edit Text dialog box is a miniword processor in a window. You can insert or delete text here. And like many of the latest word processors, the Edit Text dialog box will underline words not found in the dictionary with a wavy red line, as shown in Figure 2.8.

Just as with the fanciest word processors, you right-click on a potentially misspelled word to see a list of possible correct spellings. In Figure 2.9, I'm getting some spelling help replacing "NEWW" with "NEW."

Formatting Text Characters

So far, you have learned to apply formatting (including size) to entire text objects. You can also apply formatting to selected characters within a selected text object. An easy place to make these changes is the Edit Text dialog box.

2

Figure 2.7.

Adding text formatting in the Format Text dialog box.

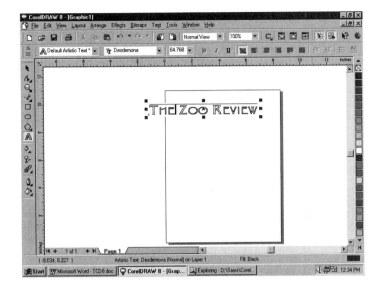

Figure 2.8.

Editing in the Edit Text dialog box.

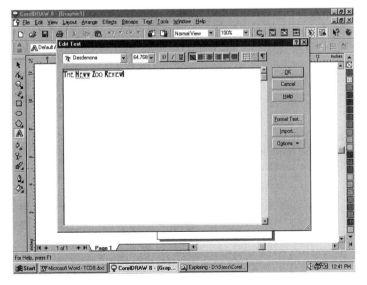

To apply formatting to selected characters within a text object, select those characters in the Edit Text dialog box, and then apply formatting. In Figure 2.10, I am changing the font size for selected characters only.

JUST A MINUTE

The Edit Text dialog box is not fully WYSIWYG (what you see is what you get). You have to click OK and view the results in the CorelDRAW window to see the exact effect of font attributes assigned to selected text.

Figure 2.9.
*Fixing spelling in the
Edit Text dialog box.*

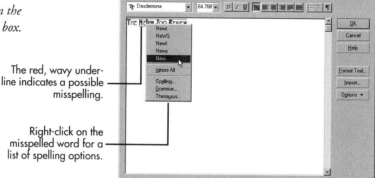

The red, wavy under-
line indicates a possible
misspelling.

Right-click on the
misspelled word for a
list of spelling options.

Figure 2.10.
*Selected text characters
can be formatted in the
Edit Text dialog box—
my favorite shortcut to
get there is Ctrl+Shift+T.*

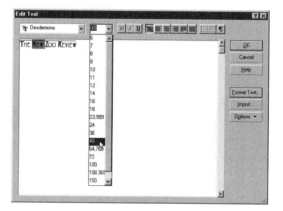

If you want more power to assign detailed formatting to selected text, click on the Format
Text button in the Edit Text dialog box. Font attributes assigned in this way will apply only
to the selected text. When you have edited and assigned formatting to any text, click on OK
in the Edit Text dialog box. The results will be visible in the CorelDRAW window.

Rotating, Sizing, and Locating Text

Earlier in this lesson, you learned to size text by dragging object handles. That works. You
can also move a selected object by dragging the X that appears in the middle of a selected
object. In Figure 2.11, I'm dragging the selected text up the page. The cross-shaped cursor
indicates the new location for the object.

To rotate text, choose the Pick tool (the one at the top of the Toolbox) and click on an object
twice. As you do, the handles change from small black squares to curved arrows, as shown
in Figure 2.12.

Drag the rotation handles in a clockwise or counterclockwise direction to rotate the selected
object.

2

Figure 2.11.
Moving text.

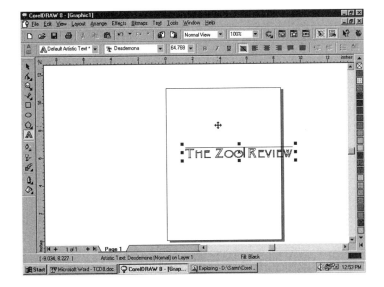

Figure 2.12.
Are you ready to rotate?

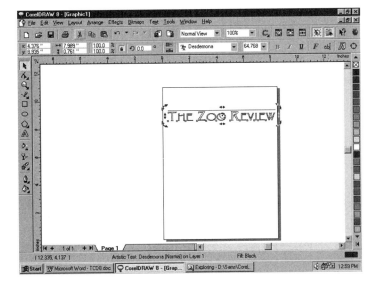

You can also precisely define the size, location, and rotation using the Property bar. To flip text to the left, enter 90 in the Rotation Angle box in the Property bar. The results are illustrated in Figure 2.13.

Figure 2.13.
Rotated 90 degrees.

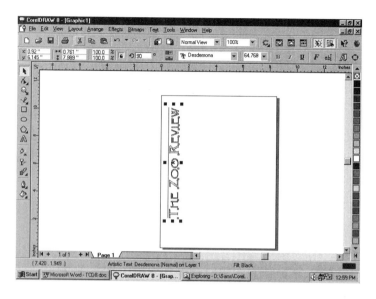

JUST A MINUTE

You can edit or reformat rotated text. It can get a little tricky to edit rotated text in the Drawing window because the text editing cursor does not rotate with the text. You might find it easier to edit rotated text in the Format Text or Edit Text dialog boxes.

To precisely locate or size a text object, you can enter coordinates or dimensions in the Position or Size boxes in the Property bar. In Figure 2.14, I have assigned a size of exactly 1" by 9" and located the text object 1" from the left side of the page and 5.5" from the bottom. The location coordinates are defined from the center of the object.

TIME SAVER

For quick, rough sizing and locating, use your mouse. For extremely precise sizing and location, use the Property bar.

Managing Fonts with the Font Navigator

CorelDRAW 8 comes with an vast assortment of available fonts. These fonts are on the CorelDRAW CD-ROM and can be added to your system using a utility provided by Corel called the Font Manager.

To add a font from the CorelDRAW 8 CD-ROM to your system, run the Bitstream Font Navigator program. You can find this program in the Productivity Tools group under the CorelDRAW 8 group.

2

Figure 2.14.

Precisely sized, rotated, and located text.

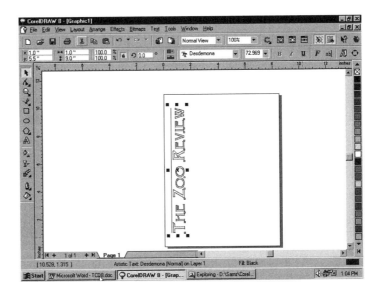

Place the CorelDRAW 8 CD-ROM that contains fonts in your CD-ROM drive, and in the Font Navigator window, navigate to the drive with your CD-ROM. Select the Fonts folder and then the Ttf (True Type fonts) folder. The Ttf folder has a series of folders named with the letters that begin the fonts they contain. So, for instance, if you want the Eras Bk BT font, open the "E" folder (see Figure 2.15).

Figure 2.15.

Finding fonts on the CorelDRAW 8 CD-ROM.

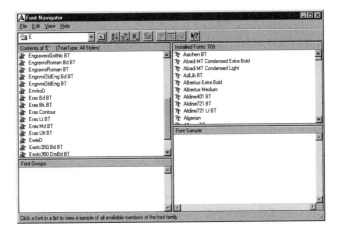

The Font Manager has an Installed Fonts window that shows how many fonts you currently have installed on your system. You can add fonts by dragging them from the Contents window (on the left) to the Installed Fonts window on the right.

JUST A MINUTE

To preview what a font looks like, simply open the Font Navigator dialog box and in the Contents window, click on the name of the font you want to preview. The preview appears in the Font Sample window.

In Figure 2.16, I'm adding the Eras Bk BT font to my system.

Figure 2.16.
Adding fonts.

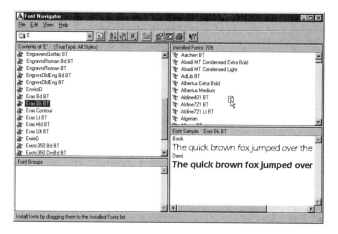

After you install additional fonts to your system, you can close the Font Navigator window.

CAUTION

If you add over 400 fonts to your system, the Font Navigator will warn you that this can affect system performance. I have over 400 fonts on my system, and I haven't noticed any ill effects. But if you find that your system runs more slowly after you add fonts, you can remove fonts in the Font Navigator by dragging them from the Installed Fonts area back into the Contents area (on the left side of the window).

Inserting Symbols

Fonts aren't just good for words. Many fonts come with a nice selection of symbols that you can use as quick and easy clip art.

2.2: Inserting Symbols As Clip Art

TO DO

1. To choose from selections of symbols, click on the Symbol Dockers tool in the Standard toolbar. This is the one that looks like a cute little star on the right side of the Standard toolbar.

2

2. Pull down the list of fonts in the Symbols window and select one. You'll have to experiment to find one with the symbol you want.

3. When you find the symbol you want, drag the symbol into the Drawing page (see Figure 2.17).

Figure 2.17.

Dragging a symbol onto the Drawing page.

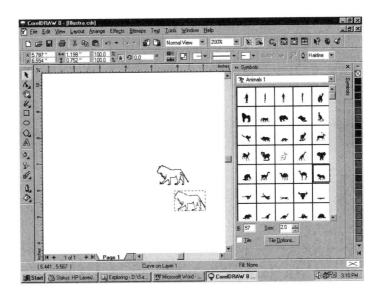

4. When you finish dragging symbols onto the Drawing page, you can close the Symbols docking window by clicking on the Close button.

CAUTION

The Close buttons in docking windows are a bit different in appearance than conventional windows Close buttons. Why? Just to be unique! But they are the small X in the upper right-hand corner of the window.

As you have seen so far, artistic text can be sized, formatted, edited, and rotated. You can add fonts from CorelDRAW's large collection and use text characters as symbols.

Next, you will see what can be done when artistic text is combined with shapes.

Summary

Artistic text is easy to enter and can be edited at any time. Shapes can be created using the Rectangle, Ellipse, and Polygon tools. Any object can have many of its attributes edited using the associated Property bar. Property bars can be used to edit the size, location, rotation, and other features of an object.

Workshop

With this workshop, you'll begin re-creating the magazine cover that Paul Mikulecky designed for us. To begin, open a new document and enter some text such as that in Figure 2.18. Locate the text at the bottom of the magazine cover.

Figure 2.18.

Enter, size, and locate text.

1. Enter a short magazine name such as "Zoo Review" and rotate that text so that it is horizontal, like the text you see in Figure 2.19. Refer to "Rotating, Sizing, and Locating Text" earlier in this chapter for more information.

2. Review your line drawing skills by adding a crosshair to the bottom of the cover, as shown in Figure 2.20.

3. Click on the Symbols Docker button in the toolbar to open the Symbols Docker window. Choose the Animals1 set of fonts. Drag the lion symbol onto the Drawing page under the crosshairs (see Figure 2.21).

4. Align the lion and the crosshairs, as you see in Figure 2.21.

5. Save your file.

Be sure to save your file when you finish. You'll need it again in Hour 3, "Working with Shapes."

2

Figure 2.19
Rotate text.

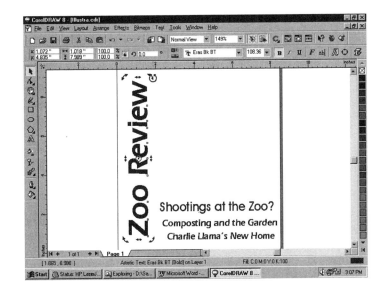

Figure 2.20.
Rotate text.

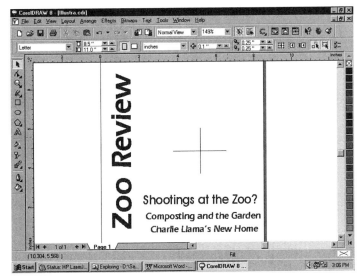

Quiz

1. How do you edit artistic text?
2. How do you rotate text?
3. Name a font set that has symbols of animals.
4. What font attributes can you assign from the Font Property bar?
5. How do you format individual text characters?

Figure 2.21.
Add a symbol.

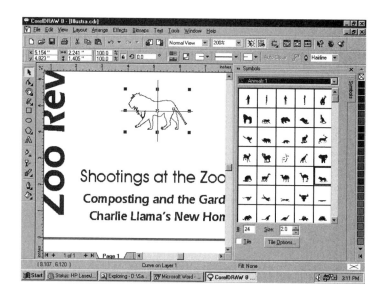

Quiz Answers

1. One easy way to edit artistic text is to select Text|Edit Text to open the Edit Text dialog box.

2. To rotate text, click twice to display rotation angle handles, and drag on one of them to rotate the text object.

3. The Animals1 font set that comes on the CorelDRAW 8 CD-ROM has symbols for many animals.

4. You can assign font type and size from the Property bar.

5. You can format specific characters in artistic text in the Edit Text dialog box (select the text with the Pick tool and press Ctrl+Shift+T). When you view your text in the Edit Text dialog box, you can drag to select characters and assign font attributes from the Edit Text dialog box toolbar. You can also format individual characters in the Drawing area. To do that, use the Text tool to select a text object, select text with the insertion point cursor, and assign font attributes from the Property bar.

2

Hour 3

Working with Shapes

CorelDRAW 8 has three different shapes tools that you use to create ellipses, rectangles, polygons, and stars. Shapes have their own rules in CorelDRAW 8. In this hour, you'll learn to create and edit shapes.

By combining artistic text with these shapes, you can create impressive designs. In Figure 3.1, our resident graphic designer Paul Mikulecky combined shapes with graphic text to complete the cover of *Zoo Review* magazine. You'll be seeing more of Paul's work in the course of this book. But here he's finishing up the magazine cover you started working on in Hour 1. Paul's cover uses techniques you've already learned (lines and artistic text) or that you are about to learn.

Although CorelDRAW 8 has a gazillion effects and combinations of effects, most graphic designs boil down to combinations of shapes and text. The sizing, locating, and rotation techniques you learned to apply to artistic text can be applied to shapes as well. So you've already learned much of what you need to know to work with shapes! All that remains is to explore the specific shape tools and then to experiment with line and fill coloring. In this hour, you learn to create and edit shapes such as the ones shown in Figures 3.2 and 3.3.

Figure 3.1.

Our goal—create a cover something similiar to Paul's.

Figure 3.2.

You will add simple shapes such as the rectangles behind the symbols.

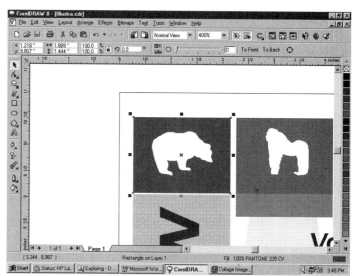

Working with Rectangles

You can use the Rectangle, Ellipse, and Polygon tools in the toolbox (on the left side of the Drawing area) to quickly and easily create shapes.

To draw a rectangle, select the Rectangle tool, and then simply click and draw anywhere in the Drawing area. In Figure 3.4, I'm drawing a large rectangle on the left side of the Drawing page.

To draw a square, select the Rectangle tool in the toolbox, but then hold down Ctrl as you drag.

Figure 3.3.

And you'll add complex shapes such as the 12-pointed star.

Figure 3.4.

Drawing a rectangle.

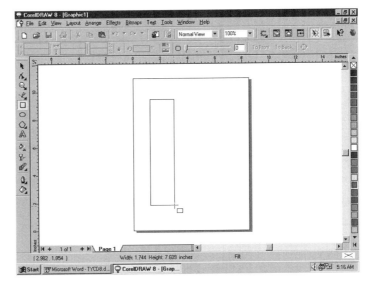

Creating Ellipses and Circles

To create an ellipse (also known as an oval), choose the Ellipse tool in the toolbox and drag. You can continue to refine the size and shape of your oval until you release the mouse button.

To draw a prefect circle, hold down Ctrl while you draw the ellipse. Figure 3.5 shows several rectangles and ellipses on the Drawing Page.

Figure 3.5.

Rectangles and squares, ellipses and circles.

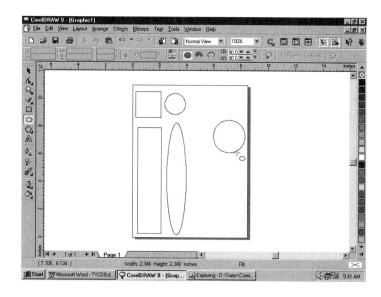

Drawing Polygons

The default shape for the Polygon tool is a pentagon: a five-sided object. To draw a pentagon, just click on the Polygon tool and drag to create the pentagon. In Figure 3.6, I'm drawing a pentagon in the Drawing page.

Figure 3.6.

This is probably how someone designed the layout of the Pentagon.

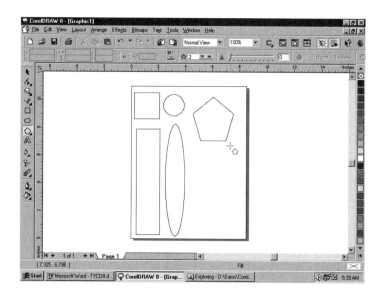

3

You can change the number of sides that you draw with the Polygon tool. If you define the polygon as a three-sided object, you'll draw triangles with it. The maximum number of sides a polygon can have assigned to it is 500, which is pretty much indistinguishable from an ellipse. To change the number of sides assigned to the Polygon tool, right-click on the Polygon tool in the toolbox, and choose Properties from the shortcut menu that appears. Then, in the Polygon tool area of the Options dialog box, enter a number of sides in the Number of Points/Sides spin box. In Figure 3.7, I'm defining an octagon by entering 8 in the spin box.

Figure 3.7.

Octagons are useful for drawing stop signs and octopuses.

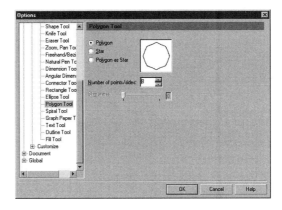

You can also use the Polygon tool to draw stars, or polygons as stars. The Polygon as Star feature is great for drawing five- or six-pointed stars, but you can also create fun little objects. What do you suppose a 13-pointed polygon-as-a-star looks like?

3.1: Creating Stars

1. Right-click on the Polygon tool in the toolbox and choose Properties from the shortcut menu.

2. Choose the Polygon as Star radio button in the Polygon tool area of the Options dialog box.

3. Enter 13 in the Number of Points/Sides spin box.

4. Experiment with the Sharpness slider. More sharpness means sharper points in stars. In Figure 3.8, I dragged the sharpness slider up to 85 to create a spindly, pointy-looking 13-point star.

5. When you are through defining your polygon-as-a-star, select OK in the Options dialog box. Even though the Polygon tool still looks like a pentagon, don't be fooled. When you drag on the Drawing area, you will create the polygon or star you defined in the Options box.

In Figure 3.9, I'm drawing a 13-point polygon-as-a-star.

Figure 3.8.

Does anyone know the name of a 13-point star?

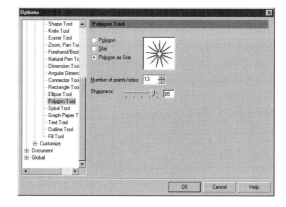

Figure 3.9.

Drawing 13-point polygons as stars.

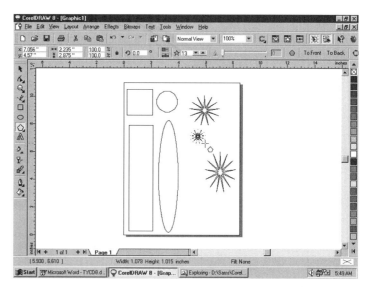

Drawing Spirals

You may have noticed that the Polygon tool has a small arrow in the lower-right corner of the tool. That little arrow indicates that this tool is a flyout, meaning it can transform into other tools. The Polygon tool can be transformed into a tool that draws spirals or a tool that draws graph grids.

To activate the flyout, click on the Polygon tool and hold down the mouse key. As you do this, the flyout pops out revealing the other tools.

Both the Spiral and the Graph tools can be adjusted by right-clicking on them and making changes in the Options dialog box.

3

You can define the number of spirals you want for your object in the Number of Revolutions spin box. You can also choose between symmetrical and logarithmic spirals by clicking on either of the two radio buttons. If you choose Logarithmic, each spiral increases its extension exponentially, as opposed to the smooth, even spirals created by symmetrical spirals. And if you select the Logarithmic radio button, you can use the Expansion slider to define just how far out you want each spiral to extend. The default setting of 100 is the maximum expansion for each spiral. A minimum setting of 1 sets you back to a symmetrical spiral.

In Figure 3.10, I'm defining a Logarithmic spiral with 5 revolutions and a 50 setting on the Expansion slider.

Figure 3.10.

Defining a logarithmic spiral.

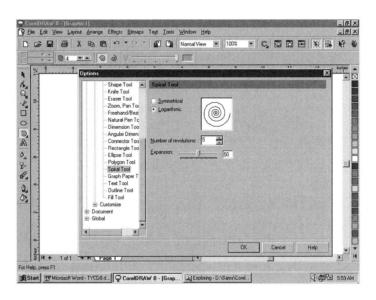

When you use the Spiral tool, you can hold down Ctrl to force the spiral to conform to a circular shape, as shown in Figure 3.11. Circular spirals have evenly spaced spirals, whereas logarithmic spirals are more compressed inside and more expanded outside.

Drawing Graph Paper Grids

To draw graphic grids, select the Graph Paper tool from the flyout. Graph Paper options can be defined by right-clicking on the Graph Paper tool and choosing Properties from the shortcut menu. The Options dialog box lets you define how many cells high and how many cells wide you want to draw with the Graph Paper tool. Figure 3.12 defines a 4 row by 4 column Graph tool.

In Figure 3.13, I'm drawing some little graphs in the Drawing Page. If you want to make your graph square, you can hold down Ctrl as you define the graph.

Figure 3.11.

Drawing a circular spiral.

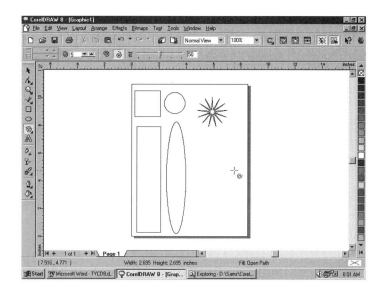

Figure 3.12.

Defining the Graph Paper tool.

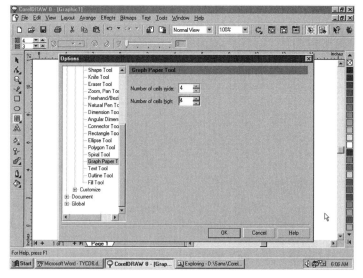

Figure 3.13.
Graphing.

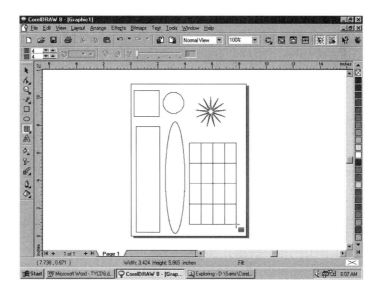

Editing Shapes

When you select a shape with the Pick tool, a corresponding Property bar appears for the shape. These Property bars vary somewhat depending on which shape you select, but most of the Property bar options are the same for all shapes.

First, let's explore the common features that are in Property bars for all shapes. Then we'll look at a few unique features that apply to either rectangles, ellipses, or polygons. Figure 3.14 shows the Property bar for a selected rectangle.

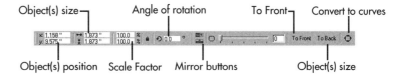

Figure 3.14.
Common features of Shapes Property bars.

Object(s) size — Angle of rotation — To Front — Convert to curves

Object(s) position   Scale Factor   Mirror buttons   Object(s) size

The Object(s) position boxes enable you to define the exact location of the selected shape. You explored this same feature earlier this hour when you worked with artistic text. You can enter x values to define the distance from the left edge of the page, or y values to define the distance from the bottom of the page. Values correspond to the distances to the center of the selected object.

JUST A MINUTE

> The reason the ToolTip reads Object(s) instead of object is that Property bar features can be applied to more than one object at a time if the objects are grouped. You can explore grouping in Hour 2, "Creating Artistic Text," of this book.

Sizing Shapes

You can size a selected shape exactly by entering values in the x and y fields in the Object Size area of the Property bar. This, too, is similar to a feature you explored working with artistic text.

You can resize a selected shape by percent by entering a value in the x or y boxes in the Scale Factor area of the Property bar. If the Nonproportional Spacing button is selected (pressed "in" on the Property bar), then changes that you make to one dimension will only reflect that dimension. If the Nonproportional Spacing button *is not* selected, then changes to one dimension will be reflected in the other dimension as well.

That can be a little confusing. Why didn't Corel just call it a Proportional Spacing button so that we didn't have to try to sort out a bunch of double-negatives? Let's look at a couple examples to make this more clear. In Figure 3.15, I have *not* clicked on the Nonproportional Spacing button in the Property bar. I am entering 50% in the x area.

When I press Enter, *both the x and y* sizing will shrink to 50% of the original. In other words, the change to the size of the selected object is proportional. The shape stays the same. My square becomes a smaller square.

If I turn on (clicked on) Nonproportional Spacing, then only the x value (width) of my selected object changes, and I end up with a rectangle. Let's walk through an example using nonproportional spacing.

3.2: Resizing Shapes Without Maintaining Proportions

TO DO

1. Select the object to be resized.
2. Make sure Nonproportional Spacing is selected (the button is "pressed in").
3. Change the x scale to 200 while leaving the y scale unchanged.

3 ▲ The object is twice as wide as it was, but the height is still the same.

Figure 3.15.

Nonproportional Spacing is not turned on.

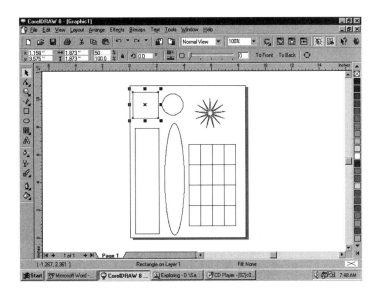

Rotating Objects

You can rotate all selected shapes using the Angle of Rotation area of the Property bar. Just enter an angle of rotation and press Enter. If you want to flip the selected shape horizontally, click on the top Mirror button. If you want to flip your shape vertically, flip on the bottom Mirror button.

Layering Objects

The To Front and To Back buttons become essential as soon as you start to add fills to shapes and move objects on top of each other. You'll explore fills in the next section of this lesson. For now, just note the To Front and To Back buttons. The Convert to Curves button transforms a shape into a curved line. You'll learn to work with curves in Hour 5, "Setting Up Page Layout," of this book.

Transforming Shapes

Each type of shape—rectangles, ellipses, and polygons—can go through its own unique transformation. Rectangles can be rounded, ellipses can be made into arcs, and Polygons can be made into stars.

These special transformations can be assigned by the different Property bars that appear when you select a shape. The Rectangle Corner Roundness slider rounds off the corners on a selected rectangle. In Figure 3.16, I've set the slider to 20, producing a rounded corners on the selected square.

Figure 3.16.

Rounding a square.

Setting a rectangle to
have rounded corners

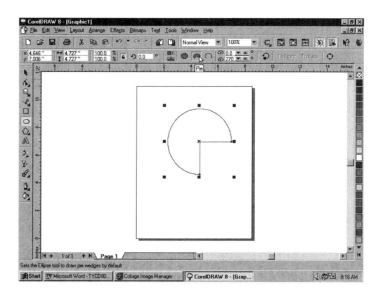

Ellipses, too, have a unique feature on their Property bar. The Pie and Arc buttons
transform ellipses to pies (as shown in Figure 3.17) and curves. These tools are only visible
when an ellipse is selected and the Ellipse Property bar is in view.

Figure 3.17.

From a circle to a pie.

An arc is a pie that is not filled in, as shown in Figure 3.18.

Figure 3.18.

A 270-degree arc.

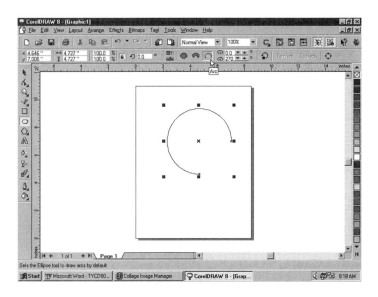

You can define the radius of a pie or an arc using the Starting Angle spin box (the top one) and the Ending Angle Spin box (the bottom one). In Figure 3.19, I am defining a pie with a starting angle of 0 degrees and an ending angle of 180 degrees.

Figure 3.19.

A semicircle.

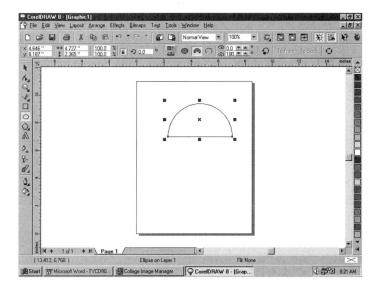

The unique Property bar features for polygons enable you to change the number of points or sides and to transform a shape from a star to a polygon, or vice versa. In Figure 3.20, I'm using the Number of Points on Polygon spin box to change my shape to an octagon.

Figure 3.20.

The Polygon Property bar used to change the number or points or sides on a polygon or star.

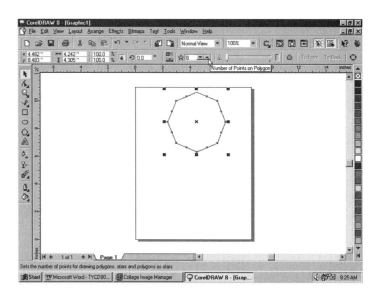

 The Polygon/Star button in the Polygon Property bar toggles between polygons or stars.

In this lesson, you learned to create and edit two of the most useful and widely used objects in graphic design: artistic text and shapes. Before ending this lesson, let's take a look at how to assign color fills and outlines to these objects.

Selecting Fill Colors from Palettes

The default CorelDRAW screen comes with a color palette on the right side of the Drawing area. This palette has a small down arrow at the bottom and an up arrow at the top. Clicking on the up and down arrows reveals more colors in your color palette. Or you can click on the small left-pointing arrow at the bottom of the palette to display the entire set of colors at once. In Figure 3.21, I've clicked on that arrow and four rows of colors are displayed. You can shrink the color palette back to one column by clicking in the lower right-hand corner of the palette.

To apply a color from the color palette to the fill of a selected object, just click on the color. That's it! Experiment by filling your screen with some shapes and artistic text and clicking on different fill colors.

You'll explore different kinds of fills in detail in Hour 4, "Controlling the CorelDRAW 8 Environment," of this book, but you've already learned to apply color fills.

Selecting Outline Colors

Outline colors are assigned the same way you assign fill colors, except that you use your right mouse button. First, select the object to which you are assigning an outline color. Then, right-click on a color in the palette.

3

Figure 3.21.

Expanding the color palette.

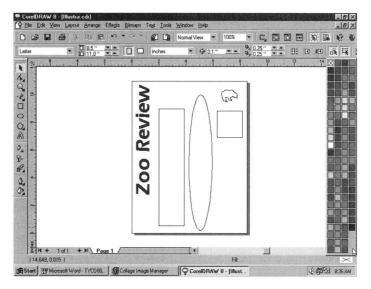

Experiment with different combinations of fills and outlines. Artistic text can have both fill and outline colors assigned to it.

To assign *no* outline color to a selected object, right-click on the X in the color palette. To assign no fill color to a selected object, click on the X in the color palette. Of course, if you assign no fill and no outline color to an object, it will be invisible.

JUST A MINUTE

> Were you wondering if invisible text can be used for "reverse" white on black writing against a dark background? It's a good idea, but it doesn't work that way. Invisible text is really invisible, not white. So if you want to place white text on top of a black shape, you need to assign a white line and/or fill to that text, not make it invisible.

Copying and Stacking Objects

You can copy a selected object by choosing Edit | Duplicate from the menu bar or by pressing Ctrl+D. You can also use the Cut, Copy, and Paste tools on the Standard toolbar to cut, copy, or paste any selected object.

When you move (or copy) an object on top of another object, you can use the To Front or To Back buttons in the Property bar to move the selected object on top of or behind other objects.

In Figure 3.22, I moved an oval on top of a rectangle. I'm in the process of using the To Back button in the Property bar to move the oval behind the rectangle.

Figure 3.22.

Moving a selected object behind another object.

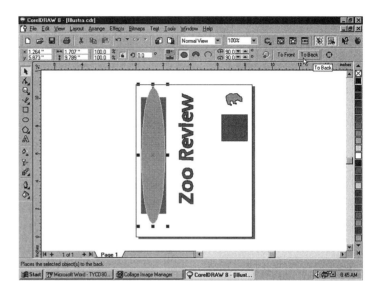

In Figure 3.23, I've moved a text object on top of both these shapes. And I moved a symbol image of a kangaroo on top of a square.

Figure 3.23.

Kangaroo jumps to top of square.

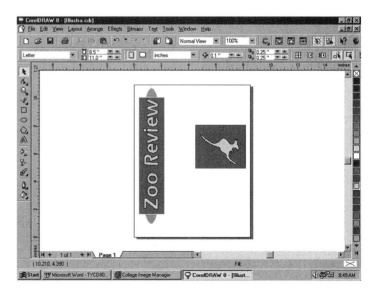

By adding fills and outlines to artistic text and shapes, and layering one object on top of another, you can create sophisticated designs.

Saving Your Drawing

CorelDRAW has extremely powerful options for printing files and for saving them in various file formats. In fact, whole lessons in this book are devoted to both printing and saving objects in other file formats. In Hour 10, "Editing Shapes and Curves," you'll explore exporting and printing options, and in Hour 11, "Masks and Lenses," you'll learn to convert CorelDRAW 8 objects into web-compatible graphics.

Although converting CorelDRAW drawings to other file formats can be complex, and working with different printing environments can be tricky, it's easy to save files as CorelDRAW 8 files and print them on your printer. Here, you'll learn to save files in the CorelDRAW format and print them using your own printer.

Saving Files

You can save your entire workspace or just selected objects by selecting File | Save from the CorelDRAW 8 menu bar.

3.3: Save Your Entire Drawing

1. Select File | Save from the menu bar. If you save an already saved file under a new name, select File | Save As instead.

2. Use the Save In drop-down menu to navigate to the folder on your computer to which you want to save the file.

3. Enter a name for your file in the File Name area of the dialog box.

4. The Save As Type drop-down menu enables you to save your file in dozens of file formats. Saving your image to non-CorelDRAW 8 file formats may result in losing some of the attributes you assigned to images. If you need to save your drawing in another file format, it's safest to save it as a CorelDRAW 8 file as well.

5. If you click on the Selected Only check box, only the objects you selected with the Pick tool will be saved. You can explore selecting multiple objects with the Pick tool in Hour 2 of this book.

6. If you click on the Embed Fonts Using Truedoc, the fonts you used in your image will be saved along with your image. Choosing this option creates text that can be edited, even if the file is opened by a program or in a system without the included font.

7. The Version drop-down menu enables you to save your file in older versions of CorelDRAW. The Thumbnail drop-down menu lets you define what kind of

thumbnail image you want to associate with your file. The thumbnail image is a small version of your file that will display in the File Open dialog box of many programs if you open the file applications other than CorelDRAW.

Figure 3.24.

*Saving a
CorelDRAW file
with embedded
fonts.*

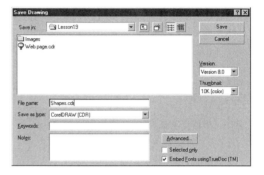

8. After you define the name, location, and type of file, click on the Save button in the dialog box.

You can ignore all the Save options and simply provide a filename. If you do that, your file will be saved as a CorelDRAW 8 file.

Just a Minute

Printing Files

Printing a CorelDRAW file is as easy as clicking on the Print tool in the Standard toolbar.

For more control over printing, choose File | Print from the menu. The General tab has all the options you need to print your file on your installed printer. (You'll explore the other options in Hour 10, "Editing Shapes and Curves.")

The All radio button in the Print Range area of the Print dialog box lets you choose to print the entire file; the Current Page radio button prints only the page on your screen. Use the Selection radio button if you selected an object with the Pick button. You can also use the Pages radio button to select which pages in a multipage file you want to print.

When you have made these selections, click on OK in the Print dialog box to print your file.

3

Summary

Fills and outline colors can be assigned from the color palette. Right-clicking on a color assigns that color to the outline of a selected object. Clicking on a color assigns that color to the fill of a selected object.

Property bars also enable you to move selected objects to the back of other objects.

Workshop

The magazine cover Paul designed for us combines shapes, artistic text, fills, outlines, polygons, and symbols. Create a cover like Paul's.

1. If you saved the file you created in Hour 2, open it now. Or start by creating a title for the magazine with artistic text and rotating it 90 degrees.

2. Add some text for the cover so that your design looks something like the text in Figure 3.25.

3. Draw a square and two circles on top of a lion symbol near the middle of the page, as you see in Figure 3.25.

4. Add four long, thin ovals as background shapes.

5. Draw a 12-pointed star as background, behind the text.

6. Use the Symbol Dockers toolbar to add some animals to the top of the page. Get the little creatures from the Animals1 font.

7. Resize, experiment with fun fills, and move objects to the back as necessary, until your magazine cover looks something like Figure 3.25.

8. Add a camera to the cover using symbol number 180 in the Webdings font.

9. Place a crosshair on the page, and move objects to Front or Back as necessary to create your unique magazine cover.

10. Save the magazine cover.

This exercise gave you a chance to experiment with all kinds of shapes, including polygons and stars.

Quiz

1. What are the three shape tools?

2. What can you create with the Polygon tool?

Figure 3.25.

Magazine cover with squares, circles, ellipses, and a star.

3. What are the unique features of the Ellipse Property bar?

4. How do you assign no outline to a selected object?

5. What's a quick, easy way to get some clip art?

Quiz Answers

1. The shape tools are the Rectangle, the Ellipse, and the Polygon tool. The Polygon tool is a flyout that can transform into the Spiral or Graph Paper tools.

2. You can use the Polygon tool to create polygons, stars, or stars-as-polygons.

3. The Ellipse Property bar has buttons that let you convert an ellipse into a pie or an arc.

4. You can assign no outline to a selected object by right-clicking on the X in the color palette.

5. You can use characters from the Symbol Docker and drag them into the Drawing area.

Hour 4

Controlling the CorelDRAW 8 Environment

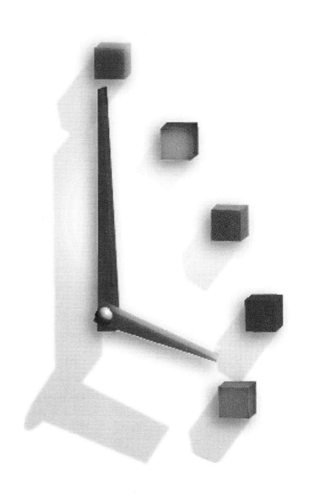

In Hour 1 of this book, you jumped right into CorelDRAW 8. You didn't need a detailed investigation into the program environment to create a wide array of text and shapes and combine them to make a fairly complex illustration.

As you continue to work with CorelDRAW, you'll find that the features that make CorelDRAW so powerful require you to customize and define the working environment. For example, if you create designs with dozens of objects, you might find working in Wireframe view faster and easier. If you create technical drawings, you'll want to use CorelDRAW's capability to attach dimensions to objects. If you design graphics for a web site, you might want to create a custom Drawing page the size of a typical monitor, defined in pixels, not inches. These are just a few examples of the wide-ranging changes you can make to CorelDRAW.

You can customize the basic look and feel of CorelDRAW 8 to serve your own specific design tasks. In this hour, you learn how to work with the Standard toolbar, place Docker windows, and work with the status bar and rollups.

Viewing and Moving Toolbars

CorelDRAW 8 comes with ten premade toolbars, but 99% of the time you will want to use the Standard toolbar. It has all the tools you need to cut, copy, and paste objects, and to control the basics of your environment, such as zoom level.

There will be times later in this book when you will view and move additional toolbars. In Hour 19, "From CorelDRAW to the World Wide Web" for example, you will use the Internet Objects toolbar. When that happens, I'll remind you how to view additional toolbars. But you can try it quickly right now just to familiarize yourself with the process of viewing and moving a toolbar.

4.1: View, Dock, and Remove the Text Toolbar

To Do

1. Select View | Toolbars from the menu bar.
2. Click on the Text check box in the Toolbars dialog box. In Figure 4.1, I am electing to display the Text toolbar.
3. Click on OK in the Options window.

Figure 4.1.
Choosing toolbars.

Figure 4.2 shows the Text toolbar displayed on the screen.

4. Dock the floating Text toolbar at the bottom of the screen by dragging it to the bottom of the CorelDRAW window and releasing the mouse button to dock the toolbar.

In Figure 4.3, I docked the Text toolbar at the bottom of the screen by moving it directly over the status bar. I'm using the Font Size List drop-down menu to choose a font size for selected text.

5. Remove the Text toolbar from your screen by selecting View | Toolbars and deselecting the Text check box in the Toolbars dialog box. Click on OK to close the Options window.

4

Figure 4.2.
*The Text toolbar is
floating and covers
part of the
Drawing window.*

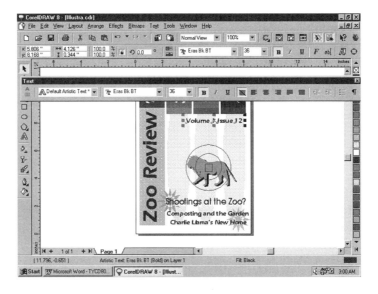

Figure 4.3.
*Using the docked
Text toolbar.*

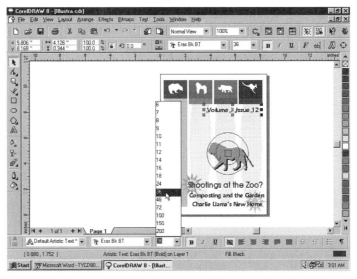

JUST A MINUTE

If you display the Text toolbar and select text on your screen, you might
have noticed that many of the features on the Text toolbar are already
displayed on the Property bar that displays automatically when you select
a text object. And you might be asking yourself, "Isn't the Text toolbar a
bit redundant." I think so. In general, you will find that Property bars

> provide easy access to the features you want to apply to a selected object, and that the default settings displaying the Standard toolbar, the Property bar, and the Status bar provide the cleanest environment in which to work.

You can display or hide and dock or float any toolbar. To pull a docked toolbar onto the Drawing area, click on a section of the toolbar in between tools (not on a tool), and drag the toolbar into the Drawing area. In Figure 4.4, I've dragged the Standard toolbar onto the Drawing area.

Figure 4.4.

The Standard toolbar can float.

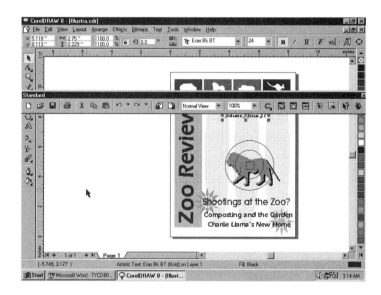

What's on the Standard Toolbar?

Many of the tools on the Standard toolbar are familiar to the user of any Windows program. Others are unique to CorelDRAW 8, and some activate features that will be explored later in this book. For your reference, the following table identifies the tools on the Standard toolbar.

4

Table 4.1. The Standard toolbar.

Tool	Tool Name	What It Does
	New	Opens a new file.
	Open	Activates the Open Drawing dialog box so you can open an existing file.
	Save	Resaves an already saved file, or opens the Save Drawing dialog box.
	Print	Opens the Print dialog box.
	Cut	Cuts selected objects and places them in the Clipboard, from which they can be pasted.
	Copy	Copies selected objects into the Clipboard.
	Paste	Pastes the contents of the Clipboard into the Drawing area.
	Undo	The icon undoes your last action; the drop-down list lets you undo a series of actions.
	Redo	The icon redoes the last undone action; the drop-down list lets you redo multiple undos.
	Import	Opens the Import dialog box from which you can import non-CorelDRAW files.

continues

Table 4.1. continued

Tool	Tool Name	What It Does
	Export	Opens the Export dialog box, enabling you to export objects or files to other file formats.
Normal View ▼	View Quality	The drop-down list lets you choose from different views, including Wireframe, Draft, and Normal.
100% ▼	Zoom levels	The drop-down list lets you zoom in or out on your drawing.
	Application Launcher	Lets you start other Corel applications.
	Scrapbook Docker window	Opens a window on the right of the screen with saved files.
	Symbol Docker window	Opens a window on the right of the screen displaying font symbols.
	Script Docker window	Opens a window on the right of the screen with wizards and automated scripts.
	Enable Node Tracking	Turns on temporary node editing when the cursor is moved over a note—see Lesson 5.
	Show Text Frames	Reveals paragraph text frames—see Lesson 8.
	What's This?	Click then point at components of the screen to get quick explanations of what the component does.

4

Tool	Tool Name	What It Does
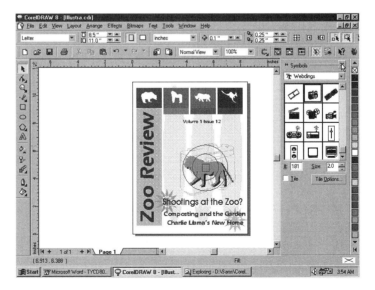	Corel Tutor	Launches online tutorials.

Working with Docker Windows

Docker windows provide another way to access features in CorelDRAW 8. In Hour 1, you used the Symbol Docker window to drag symbols from font lists onto the Drawing area. The Scrapbook, Script, and Present Docker windows are also useful. But before we examine them, let's explore how you can control Docker windows in general.

Managing Docker Windows

The Symbol Docker window you used in Hour 1 is great for pulling symbols onto your Drawing area. The problem is, it takes up about a third of your screen, reducing your work area. You can solve that problem by simply closing the Docker window. You do that by clicking on the small X in the upper-right corner of the window. In Figure 4.5, I am closing the Symbol Docker window.

4

Figure 4.5.

Click on the X in the upper-right corner of the rollout to close the Symbol Docker window.

x:	3.617 "
y:	8.488 "

A less extreme solution is to shrink the Docker window by clicking on the two right arrows on the left side of the top of the Docker window.

When you shrink a Docker window, the window zips up into a vertical bar that you can reopen by clicking on the two left pointing arrows at the top of the compacted window. In Figure 4.6, I am expanding a Docker window.

Figure 4.6.

Expanding a compacted Docker window.

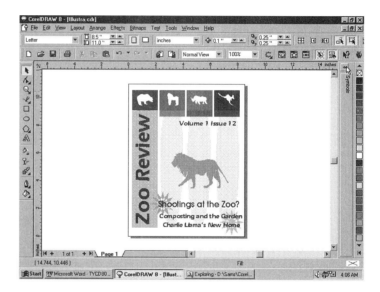

Using the Script and Preset Docker Window

The Script and Preset Docker window makes available a number of predefined wizards that create calendars and apply effects to selected objects. The Calendar Wizard is great for creating customized calendars, like the one I do every year with embarrassing pictures of family members. The Calendar Wizard takes a while to generate a 12-month calendar, but it does a lot of work for you.

A simpler script is the one that applies shadows to a selected object.

4.2: Apply the Shadow Script

To Do

1. Draw or select an object in the Drawing window.
2. Click on the Script and Preset Docker tool in the Standard toolbar.

In Figure 4.7, I've selected a lion symbol, and I am about to double-click on the Shadow script.

3. Double-click on the Shadow icon in the Docker window.

4

Figure 4.7.
Shadowing a lion.

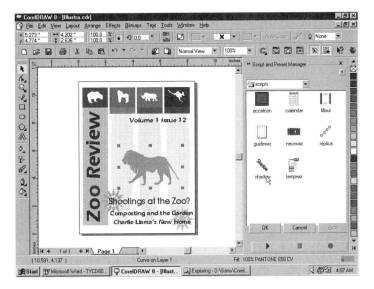

4. In the Drop Shadow Maker dialog box, change the Horizontal spin box to 150 and the Vertical spin box to -90 to increase the depth of the shadow.

5. Click on the check box in the Special Effects area of the dialog box, and use the Make Shadow Transparent spin box to set the shadow to 50% transparency.

In Figure 4.8, I used the location spin boxes to slightly increase the distance of the shadow from the selected lion.

Figure 4.8.
Defining a drop shadow.

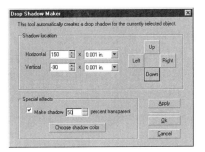

6. When you have defined your drop shadow, click on the Apply button in the dialog box. Figure 4.9 shows the drop shadow applied to the lion.

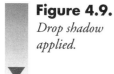

Figure 4.9.
Drop shadow applied.

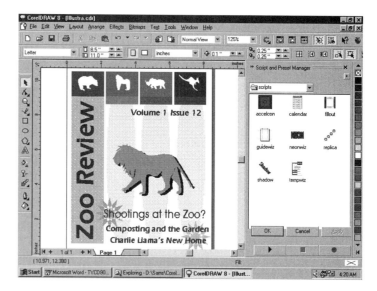

Using the Scrapbook Docker Window

The CorelDRAW Scrapbook is a visual version of the Windows Explorer. It enables you to pull objects off your system drives and into an open drawing. It also enables you to drag objects off your drawing and into the Scrapbook.

In Figure 4.10, I am dragging the camera image off the Drawing page and into the Scrapbook so that I can find it and use it easily. If you drag an object off the Drawing page, it will save as part of your CorelDRAW file, but it will not be available for *other* CorelDRAW files. If you place an object in the Scrapbook, it will be available there to drag back into *any* open CorelDRAW file.

The drop-down list at the top of the Scrapbook Docker window enables you to navigate your system drives and folders to find files. The tabs on the right side of the window help you sift through objects.

You rename files in the Scrapbook by right-clicking on the icon and choosing Rename from the shortcut menu. In Figure 4.11, I'm renaming the camera symbol I dragged into the Scrapbook and assigning the filename Camera2.cdr to that image.

Objects stored in the Scrapbook are easy to find and place in CorelDRAW designs. You can also import files, but the graphical interface of the Scrapbook makes it a handy way to manage files.

4

Figure 4.10.
Placing a graphic object in the Scrapbook.

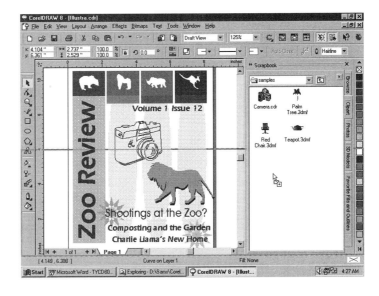

Figure 4.11.
Renaming a file in the Scrapbook.

Interpreting the Status Bar

The status bar located underneath the Drawing area tells you a couple important things about a selected object. No, one of them is not the object's "social status." The Status bar tells you the type of object you have selected and the type of fill. In Figure 4.12, the Status bar is advising me that the object I selected is a rectangle and that the fill color is yellow.

Figure 4.12.

Selecting a yellow rectangle.

The status bar also identifies the location of the cursor in x and y coordinates. The x value (the first one) represents the distance from the left edge of the Drawing page. The y value (the second one) represents the distance your cursor is from the bottom of the Drawing page.

Finally the status bar tells you what layer you are working with. Complex CorelDRAW files can have more than one layer. Layers are explored in detail in Hour 16, "Managing Layers and Pages."

Controlling Rollups

As you explore more advanced formatting tools and effects, you will encounter CorelDRAW's *rollups*. These are miniwindows that hang out over your Drawing area that provide quick and easy access to groups of tools. You'll learn to use these tools in the rest of this book, but for now let's take a quick look at how rollups work.

You can open rollups in a variety of ways. You can select View | Rollups from the menu bar and choose from a list of rollups in that menu. Some tool flyouts also enable you to activate rollups. To open the Pen rollup, click and hold the mouse button on the Pen tool in the toolbox, as I am doing in Figure 4.13.

From the flyout, select the Pen rollup (the third tool on the flyout).

The Pen rollup that appears on your Drawing area holds all kinds of tools for defining outline size, style, color, and arrows. You explored these tools fully in Hour 3, but for now experiment with controlling the rollup itself.

4

Figure 4.13.

Selecting the Pen rollup.

To roll up the rollup, click on the small, up-pointing triangle at the top of the rollup. The rolled up rollup doesn't take much space, but it is easily accessible if you want to use it. Want to get the rollup back on your screen? Just click on the small down arrow in the rolled up rollup to see the whole thing again.

If you click on (depress) the little thumbtack at the top of a rollup (see Figure 4.14), the rollup will stay on your work area after you apply an effect from it. If you deselect the thumbtack (so that it is not in the depressed position), the rollup will disappear after you apply an effect.

Figure 4.14.

Sticking a rollup on the screen with a thumbtack.

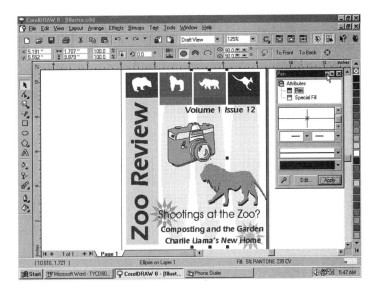

Throughout the course of this book, you'll use many rollups. Now you know how to make them behave.

Summary

The CorelDRAW 8 environment can be somewhat overwhelming with at least three ways to apply many effects to objects: the menu bar, the toolbar, and the Property bar. And many features can be applied by rollups and toolbox tools as well. As you experiment with CorelDRAW, you will settle on ways you like to assign properties to objects. You'll find the Property bar is a useful jack-of-all-trades that enables you to define the properties you use most frequently to objects.

CorelDRAW can be any kind of environment you want it to be. You can define measurement units in anything from pixels to meters. You can select from dozens of predefined page sizes or define your own custom page sizes.

Properties you learned to apply to one object in Hour 1, such as size, fill color, and line color, can be applied to many selected objects or to grouped objects.

Workshop

In this workshop, you will use your new environment-control skills to look at a drawing in different ways.

1. Open the magazine cover you designed in this hour. View your project with no toolbars or property bars displayed.
2. View both the Standard toolbar and the Property bar.
3. Drag the toolbox to the right side of the Drawing area and dock it there.
4. Organize your workspace with the toolbox, toolbar and Property bar set in a way you want to work with them.

Quiz

1. How do you set the toolbar display?
2. What button on the toolbar cancels your most recent action(s)?
3. How do you close those Docker windows?
4. What does the x value in the status bar represent?

Quiz Answers

1. Set the toolbar display by selecting View | Toolbars from the menu bar, and use the available check boxes to define the toolbar display.
2. The Undo button reverses your previous action(s).
3. You can close a Docker window by clicking on the small x in the upper-right corner of the window.
4. The x value in the status bar represents the distance from the left edge of the Drawing page to the center of the selected object.

4

Hour 5

Setting Up Page Layout

CorelDRAW can be all things to all folks. Laying out a tabloid newspaper? A magazine? A fan-fold brochure? A business card? Or a web page? The Page area can be all these things and more. CorelDRAW predefines many popular page sizes, and you can easily assign them to your project. You can custom define others.

After you have defined your page, other layout tools help you work on it. Grids, guidelines, and the ability to snap objects to grids or guidelines are very handy features for laying out your design. In this lesson, you learn how to define different sizes of page layout. You also learn to use guidelines, grids, and alignment features to place objects on your page. And you learn to work more quickly by using less-detailed views when possible.

Defining Page Size

The easiest way to define your page size is to click on a blank part of the Drawing area. When you do, the Page Layout Property bar becomes active. You can use this Property bar to define the size and orientation of your page, as well as many other attributes.

5.1: Define a Page Size

1. Click anywhere except on an object.

2. Pull down the Paper Type/Size drop-down list from the Property bar. In Figure 5.1, I am selecting an envelope size Drawing page.

Figure 5.1.

Defining an Envelope page.

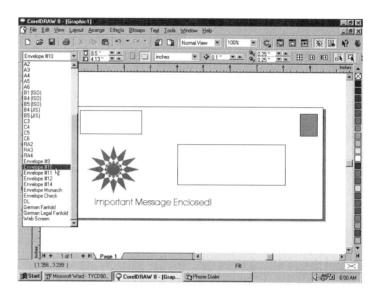

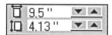 You can manually define custom page sizes using the Paper Width and Height spin boxes in the Property bar.

If you plan to use a custom page size quite a bit, you can define that page and include it in the list of predefined page sizes. Because I create many web graphic images, I often define a custom page size fitted to a 640 × 480 pixel monitor screen.

5.2: Define a Custom Page Size to Fit a 640 × 480 Pixel Monitor Screen

1. Select Tools | Options from the menu bar, and double-click on Page in the Options dialog box.

2. Double-click on Document, and then double-click on Size in the left side of the Options dialog box.

3. When the Size section of the Options dialog box becomes active, pull down the Paper list and select Custom.

5

4. Select Pixels from the drop-down list of measurement options. In the Resolution drop-down list, select Other and enter 72 as the resolution. This is the pixel/inch resolution of most monitors.

5. Enter 640 in the width spin box, and 40 in the height spin box. The small preview screen in the right half of the Size area of the dialog box displays a thumbnail of your page size. Figure 5.2 shows a web screen being defined.

Figure 5.2.

Defining a custom page size.

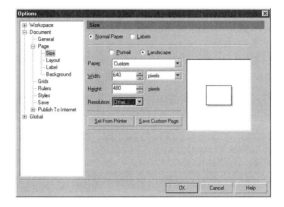

Another popular monitor resolution is 800 × 600. You can also create a predefined page size for that screen resolution.

TIME SAVER

6. After you define your custom page size, you can save that definition by clicking on the Save Custom Page button in the dialog box. Name your page definition. Then, click on OK in the Custom Page Type dialog box. In Figure 5.3, I have named my custom page 640 × 480 Web Screen.

Figure 5.3.

Naming a custom page definition.

In Figure 5.4, I'm selecting a custom-defined page size from the Paper Type/Size drop-down list.

5

Figure 5.4.

Applying a custom page size.

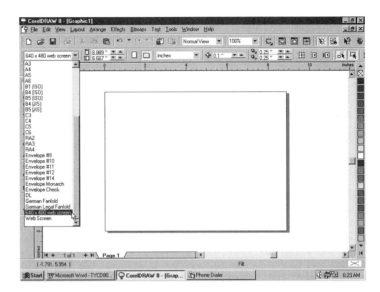

Customizing Your CorelDRAW 8 Page Layout

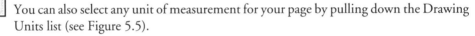
The Portrait and Landscape buttons in the Property bar enable you transform many page layouts from portrait (pages that are taller than they are wide) to landscape (pages that are wider than they are tall).

You can also select any unit of measurement for your page by pulling down the Drawing Units list (see Figure 5.5).

Figure 5.5.

Selecting pixels as the unit of measurement.

5

The Nudge Offset box defines how far a selected object moves when you "nudge" it by pressing the right, left, up, or down arrows on your keyboard. If you set the distance to 1", for example, you can choose any object with the Pick tool, press the down arrow on your keyboard, and that object moves one inch down. Exactly. Custom-defined nudge offsets can be a big time-saver. One scenario is that you have four rectangles sitting on top of each other and you want to space them one inch apart. A custom-defined nudge value makes this as easy as pressing the right arrow one, two, three, or four times.

The Duplicate Distance value boxes define how much offset will be applied to a selected object when you duplicate it by pressing Ctrl+D, or by choosing Edit | Duplicate from the menu bar.

Using Guidelines & Grids

Grids and guidelines work like invisible magnets on your screen and allow you to easily locate a selected object to a horizontal or vertical location, or both.

When you select View | Grid from the menu bar, dots appear on your screen. They won't print; they're only there as location points. When you click on the Snap to Grid button in the Page Property bar, the grid coordinates act like magnets that attract the object you are moving. If you want to move an object to a location not on a grid coordinate, you'll find that difficult with Snap to Grid turned on.

Snap to Objects works in a similar way, but instead of grid coordinates, it is other objects that act like magnets. When you click on the Snap to Objects button in the Page Property bar, objects on your page attract the object you are moving.

Finally, you can place custom-defined guidelines on your page and use them as snap-to objects. To place a horizontal guideline, drag on the ruler on the top of the screen, and drag down to a location on your page. In Figure 5.6, I am dragging the top ruler to the 10.5 inch mark on the vertical ruler to create a guideline there.

Vertical guidelines are created pretty much the same way horizontal ones are, except that you drag from the vertical ruler on the left side of the Drawing window to create them.

5.3: Define a Vertical Guideline at Six Inches, and Align a Rectangle at the Guideline

To Do

1. Drag on the ruler on the left side of the Drawing window, and pull it until the top of the ruler is aligned with the six-inch mark on the horizontal ruler on the top of the page.

2. Click on the Snap to Guidelines button in the Page Property bar. This guideline acts as a magnetic border.

3. Draw a rectangle. Select that rectangle and drag it near the guideline you defined. Let the magnetic attraction of the guideline pull the right side of your rectangle right to the 6-inch point.

4. Click on a blank part of the page to make the Page Property bar active. Click again on the Snap to Guidelines button in the Page Property bar.

You can remove guidelines from the Drawing area by selecting them with the Pick tool and pressing the Delete button.

Figure 5.6.

Defining a horizontal guideline.

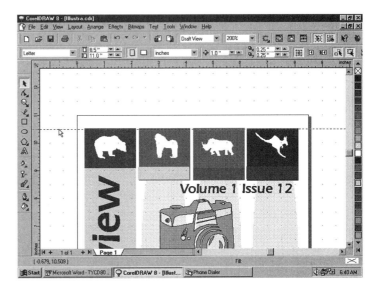

Working with Views

You can zoom in and out in CorelDRAW, and you can use the Pan tool to drag parts of your drawing into the viewable window. The Zoom tool works as an interactive magnifying (or telescoping lens) enabling you to focus on a small part of your page or zoom out to see the entire Drawing area.

You can also control how you see and work with your page by selecting from five different view quality options. CorelDRAW objects take quite a bit of system resources, and when you fill a screen with them, editing can slow to a crawl. Lower quality views can speed up that process. View quality settings from lowest to highest are: Simple Wireframe, Wireframe, Draft view, Normal view, and Enhanced view.

Zooming and Panning

You can select different zoom magnifications from the Zoom Levels drop-down list in the Standard toolbar. Or you can zoom in and out interactively by clicking on the Zoom tool in the toolbox and then clicking on a portion of your drawing that you want to magnify. You can zoom back out by pressing the F3 function key on your keyboard.

5

You can also define zoom level by choosing the Zoom tool and right-clicking on the Drawing area. The shortcut menu that appears provides a list of zoom options. In Figure 5.7, I am using the Zoom tool to zero in on my lion and camera.

Figure 5.7.

Zooming in.

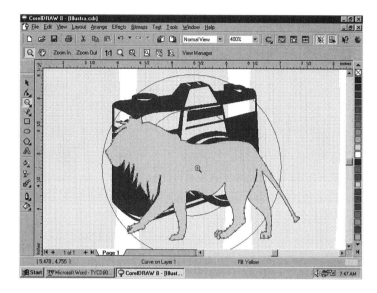

The Zoom tool is a flyout, and when you click on it and hold down the mouse button, you can choose between the Zoom tool and the Pan tool.

The Pan tool enables you to click on a section of an image and drag that section of the image into view. The Pan and Zoom tools have no effect on the actual appearance of your finished image; they simply enable you to view your image from different perspectives.

In Figure 5.8, I'm using the Pan tool to drag the bear into the center of my screen.

Defining View Quality

The View menu provides commands for changing five levels of the view quality. The lowest level, Simple Wireframe view, provides the fastest redrawing of your screen. I like Simple Wireframe view because you can easily select objects in a crowded design. Simple Wireframe view won't display fills or outline color or style, so you see just the bare bones of objects. But Simple Wireframe view works fine for defining size, rotation angle, and location of objects.

The Wireframe view is very similar to the Simple Wireframe view. The Wireframe view displays object outlines but not fills or outline attributes.

Figure 5.9 shows a page in Wireframe view. If you don't need to see fills and effects, Wireframe view is a fast environment in which to edit your objects.

Figure 5.8.

Using the Pan tool to drag a bear.

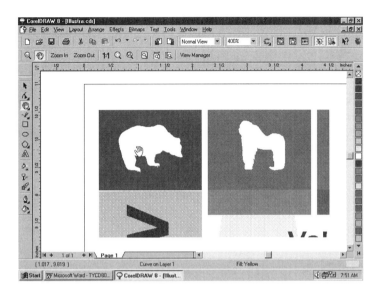

Figure 5.9.

Wired into Wireframe view.

Draft view displays regular color fills and many effects. Some effects appear in a simplified view. Normal view shows all fills. Enhanced view is like Normal view, except that it also displays Postscript style fills. (You investigated fills in Hour 4.)

5

Controlling Objects

You learned to control many properties of a selected object: size, fill, outline, location, rotation, and more. Now it's time to learn to control the attributes of more than one object at a time.

With CorelDRAW, you can select and edit many objects at once. You can temporarily bind objects together as a Group and edit them collectively. CorelDRAW also makes it easy to define the relationships between objects; they can be aligned with each other in a variety of ways.

Selecting Multiple Objects

The first step in editing many objects at once is to select more than one object. In Lesson 1, you learned to select a single object by choosing the Pick tool from the toolbox and clicking on an object you want to select.

To select more than one object, you can click on the Pick tool and then draw a marquee around a number of objects you want to select. Or you can hold down Shift while you click on more than one object. In Figure 5.10, I am selecting four of the animal symbols and the background rectangles behind them.

Figure 5.10.

Selecting several objects with the Pick tool.

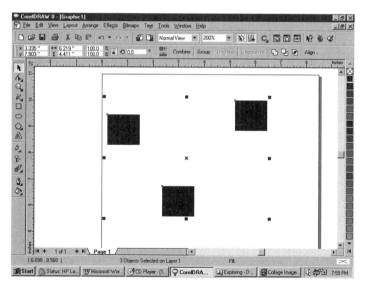

You can move, cut, copy, paste, and resize selected objects the same way you edit a single selected object. You can also select noncontiguous objects—objects that aren't touching each other. By selecting the Pick tool and holding down Shift, you can select any number of objects. In Figure 5.11, I selected the two 12 stars in my illustration and I'm dragging them out of the Drawing page.

Figure 5.11.

Moving two noncontiguous stars.

Grouping Objects

You can edit grouped objects the same way you edit groups of selected objects. But the advantage of grouping is that the objects appear as one, and you don't need to select them each time you want to edit them as a group.

To group objects first select them. Then choose Arrange | Group from the menu bar. You can ungroup objects by clicking on the grouped objects with the Pick tool and choosing Arrange | Ungroup.

Figure 5.12 shows two objects grouped, combined, and welded.

Combining Objects

Combining objects is a whole different thing than grouping them, even though the terms sound similar. Grouping lets you work with several objects at once. But the simple act of grouping objects does not change them. That's not true when you combine objects.

Combining objects, actually transforms the objects that are combined, as you can see in Figure 5.12. You combine objects by selecting them with the Pick tool and choosing Arrange | Combine from the menu bar. Combined objects can be broken back apart (Arrange | Break Apart). However, the objects do not revert to their original shape and fill but retain changes made when they were combined. Use combining for effect but not to temporarily join objects.

Welding

Welding is the most drastic way to join objects. The welded objects take on the outline and fill of the object that was selected last. Welded objects can revert to their original individual objects only by using the Undo button (or selecting Edit Undo).

5

Figure 5.12.

Grouping versus combining versus welding.

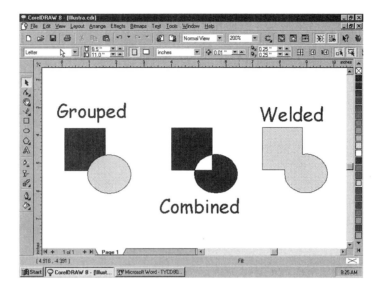

JUST A MINUTE

Grouped objects can be rotated, resized, and moved as a single object. Earlier in this hour, you examined the Mirror buttons in the Standard toolbar that are available to any selected object(s). You can also flip objects vertically and horizontally by dragging a side or top handle past the opposite side. This is easier to show than explain. In Figure 5.13, I dragged the left side handle of the middle grouped object to the right, past the right edge of the object. The result, displayed as a dotted line while I drag, is an object that is not only resized but horizontally flipped.

Aligning Objects

CorelDRAW 8 offers an almost unlimited array of alignment options for selected objects. Want to align the tops of objects, space them evenly, and place the whole collection in the center of your page? It can be done. How about aligning objects on their centers? No problem, as you can see in Figure 5.14.

Let's take those two examples—evenly spaced objects aligned by their tops and center-aligned objects—and walk through them.

To align objects to their centers, select all the objects with the Pick tool, and then choose Arrange | Align and Distribute from the menu bar. In the Align and Distribute dialog box, choose both Center check boxes, as shown in Figure 5.15.

5

Figure 5.13.
*Flipping while resizing
grouped objects.*

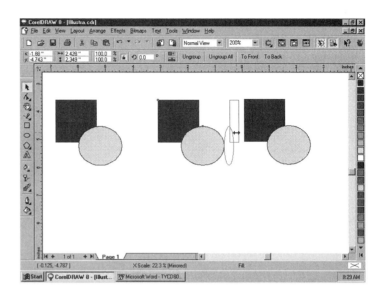

Figure 5.14.
Aligned centers.

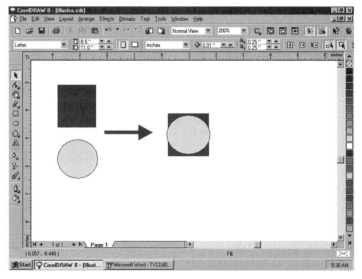

Figure 5.15.
*Centering horizontally
and vertically.*

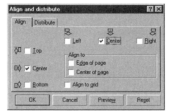

5

Click OK in the Align and Distribute dialog box to apply the alignment to your selected objects.

To align objects by their tops, space them evenly, and place them in the center of your page, follow these steps:

1. Select all the objects with the Pick tool.

2. Choose Arrange | Align and Distribute from the menu bar.

3. Click on the Top check box on the left side of the Align tab of the Align and Distribute dialog box. Click on the Center check box in the right side of the tab.

4. Click on the Center of Page check box.

5. Click on the Distribute tab and click on the Spacing check box in the right/top section of the tab. Click on the Extent of Page radio button in the Distribute section of the dialog box to distribute the objects across the page. The settings I am applying in the Distribute tab are shown in Figure 5.16.

Figure 5.16.

Defining Distribute settings.

6. When you have defined alignment and distribution settings, click on OK .

Figure 5.17 shows the objects centered on the page, stretching from one edge of the page to the other and evenly spaced.

Defining Default Fill and Line Colors

The last aspect of defining the CorelDRAW environment that you examine in this chapter is setting default fill, and line and text colors. Don't worry—this is easy. Simply click on a color in the color palette without any objects selected, and the Uniform Fill dialog box appears. This is where you define default color fills assigned to graphics, artistic text, or paragraph text—in any combination.

Pick the objects you want affected by the default fill color by clicking on check boxes in the Uniform Fill dialog box. In Figure 5.18, I'm assigning my default color to all three.

Figure 5.17.

Centering horizontally and distributing across the page.

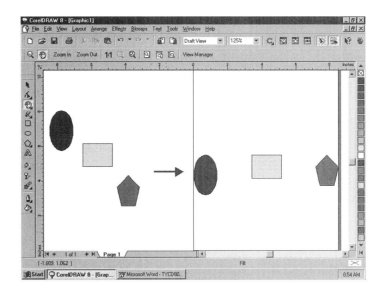

Figure 5.18.

Assigning a default fill color.

You can define default outline colors the same way except that you right-click on a color in the palette with no object selected. Use the check boxes in the Uniform Fill dialog box to assign the selected color to Graphic, Artistic Text, and/or Paragraph Text.

Summary

The CorelDRAW 8 environment can be somewhat overwhelming. There are at least three ways to apply many effects to objects: the menu bar, the toolbar, and the Property bar. And you can apply many features using rollups and toolbox tools as well. As you experiment with CorelDRAW, you settle on ways you like to assign properties to objects. You'll find the Property bar is a useful jack-of-all-trades that enables you to define the properties you use most frequently to objects.

CorelDRAW can be any kind of environment you want it to be. You can define measurement units in anything from pixels to meters. You can also select from dozens of predefined page sizes or define your own custom page sizes.

5

Properties you learned to apply to one object in Lesson 1, such as size, fill color, and line color, can be applied to many selected objects or to grouped objects.

Workshop

In this workshop, you open the magazine cover you have been working on in previous lessons. You zoom in on, and edit, different objects within the illustration.

1. Open the CorelDRAW file with the magazine cover you have worked on in earlier hours.

2. Switch to Wireframe view. Try Draft view. Continue to work in Draft view.

3. Zoom in on the center of your drawing. Use the Pan tool to move the drawing around on the screen so that you can see the lion in the middle of your illustration.

4. Apply a shadow to an object using the Script and Preset Manager window.

5. Select several objects such as the circles, the lion, and the camera.

6. Align all your selected objects on their horizontal and vertical centers, as you see in Figure 5.19.

Figure 5.19.

Centering the camera, the circles, and the lion.

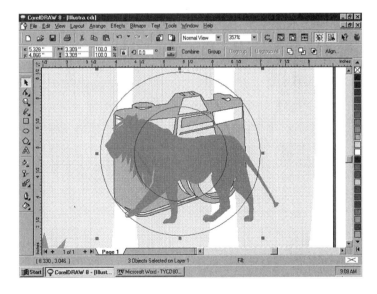

JUST A MINUTE

Your illustration might be different, but find several objects in it to align on their centers.

7. Select several objects such as the symbol-animals, and assign fill colors and outline colors to them all at once, as shown in Figure 5.20.

Figure 5.20.
Editing grouped objects.

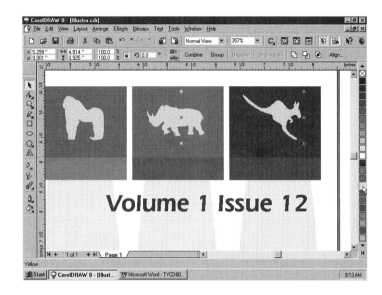

8. Save your file.

You just practiced viewing your drawing using both Wireframe and Draft views, and you used Align tools to arrange objects on your page.

Quiz

1. How do you select more than one object?
2. How do you select a page size?
3. How do you delete a guideline?
4. Name two ways to align the tops of objects.

Quiz Answers

1. You can select multiple objects by choosing the Pick tool in the toolbox and drawing a marquee around them. Or you can use Shift and click on the objects one at a time.
2. The easiest way to define page size is to click on a section of the Drawing area that does not have an object on it, and choose the page size from the Property bar.

5

3. You can delete a guideline by clicking on it and pressing Delete. Remember, though, guidelines do not print.

4. You can align the tops of objects using the Align and Distribute dialog box (Arrange | Align and Distribute). Or you can place a horizontal guideline and turn on the Snap to Guidelines button in the Page Property bar.

5

Hour 6

Defining Outlines

In Hour 1 you discovered the quick and easy way to assign or change the color of the outline of any selected object(s). Just choose the Pick tool to select the object(s) and then right-click on the color palette to assign an outline color.

Ah, but there's so much more! CorelDRAW 8 provides a plethora of outline styles, such as thick and thin, dashed and dotted. In Figure 6.1, our resident artist Paul Mikulecky from Electronic Design Studio has taken the magazine cover for *Zoo Review* and spiffed it up with a custom outline around the lion, as well as some interesting fills. (You'll learn to apply special fills in Hour 7, "Mixing Up Fills.")

Figure 6.2 zooms in on the lion to show off a couple of the techniques Paul applied. You can see that the lion now has a thick, broken line for an outline instead of the original, default solid thin line.

Now that you have a taste of what outlines can do, time to dive in and examine how to apply these effects. This lesson shows you how to create various outlines as well as to set default outline styles.

Figure 6.1.
Adding outlines and fills to the magazine cover.

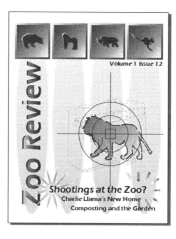

Figure 6.2.
The lion outfitted with a dashed line outline.

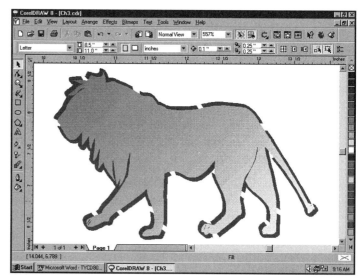

Creating Outlines

You can assign outline styles in several ways in CorelDRAW 8. As you saw in Hour 4, the CorelDRAW 8 environment usually supplies you with multiple options for accomplishing almost any task, and that is true of assigning outlines as well. You can define outlines from a rollup, from a flyout, or from a Property bar.

6

Defining Outline Width from the Outline Flyout

The quickest way to assign an outline width to a selected object (or objects) is to click on the Outline tool in the toolbox and choose from one of the preset widths. The options are $1/4$ point, $1/2$ point, 2 points, 8 points, 16 points, or 24 points (the widest).

6.1: Assign an 8-Point Outline to a Rectangle

To Do

1. Draw a rectangle.

2. Click on the Pick tool. The rectangle is still selected.

3. Click on the Outline tool, and click on the 8 point line—the one I'm selecting in Figure 6.3.

Figure 6.3.

When you assign line widths from the Outline flyout, the line width is indicated in the status bar.

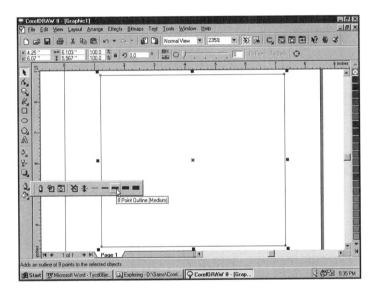

Defining Outline Options with the Pen Rollup

The Pen rollup is a bit of a holdover from older versions of CorelDRAW, but it still has advantages. In Figure 6.4, I'm selecting the Pen rollup from the Outline tool flyout. The rollup is over on the right side of the screen in Figure 6.4.

One advantage of the Outline rollup is that you can tack it onto the Drawing area so that it's always available. (For more information about working with rollups, see Hour 4, "Controlling the CorelDRAW Environment.") The Pen rollup enables you to assign line width, starting and ending arrows, line style, and line color. That's quite a bit.

Let's explore assigning these various options by starting with an oval transformed into an arc. The following steps add an arrow to the end of that arc, transform it into a red, dashed line, and make it about 7 points thick.

Figure 6.4.

Selecting the Outline rollup from the Outline Tool flyout.

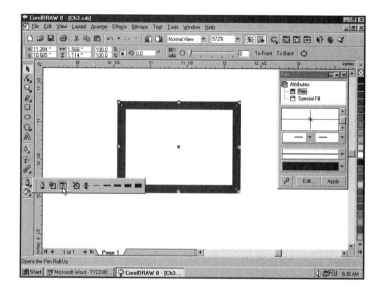

6.2: Assigning Outline Options with the Pen Rollup

1. Open a new document in CorelDRAW and create an arc. (If you don't remember how to create an arc, refer back to the section "Editing Objects" in Hour 1.)

2. After you create the arc, open the Pen rollup. Figure 6.5 the pen rollup.

3. Click on the Outline Color drop-down list in the Pen rollup and select red, as shown in Figure 6.6.

Figure 6.5.

The Pen rollup.

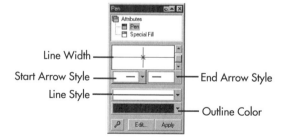

4. Pull down the Line Style drop-down menu, and choose the dashed line (see Figure 6.7).

5. Pull down the End Arrow Style drop-down menu, and assign an arrow of your choice to the end of the line as I have in Figure 6.8.

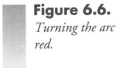

Figure 6.6.
Turning the arc red.

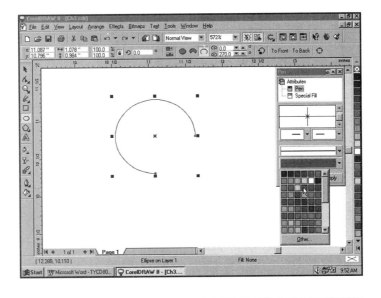

Figure 6.7.
Changing the line style to dashes.

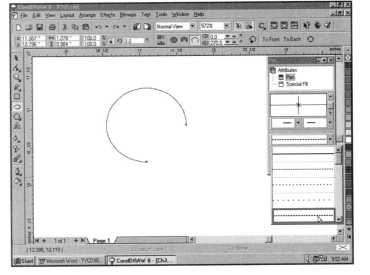

6. Finally, click on the up arrow in the thickness area of the Pen rollup, until the line width is 7.2 points, as shown in Figure 6.9.

7. When you have finished defining the outline properties in the Pen rollup, click on the Apply button.

Figure 6.8.
*Adding an arrow
to the end of the
line.*

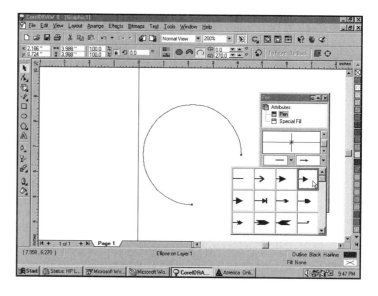

Figure 6.9.
*Defining outline
thickness in the
Pen rollup.*

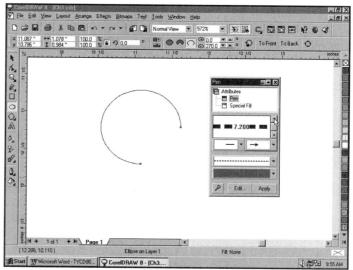

You should now have an arc similar to the one on the bottom of Figure 9.10.

One of the cool things about working with the Pen rollup on your screen is that after you
define settings, you can apply them to any selected object(s). For example, in Figure 6.10,
I tweaked the outline we just defined by getting rid of the end line, and then I applied it to
the lion.

6

Figure 6.10.
Applying the settings in the Pen rollup to a lion.

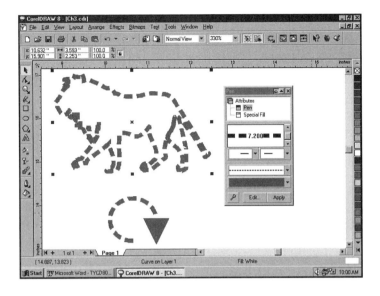

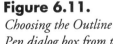

JUST A MINUTE

Because the lion is a *closed curve*, he doesn't actually have a beginning or end, and we cannot apply an arrow to his outline even if we want to. You'll explore closed and open curves in more detail in the next hour in the section "Open and Closed Curves."

The Outline Pen Dialog Box

To define outline details you never dreamed existed, use the Outline Pen dialog box. You can open the Outline Pen dialog box by clicking on the Edit button in the Pen rollup, or by choosing the dialog box from the Outline tool flyout (it is the first tool in flyout). In Figure 6.11, I am selecting the Outline Pen dialog box.

Figure 6.11.
Choosing the Outline Pen dialog box from the Pen flyout.

JUST A MINUTE

As an alternative, you can right-click on an object and choose Properties from the shortcut menu. When you do, yet another Object Properties dialog box appears. Select the Outline tab. This dialog box is a stripped down version of the Outline Pen dialog box. The larger Outline Pen Property Box is shown in Figure 6.12. It has all the features in the Outline tab of the Object Properties dialog box. After you explore the features in the larger Outline Pen dialog box, you can select some of those same features in the Object Properties dialog box.

Figure 6.12.
The Outline Pen dialog box.

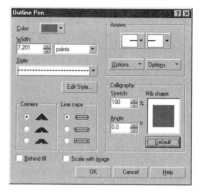

The Outline Pen dialog box repeats some of the features you explored in the Pen rollup, but in some cases in more detail. In Figure 6.13, I've defined outline width in points to an insanely detailed four decimal places.

Figure 6.13.
Microdefining line width.

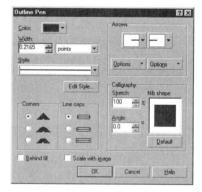

You also get tremendous control over dashed and dotted lines in the Outline Pen dialog box. By clicking on the Edit Style button, beneath the Style drop-down menu in the dialog box, you open the Edit Line Style dialog box. Here you pull on the I-beam cursor to define the number of squares in your pattern and then click on white squares to turn them colored. In Figure 6.14, I have defined a dashed line style with eight squares, five of them darkened.

Figure 6.14.
Defining a customized dashed line.

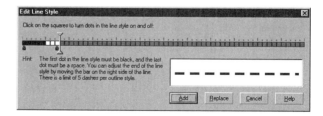

6

After you define a custom line style, click on the Add button in the Edit Line Style dialog box to add that custom style to the list of available line styles.

CAUTION

If you click on the Replace button in the Edit Line Style dialog box, you exit the dialog box and apply the defined line style to any selected object(s).

The Arrows section of the Outline Pen dialog box doesn't do much that you didn't just explore in the Pen rollup. The Corners area of the dialog box lets you assign a couple variations of rounded corners, which you'll learn more about in Hour 10, "Working with Shapes and Curves." The Line Caps section of the dialog box defines the appearance of the ends of lines. The options are Square Line Caps, Rounded Line Caps, or Extended Square Line Caps. In Figure 6.15, I have assigned (from left to right) square, rounded, and extended square line caps to the three arc ends, and rounded corners to the rectangle.

Figure 6.15.

The three Line Cap options provide subtle control over line appearance, from extended squares to rounded line ends.

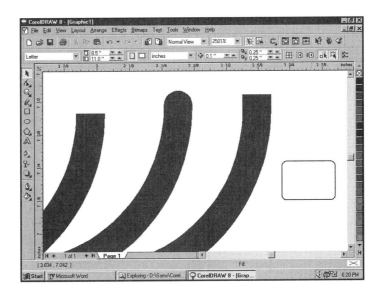

CAUTION

Adding line caps extends the length of lines. If you attach Line Cap options to dashed lines, you extend those lines and might ruin your dashes by filling in the spaces between them.

The Outline Pen dialog box also lets you define Calligraphy styles for outlines. In the enhanced lion that Paul created for this lesson, he defined the Calligraphy Stretch spin box at 50% and the Angle at 45 degrees. You can try that yourself on the lion in the Animal1 font set, and see Paul's results by looking back at Figure 6.2 near the beginning of this hour.

Defining Default Outlines

You can set default outline attributes by defining outline properties in the Outline Pen dialog box with no object selected. When you do, the Outline Pen dialog box (shown in Figure 6.16) presents you with three check boxes. These check boxes define what kinds of objects will be subjected to the outline you define. If you choose all three, as I am in Figure 6.16, then the outline attributes you assign in the dialog box will apply to the outlines of every object you draw.

Figure 6.16.

Choosing objects to which you will apply custom-defined default outline attributes.

Are custom default outline settings useful? Probably not for artistic and almost certainly not for paragraph text (you'll explore paragraph text in Hour 8, "Drawing and Editing Freehand Curves," and then you can decide for yourself). However, if you have an ornate, unique custom outline you want to apply to many objects, it is worth it to define a custom outline. When defined, custom outline defaults apply only to the drawing in which they were created.

CAUTION

One potential source of chaos is if you accidentally redefine outline defaults. It's easy to do. If you open the Outline Pen dialog box and define line attributes with no line selected, those attributes become the default settings for lines.

Summary

Outlines can be any thickness or color. You can define outline properties for any object in CorelDRAW 8. Outlines can be assigned from defined styles or created by customizing an outline style.

Workshop

In this workshop, you enhance the magazine cover you created in previous lessons by adding outlines to the objects. To begin, open the document you worked on in the previous three lessons.

1. Modify the outline for the camera in the background by defining an outline width of 2 points.

2. Assign a dashed line outline style to the selected line.

3. Experiment with Nib Shape in the Outline Pen dialog box. Define a Nib Shape set to 45 degrees, with a Calligraphy Stretch setting at 100%. These settings define the shape of the dashes in your dashed line.

4. Define a dark outline (you can choose Other from the color drop-down menu and pick Pantone 235 CV) for the lion with a width of 9 points.

5. Set a dashed line (11th selection on Style), and select Behind Fill.

6. Save the changes to your illustration.

Feel free to experiment with additional outline properties.

Quiz

1. How do you define a default outline?

2. How do you define an outline width to four decimal places?

3. Name five attributes that you can assign to an outline.

4. Does an object need an outline to be visible?

Quiz Answers

1. Define an outline with no object(s) selected.

2. Open the Outline Pen dialog box. In the Width spin box, you can type a width setting with four decimal places (or more).

3. You can assign outline color, thickness, style, corners, and arrows.

4. No. Objects with fills can be seen, even if they do not have an outline. However, objects with no fill or outline will not print and are not visible unless they are selected, or in Wireframe view.

Hour 7

Mixing Up Fills

CorelDRAW 8 enables you to assign five basic types of fills to any selected closed object. They are:

- [ ] **Uniform fills**. Single color fills, although that single color can be applied.
- [ ] **Fountain fills**. Fills that fade from one color to another.
- [ ] **Pattern fills**. Fills made from bitmap or vector files.
- [ ] **Texture fills**. Fills made from bitmap image files and can be edited.
- [ ] **PostScript fills**. Fills that use the PostScript programming language to generate patterns.

Pattern fills, Texture fills and PostScript fills are fun for special, spectacular effects. Most of the time you will use Uniform fills to assign a single color or Fountain fills to assign colors that merge into each other.

I mentioned that you can apply fills to *closed* objects. What does that mean? A closed object is a shape—such as the ones you have worked with in the previous two lessons (a rectangle, an oval, or a polygon)—or a free-form drawing with a continuous (connected) outline. You'll explore freehand drawing in the next lesson in this book.

A Uniform Color fill is Corel's way of describing a fill that consists of just one solid color, such as the one I applied to the lion in Figure 7.1.

Figure 7.1.

A uniformly filled lion.

Fountain fills combine two colors that fade into each other within an object. In Figure 7.2, our friendly lion is illustrating a Fountain fill that fades from a dark color in the upper-left corner of the object, to a light color in the lower-right corner.

Figure 7.2.

A Fountain-filled lion— note that the status bar identifies the type of fill.

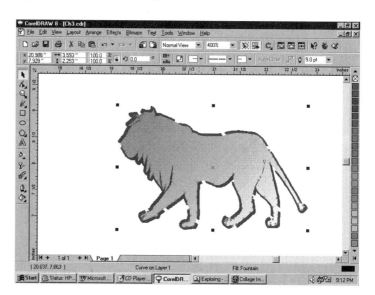

7

You can insert Pattern fills into an object from either bitmap graphic images or from vector images. Figure 7.3 shows both our Pattern-filled lion and the graphic file that provided the fill.

Figure 7.3.
A balloon-filled lion.

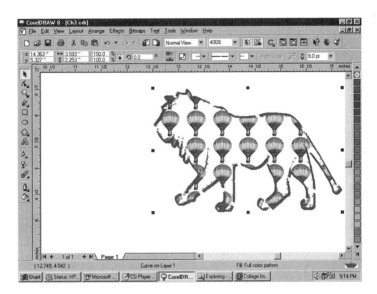

Texture fills enable you to start with several lists of wild and trendy designs and then play with them. The surreal lion in Figure 7.4 has been transformed with a Texture fill.

Figure 7.4.
Lion plus Texture fill.

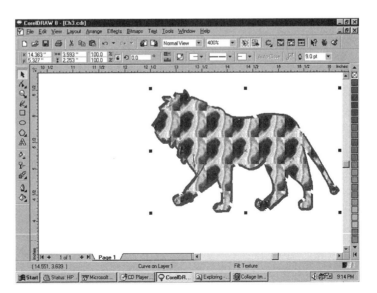

PostScript fills are fills-created patterns defined using the PostScript page-description language. These patterns can be viewed only if you select Enhanced view from the View drop-down menu in the Standard toolbar.

Okay, you have a taste of what CorelDRAW fills can do; now you'll learn to apply them.

Uniform Color Fills

You already know how to assign a color to a selected object. You just click on the color in the color palette to the right of your Drawing area. If you work with a printer that requires you to select colors from a fixed color palette, such as PANTONE Matching System colors, you can assign those colors to your color palette by choosing View | Color Palette from the menu bar, and then choosing from the options for preset colors.

If you are not constrained to a fixed color palette, you can mix up custom colors from the Uniform Fill dialog box or from the Color rollup.

JUST A MINUTE

> I'll explain the distinction between *fixed* and *mixed* color palettes in the section "More on Color Palettes."

Mixing Colors for Uniform Fills

The process of mixing colors is similar in the Uniform Fill dialog box and the Color rollup. The dialog box has more features, and the rollup stays on the Drawing area while you work.

Figure 7.5 shows the Color rollup being selected from the Color flyout and displayed on the screen as well.

Both the Uniform Fill dialog box and the Color rollup have similar features. We'll use the Uniform Fill dialog box to explore them. Figure 7.6 shows the Uniform Fill dialog box being selected from the Color flyout.

The four buttons in the upper-left corner of the Uniform Fill dialog box switch between four different ways of defining colors. The first two buttons (Color Viewers and Mixers) enable you to mix up custom colors. Use the other two buttons to select colors from fixed color palettes. The More>> button exposes the entire dialog box, which can help define custom colors.

Of the four buttons, the Mixers button opens a tab of the Uniform Fill dialog box that enables you to mix up colors using the three widely used methods for defining custom colors. The three methods for defining mixed colors are CMYK, RGB, and HSV.

7

Figure 7.5.
The Color rollup.

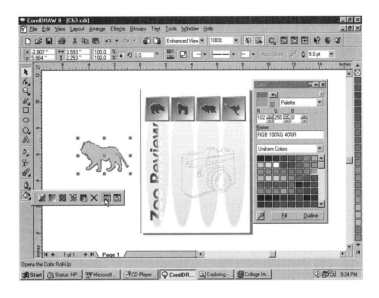

Figure 7.6.
*Selecting the Uniform
Fill dialog box.*

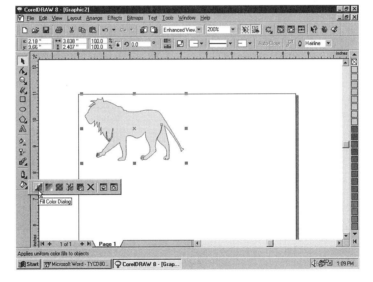

Mixing Colors Using CMYK Definitions

Use the Model drop-down menu in the Mixers view of the Uniform Fill dialog box to choose
between the RGB, CMYK, or HSV methods of defining colors.

In Figure 7.7, I'm choosing the CMYK method for defining colors. This method defines
colors as a mix of Cyan (a shade of green), Magenta (a bluish purple), Yellow, and blacK
(represented with a K in the CMYK acronym).

7

Figure 7.7.

*Mixing custom colors,
CMYK style.*

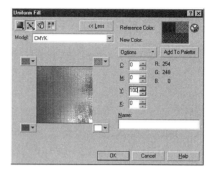

You can use the CMYK method of mixing colors for four color printing. You can separate colors defined using CMYK into four different masters—a technique you'll explore in Hour 10, "Working with Shapes and Curves."

Defining Colors with RGB or HSV Definitions

The RGB and HSV color definition systems are useful for defining web graphic image colors. RGB stands for Red, Green, and Blue and enables you to define a mix of those three colors. For example, say you are designing a web image and getting coloring advice from Lynda Weinman and Bruce Heavin's *Coloring Web Graphics* book. If Lynda advises you to use a background tile color of R 204, G 204, and B 0, you can define that color using the RGB model as I'm doing in Figure 7.8.

Figure 7.8.

*Defining colors using
RGB model.*

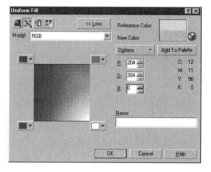

The HSV model defines colors in terms of Hue, Saturation, and Value. Hue is the location of a color on a color wheel or ramp, with 0 and 359 representing red and 240 representing blue. Saturation controls the amount of hue, and Value defines brightness. A Saturation setting of 50 mixes white pixels into your color at a ratio of 50/50. A Saturation value of 0 mixes no color pixels in with 100 white pixels to produce white no matter what value you enter for Hue. A Value setting of 0 produces black no matter what hue you define, and a Value of 100 produces the brightest possible color for your Hue.

7

Assigning Colors Without Worrying About Definitions

At this point, you might be saying to yourself, "Do I really need to know all these color definition systems?" The answer is maybe not. If you create images that you want to view on a color monitor, just rely on your visual good sense and click on colors in the color grid in the Uniform Fill dialog box.

When you select custom colors by clicking on the color grid on the left side of the Uniform Fill dialog box, you automatically generate CMYK, RGB, and HSV values on the right side of the dialog box.

This becomes more relevant when you decide to send your CorelDRAW illustration to a printer or to a web site. Both of those forms of output have different limitations as to which color definition systems they accept. You'll return to color definition issues in Hour 18, "Printing," and Hour 19, "From CorelDRAW to the World Wide Web."

After you select a color in the Uniform Fill dialog box, click on OK to assign that color to all selected objects.

Fountain Fills

Fountain fills, which fade one color into another, are some of the coolest effects you will apply to an object.

You can define Fountain fills using the Fountain Fill dialog box (the second tool in the Fill tool flyout), or you can use the Special Fill rollup (the last tool in the Fill tool flyout). But the easiest and most intuitive way to define Fountain fills is to use the Interactive Fill tool. In Figure 7.9, I have selected the lion object, and I'm choosing the Interactive Fill tool from the toolbox.

Figure 7.9.

Selecting the Interactive Fill tool.

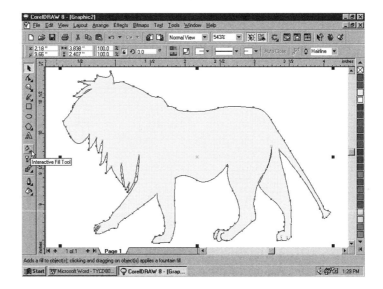

From the Fill Property bar, pull down the Fill Type drop-down menu and select Fountain Fill. When you do, the Property bar displays two different color drop-down menus: the First Fill Picker and the Last Fill Picker. These two drop-down menus define the starting and ending color for your Fountain fill.

Choose a starting and ending color, and then drag from one part of your selected object to another to define the Fountain fill pattern. In Figure 7.10, I've chosen a dark color for my first color and a light color for my end color. I'm using the Interactive Fill tool to drag from the lion's head to his tail, directing the flow of the fill pattern.

Figure 7.10.

Defining a Fountain fill interactively.

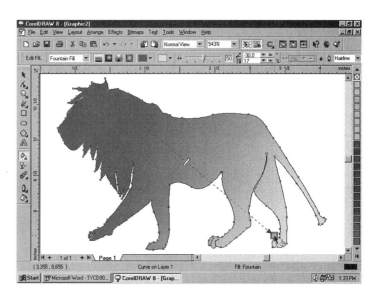

The Fountain Fill Midpoint slider in the Property bar enables you to shift the transition point between your two colors. In Figure 7.11, I've dragged the midpoint far to the left, creating an effect where the ending color fills more of the lion. You can adjust the slider while you have the fill selected, or you can use the Interactive Fill tool again to select the object later to change the slider settings.

 The Fountain Fill Property bar also includes buttons to transform Fountain fills from Linear to (from left to right) Radial, Conical, or Square fills.

 In Figure 7.12, I applied each of the four types of gradient fills to the lions on the top of the page. Then, for the lion on the bottom of the page, I selected a radial fill. To create the radial fill, I drew a line down from the top of the lion to define the fill, and I adjusted the slider on the radius line toward the first (light) colored handle to adjust the flow of the fill in favor of the ending (dark) color.

7

Figure 7.11.
Adjusting the Fountain fill midpoint.

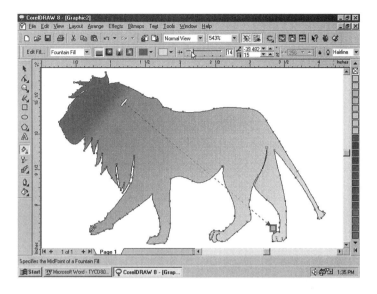

Figure 7.12.
Tweaking a Conical Fountain fill.

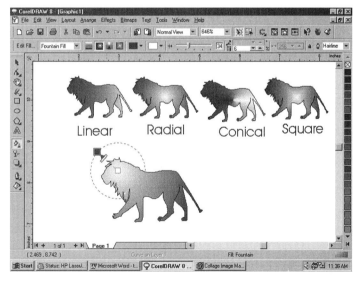

There's really no way to describe the fun of applying and tweaking Fountain fills. Experiment with different colors, using the Linear, Conical, Radial, and Square Fountain fills.

Pattern and Texture Fills

The easiest way to experiment with Pattern and Texture fills is to open the Special Fill dialog box. You can do that from the Fill flyout (it's the last tool) or by choosing View | Rollups | Special fills from the menu bar.

Three tools are in the middle of the Special Fill rollup: From right to left they are the Fountain Fill, Pattern Fill, and Texture Fill tools. The Pattern Fill and Texture Fill tool buttons each open up a different gallery of fill patterns you can apply to selected objects. (The Fountain Fill tool is another way to define Fountain fills.) If you choose the Pattern Fill tool in the Special Fills rollup, you can select from galleries of Two Color, Full Color, or Bitmap images from the drop-down menu.

Each type of fill has a gallery of images that you can choose by clicking on the down button in the bottom half of the rollup. A nice selection of fills is built into CorelDRAW 8; there's no need to create them. In Figure 7.13, I'm choosing one of the Full Color patterns from the gallery of images.

Figure 7.13.

Assigning a Pattern fill.

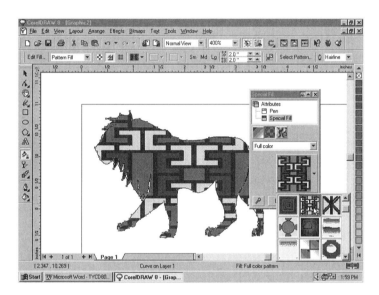

The Texture Fill Tool (the third tool) in the Special Fills rollup shows a list of Texture fills available.

The Edit button in the rollup opens up the Fountain Fill, Pattern Fill, or Texture Fill dialog box, depending on which of the three tools you select in the rollup. Each of those three different dialog boxes enables you to fine-tune each specific fill pattern. Each of these dialog boxes has a Preview button that enables you to test the effects you apply to a fill. In Figure 7.14, I'm using the Preview button to see how my distorted fill will look. When you define just the right fill, click on OK in the Texture Fill dialog box.

After you define a fill, click on the Apply button in the Special Fill rollup to apply that fill to selected objects.

7

Figure 7.14.
You can edit any fill.

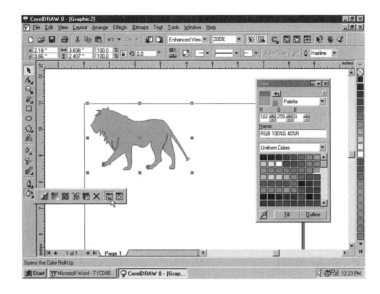

PostScript Fills

You define PostScript fills using the PostScript Texture dialog box. Use the PostScript Texture (fifth) tool in the Fill tool flyout to open that dialog box. The PostScript page description language, which is basically a programming language, creates PostScript fills. They are not easy to edit—and rarely used. You might use a PostScript fill if a graphic image file was given to you in PostScript format, and you were assigned to use it as a fill in an object.

Fill Defaults

You can define a default fill for your drawing by using any of the techniques you learned in this chapter to define a fill. Just define the fill without selecting any objects. This process is similar to defining a default outline that you learned earlier in this hour.

Spot Colors Versus Process Colors

CorelDRAW provides two methods for defining colors that produce their own color palettes on your screen.

☐ Fixed palettes (also referred to as color matching systems or spot colors)

☐ Process color (also referred to as color models or mixed colors)

If you are designing an illustration to appear on your monitor, you don't have to worry about which method you use to define colors. However, if want to print or display your illustration on a web page, you need to figure out a way to tell those output destinations how you want your colors defined.

Fixed palettes (also known as spot colors) are used in printing and to define colors on web sites. Mixed color is also used in color printing. These options are discussed more in Hour 18, "Printing" and web sites Hour 19. But as you work in CorelDRAW, you do have the option of deciding which way you want to define your colors.

Fixed Palettes

Fixed palettes have a number of preset colors. You can create a custom color by mixing these preset colors. When your file is reproduced by a printing process that uses the same fixed color palette you used when you created your image, the final output will match the colors you assign. An example of using a color matching system is when you are designing a two-color brochure. Your printer might tell you that he can handle any spot color you select from the PANTONE color palette. In that case, select your colors from the PANTONE color palette. If your printer allows you to save money by creating your own color separations, explore this process in Hour 10 "Working with Shapes and Curves."

Process Color

Process, or mixed, color models enable you to define colors by combining primary colors or by using systems that attach values to colors. The most popular mixed color model is CMYK, which enables you to mix percentages of Cyan, Magenta, Yellow, and blacK. An example of using the CMYK palette is if you prepare illustrations for four-color printing processes. Again, you can provide your printer with a CorelDRAW file, or you can produce your own color separations for each of the four colors. (Again, you'll learn to create your own color separations in Hour 18.)

JUST A MINUTE

For more information about working with color palettes for web site design, see Hour 19.

When you know which color palette you need to match your output, you can replace the default CorelDRAW 8 palette with one that matches the colors available to you.

Summary

You can define outline and fill properties for any closed object in CorelDRAW 8. Closed objects include shapes. Outlines can be assigned from defined styles or created by customizing an outline style and can be any thickness or color.

7

You can mix any color imaginable and apply it to a color fill. You can also fill objects with Fountain fills that fade from one color to another, or with patterns from a large selection of Pattern fill files. You can edit these Pattern fills to create unique fills for objects.

Workshop

Open and enhance the magazine cover you enhanced in the previous hours by adding special outlines to the objects.

Fill all animals with PANTONE 235CV. This color is available from the PANTONE Matching System palette. Use PANTONE 235 CV as the dark color for all the fills on the magazine cover.

1. Open the document you saved from the workshop in Hour 2.

2. Select the first square (behind bear) and apply a Linear Fountain fill using a start color of PANTONE 235CV (or a brown) and an end color white. Use the Interactive Fill tool to place the fill at an angle.

3. Duplicate the square with the Fountain fill, and place it behind each animal at the top of the page.

4. Modify Zoo Review Title by assigning an angled Fountain fill, as shown in Figure 7.15.

Figure 7.15.

Assigning a Fountain fill to text.

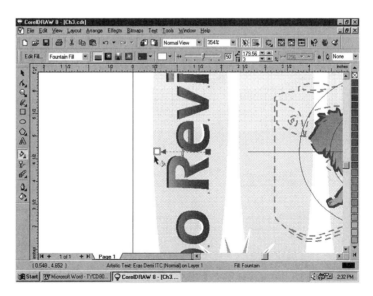

5. Assign a radial Fountain fill to the background ellipses, as shown in Figure 7.16.

Figure 7.16.

Assigning a Conical fill to the top of the back-ground ellipses.

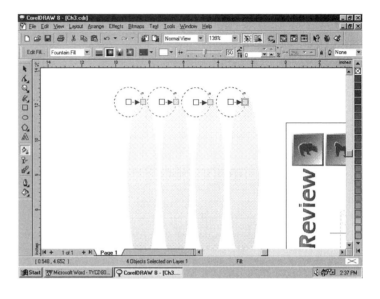

TIME SAVER

In Figure 7.16, I dragged all the ellipses off the Drawing page so that you can see the Conical Fountain fill more clearly. Another tip: You can select all the ellipses and apply the Fountain fill to them all at once.

6. Modify the fill for the camera in the background by defining no fill. The camera with an invisible fill is shown in Figure 7.17.

Figure 7.17.

Camera with no fill.

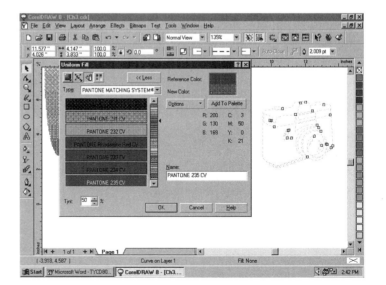

7

7. Fill the lion with a Linear Fountain fill, starting with white and ending with a dark color. See Figure 7.18 for ideas on how to set the Fountain fill angle and midpoint.

Figure 7.18.

The Fountain fill midpoint for the lion set at 89.

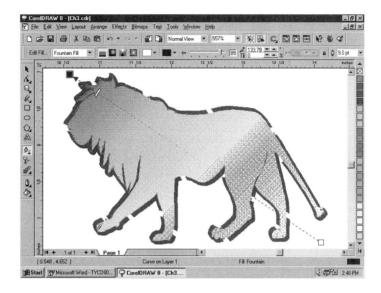

Figure 7.19.

Adding a Conical Fountain fill.

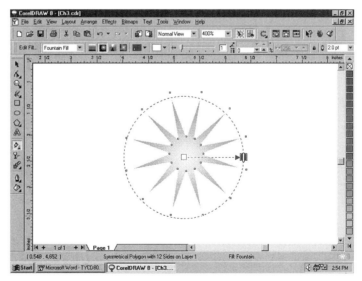

8. Define a dark outline (you can choose Other from the color drop-down menu and pick PANTONE 235 CV) for the lion with a width to 9 points. Set a dashed line (11th selection on style) and select behind fill.

9. Experiment with adding Radial fills and Texture fill patterns to the 12-sided polygon/star(s) in the illustration, as shown in Figure 7.19. Try cranking the Fountain fill midpoint all the way down to 1.

10. Save your figure so that you can use it again in the next lesson.

Quiz

1. How do you define a default fill?

2. How do you define a Fountain fill path?

3. Can a pattern be used for a fill?

4. What are three popular methods for defining mixed colors in CorelDRAW 8?

5. How do you select a color palette?

Quiz Answers

1. To define a default fill, define a fill with no objects selected.

2. You can define the trajectory of a Fountain Fill using the Interactive Fill tool.

3. Yes—you can apply Pattern fills from the Special Fills rollup.

4. You can define mixed colors using CMYK, HSV, or RGB settings.

5. You can assign a color palette by selecting View | Color Palette from the menu bar and then selecting a palette.

Hour 8

Draw and Edit Freehand Curves

You can use freehand curves to draw designs on your screen in CorelDRAW 8. Even skilled artists find it difficult to draw complex designs with a mouse, but the ability to add to or enhance a design with freehand curves is a powerful tool in creating illustrations.

In Figure 8.1, you can see a few uses for freehand lines. The mountains in the logo were drawn freehand and then edited and filled. The shape surrounding the lizard was drawn freehand. And even the letters "TE" were touched up using freehand drawing editing tools.

Freehand curves are drawn with the Freehand Drawing tool. This tool is part of a flyout that also includes the Bézier tool, the Natural Pen tool, the Dimension tool, and the Connector Line tool. These tools are shown in Figure 8.2.

Figure 8.1.

You can use freehand lines many ways in illustrations.

Figure 8.2.

The Freehand tool flyout.

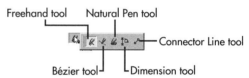

The Natural Pen tool is similar to the Freehand tool, except that it draws a "filled-in" line. You can adjust the width at different parts of the line. In Figure 8.3, I drew the first letter of my name with the Natural Pen tool and tweaked the thickness of the resulting "line," which is really a shape.

Figure 8.3.

The Natural Pen tool draws lines that are shapes.

In this Lesson, you focus on the Freehand Line tool. To be honest, nobody draws great-looking shapes with a mouse or even a more sophisticated computer drawing device. The trick is to sketch out a crude drawing that is close to what you want, and then touch it up by editing the resulting nodes.

Because nodes are very powerful, you will explore different aspects of them in this lesson, and in the next two lessons as well.

Don't become frustrated trying to draw smooth, gracious curves with the Freehand tool. That's not going to happen. Your shapes will turn out nicely as you learn to edit nodes.

JUST A MINUTE

There are other tools in the Freehand flyout in addition to the Natural Pen tool. The dimension tools, which are for adding measurements to objects for technical drawings or for callouts, are beyond the scope of this book. You'll spend a whole lesson on the Bézier tool in the flyout in Hour 9, "Creating Bézier Curves."

JUST A MINUTE

Draw Freehand Curves

In Hour 1 of this book, you learned to draw straight lines by clicking once, holding down the Ctrl key, and clicking and clicking again. With that technique, you can draw horizontal or vertical lines, or lines at 15-degree increment angles (such as 45 degrees or 30 degrees). You also learned to create objects composed of several line segments by double-clicking to add new nodes to your object.

The process of drawing freehand curves is more freestyle. You simply click on the Freehand tool and then click and draw on the Drawing area. As previously mentioned, your first, and even 100th, attempts are not likely to produce smooth and elegant curves. That's okay. Try drawing a curved line such as the one in Figure 8.4 for practice.

Figure 8.4.

Freehand lines never look good before you touch up the curves.

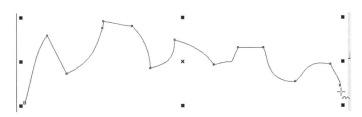

After you draw a curved line, you can apply any outline attribute to that curve. Refer to Hour 6, "Defining Outlines," to refresh your outline skills.

8.1: Draw and Shape a Curved Line

To Do

1. Draw a freehand curve.
2. Select the Pen rollup from the Outline Pen flyout.
3. Choose a thick line width in the Line Width slider (looks like a vertical scrollbar).
4. Choose a dashed line from the Line Style drop-down list.
5. Click on the Apply button in the Pen rollup.

In Figure 8.5, I've defined a custom dashed line and line thickness, and applied it to my freehand curve.

Figure 8.5.

You can apply any outline attributes to a curved line.

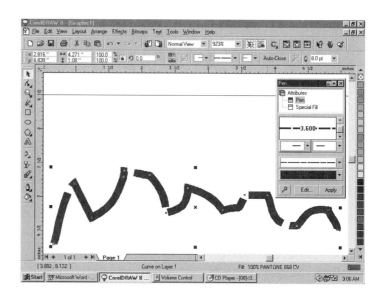

Closed Curves

You can transform curves into closed curves. These closed curve objects can have fills assigned to them. Sometimes it is difficult to tell if an object is a closed curve. One way to tell is to look at the Property bar and see if the Auto-Close button is grayed out. If the button is grayed out, your curve is already closed.

You can also tell if a curve is closed by selecting it and checking the Curve Property bar. If the Auto-Close button is available, the curve is not closed.

Manually Close Curved Objects

You can create a closed curved object by having the curve end where it started. For example, if you try your best to draw a circle, it might not look too round, but if you end at the point where you started to draw, your circle will be a closed object.

8

CorelDRAW assists you a bit in creating closed objects. If you come pretty close to ending your curve at the starting point, CorelDRAW will assume you wanted to end exactly where you started and close your object.

Later in this lesson, when you start to use the Shape tool, you'll learn to convert closed curves to curves that are not closed.

Auto-Close Curves

If you have a curve that you want to convert to a closed object, you can use the Auto-Close button in the Property bar. To do this, select a curved object and click on Auto-Close in the Property bar. That's it! The first and last point (or *node*) in the curve automatically connects with a straight line.

Figure 8.6 shows two different curved lines that I transformed into closed curves. Each of the closed curves has a fill applied.

Figure 8.6.

Any curve can be closed using Auto-Close.

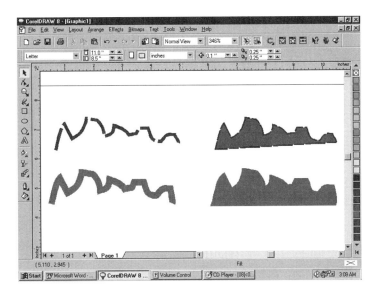

Edit Curve Nodes

You have already seen how every selected object displays eight handles. These black squares on the corners and sides of a selected object enable you to resize the object by pulling on them.

Selected objects also display much smaller control points called *nodes*. These nodes enable you to edit the shape of a selected object with tremendous detail. In this lesson, you learn to use nodes to edit the shape of curves and to edit text in micro-detail.

Some node editing is possible using the Pick tool, whereas more complex node editing requires the Shape tool. In this next section, you start by editing nodes using the Pick tool.

Examine Nodes

When you select a single object and examine it closely, you see tiny nodes. These nodes are smaller than the handles around the selected object and are only visible when you select one object.

Another difference between nodes and handles is that nodes actually appear on the outline of the actual shape or curve, whereas handles appear on the corners and sides of a rectangle around the object.

Nodes do different things under different conditions. They behave differently in Artistic Text, shapes, and curves. Here you learn to edit nodes on curves and artistic text. For now, you need to know that every shape has nodes. When you draw a shape, CorelDRAW automatically generates nodes and curves that, together, compose your object.

In Figure 8.7, you can see that my somewhat crudely drawn lizard is composed of many nodes that separate curves. Together, these curves and nodes make up the curved object.

Figure 8.7.

Every curve is broken up by nodes.

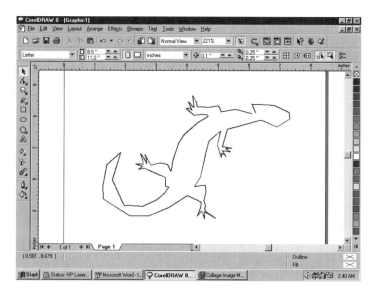

If you click on the Curve tab in the Object Properties dialog box, you can see whether your curve is closed, as shown in Figure 8.8.

8

Figure 8.8.

Counting nodes in the Object Properties dialog box.

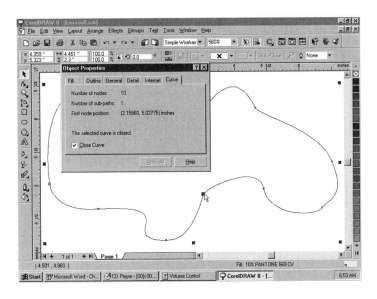

Edit Nodes

The first step in editing a node is to select it by clicking on the node with the Pick tool.

You can move a selected node by dragging on it. In Figure 8.9, I am dragging one of the lizard's nodes and, in the process, reshaping the lizard.

Figure 8.9.

Reshaping a curve by dragging a node.

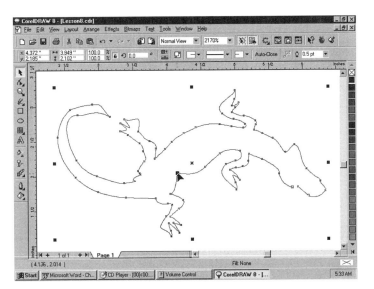

Add and Delete Nodes

You can add and delete nodes by right-clicking on a node with the Pick tool and choosing Add or Delete from the shortcut menu that appears. In Figure 8.10, I am adding a node to my curve.

Figure 8.10.

Adding a node to a curve.

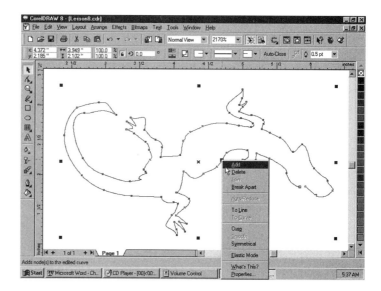

By adding or deleting nodes and moving them around, you can tweak the shape of your freehand drawing.

Edit Artistic Text Nodes

Text nodes behave differently than curve nodes; for example, you cannot edit them using the Pick tool. However, if you select an artistic text object with the Shape tool, you can edit individual text nodes, and you can control spacing between characters.

Edit Text Spacing

Selecting Artistic Text with the Shape tool also displays the vertical and horizontal shape-sizing handles. The vertical shape-sizing handle appears on the left edge of the selected text, and the horizontal shape-sizing handle appears on the right of the selected text (see Figure 8.11).

The vertical shape-sizing handle is only useful if you have more than one line of text. If you do, the vertical sizing handle increases line spacing when it is pulled down and compresses spacing when it is pushed up.

8

Figure 8.11.
Shape-sizing handles.

You can expand the spacing between letters by dragging the horizontal shape-sizing handle to the right or compress letter spacing by dragging it to the left. In Figure 8.12, I've stretched out the letter spacing.

Figure 8.12.
Increasing spacing between characters.

You can also edit the horizontal and vertical location of individual characters with the Shape tool. When you drag on the node attached to any characters (the node to the left of the character), you can move it. In Figure 8.13, I am rearranging my text.

Figure 8.13.

Move individual artistic text characters using the Shape tool.

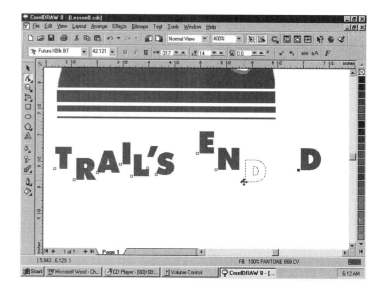

Convert Text to Curves

You can edit the shape of individual text characters by transforming text to curves. After you do that, you can no longer edit the content of the text in the Text Edit dialog box. But you can reshape individual characters.

8.2: Editing the Shape of Text Characters

1. Type artistic text. I like to use a very solid, thick font such as Impact if I am going to edit the shape of characters.

2. Select the Pick tool, then right-click on the text, and choose Convert to Curves from the shortcut menu.

3. If you want to edit each character as a separate object (useful if you want to move them in relation to each other), select Arrange | Break Apart from the menu bar.

4. Click on one of your characters if you have broken your text object apart.

5. After you convert text to curves, you can use the Pick tool to reshape the text by dragging the nodes. In Figure 8.14, I am reshaping the letter "E."

Summary

By combining freehand lines and editing nodes, you can create curves from scratch. Your first try to draw a freehand line will be crude, but CorelDRAW offers many options for editing your drawing.

Figure 8.14.
Reshaping text.

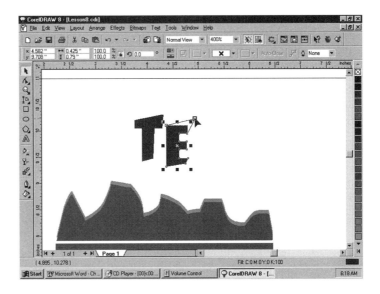

Selected objects have handles that you explored in earlier hours. They also have nodes. You can move curve nodes using the Pick tool, to edit the shape of a selected object.

Artistic text nodes move the location of individual characters. Use the shape-sizing handles to edit text spacing.

Workshop

Create the beginning of a logo such as the one in Figure 8.15.

Figure 8.15.
Try creating this logo with the Freehand and Shape tools.

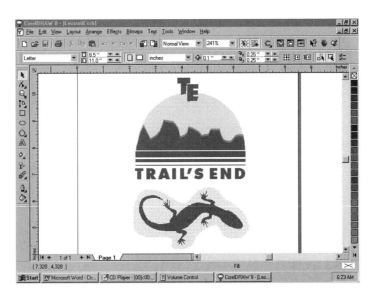

1. Use the Freehand tool to create the mountain silhouette.
2. Use the Auto-Close button to transform the mountain into a closed shape.
3. Assign a fill to the mountains.
4. Draw some horizontal lines under the mountains.
5. Create the sun in the background of the logo by drawing an ellipse, converting the circle to an arc, and moving the arc to the back of the other objects. (Review Hour 3 to remember how to draw arcs.) Assign a yellow fill to the sun.
6. Create the "Trails End" Artistic text, and use the shape-sizing handle to stretch the space between characters.
7. Create the "TE" logo by starting with artistic text. Convert the text to a curve, and customize the shape and location of the letters using the Shape tool.
8. Create the lizard by using characters #77 from the Animals font set. (Lesson 2 covers the use of symbols.)
9. Create a contour around the lizard with the Freehand Drawing tool.
10. Touch up the contour around the lizard by moving nodes.
11. Assign a thick line width to the contour around the lizard.
12. Touch up the logo with your own touches.

Quiz

1. How do you expand the spacing between letters?
2. How can you tell if a curve is closed?
3. How do you create a closed curved object while you are drawing it with the Freehand tool?
4. How do you add and delete nodes to or from an object?
5. How do you convert artistic text to curves? And why would you want to? What's the drawback in converting text to curves?

Quiz Answers

1. You can expand the spacing between letters by dragging the horizontal shape-sizing handle to the right.
2. You can tell if a curve is closed by selecting it and checking the Curve Property bar. If the Auto-Close button is available, the curve is not closed.
3. You can create a closed curved object by having the curve end where it started.
4. You can add and delete nodes by right-clicking on a node with the Pick tool, and choosing Add or Delete from the shortcut menu that appears.
5. Right-click on the text and choose Convert to Curves from the shortcut menu. After you convert text to curves, you can edit the shape of individual text characters. You cannot, however, edit the content of artistic text in the Edit Text dialog box after you convert it to curves.

8

Hour 9

Bézier Curves

Create Bézier Curves

There are two main drawing tools in CorelDRAW: the Freehand tool and the Bézier tool. The Bézier tool is named after a French engineer who developed a system of mathematically generated curves.

The Bézier tool behaves differently than the Freehand tool by creating curves composed of many line segments. In Hour 1 you learned to create multisegmented lines using the Freehand tool, but it was necessary to double-click each time you wanted to add a node. The process of creating multisegmented lines with the Bézier tool is much easier, as you will see in this lesson.

The real power of the Bézier tool comes from drawing smooth curves. Just like your experience with the Freehand tool in Hour 8, you'll find that wielding the Bézier tool to draw curves is awkward and challenging. However, just like designs drawn with the Freehand tool, you can easily move nodes around to adjust the curves you draw.

One of the fun things you can do with the generated curves is use them as paths for text. In Figure 9.1, I fit text to a curve and then delete the curve.

Figure 9.1.
You can fit text to a curve and then delete the curve.

In Figure 9.2, you can see how Paul Mikulecky used parallel Bézier curves in the background of his illustration, combined with text fit to a curve.

Figure 9.2.
Paul's Trail's End logo combines parallel Bézier curves and text fit to a curve.

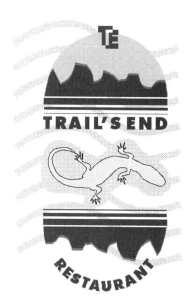

Trace with the Bézier Tool

Nobody can draw nice, smooth freehand drawings with the Freehand tool. As you have already seen, the goal is to create a rough sketch and then enhance that by editing node location.

The Bézier tool makes it easier to draw more detailed sketches. You can draw straight lines with the Bézier tool by clicking once, and then clicking a second time. The result is a straight line between the two nodes.

9

9.1: Use the Bézier Curve Tool to Trace the Lizard Symbol

1. Open the Symbols Docker window (click on the star-shaped tool in the toolbar). Select the Animals1 font set, and drag the lizard onto the Drawing window.

2. Select the Bézier tool from the Freehand flyout; it's the second tool in the flyout.

3. With the Bézier tool, you can continue to click and add nodes as long as you want. There's no need to double-click.

4. When you finish creating your shape, press the Spacebar on your keyboard. That ends your Bézier drawing and selects the Pick tool.

If you want to finish drawing a Bézier curve and start a new one, you can press the Spacebar twice.

In Figure 9.3, I used the Bézier tool to trace the lizard.

Figure 9.3.

The Bézier tool is useful for tracing because it's easy to add nodes to curves.

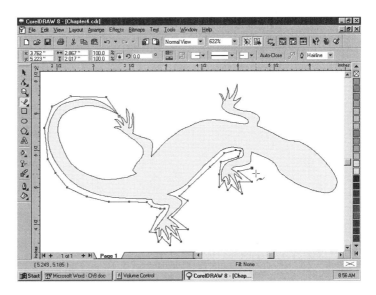

You can edit nodes while you add line segments with the Bézier tool. Just hold down the Alt key and edit existing nodes. In Figure 9.4, I'm moving a node.

Draw Curves with the Bézier Tool

You generate curves with the Bézier tool by selecting key points and directions for the curve. The key to having fun with Bézier curves is to remember that they can be edited. Bézier curves can be resized and rotated, so don't worry about the size or wavelength of your Bézier curve when you generate it.

Figure 9.4.

Hold down Alt to edit nodes while drawing Bézier curves.

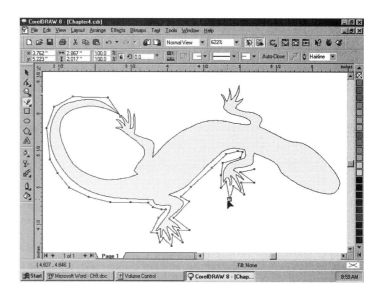

Bézier curves are also not the way to draw a complex shape. To do that, define the rough outline for the shape or curve, and then edit nodes. In Hour 10, "Editing Shapes and Curves," you'll learn to edit the curve nodes so that you don't need to worry about when you generate Bézier curves.

The most commonly used Bézier curve is a basic wave. Waves are easy to edit, but it's helpful when you create them to make them symmetrical. One way to do that is to utilize the Snap to Object feature to locate wave nodes that are evenly spaced.

9.2: Draw a Wave

1. Draw a rectangle (using the Rectangle tool).

2. Select the Bézier tool from the toolbox.

3. From the Layout menu, turn on Snap to Objects.

4. Draw with the Bézier tool from the top-left corner of the rectangle to the bottom-left corner, as I'm doing in Figure 9.5.

5. Next, drag from the top-right corner of the rectangle to the bottom, I'm doing as in Figure 9.6, to finish the curve.

6. After you finish the curve, press the Spacebar to select the Pick tool.

7. Because the whole point of the rectangle was to provide a fixture to keep the curve symmetrical, delete it.

9

Figure 9.5.

Step one in drawing a symmetrical Bézier curve.

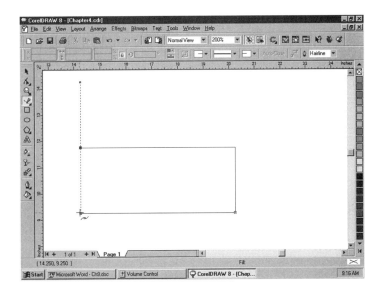

Figure 9.6.

Finishing a wave-like curve.

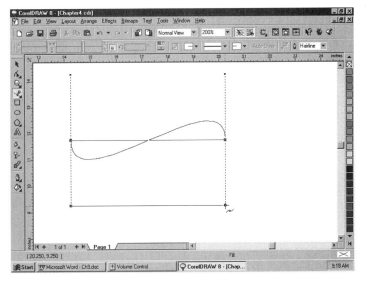

JUST A MINUTE

After you create a wave-like curve, you can rotate it 45 degrees or 90 degrees. You can compress it to make the curves steeper or stretch it to make the curve smoother. You can flip the curves horizontally or vertically, and match them next to each other. (See Figure 9.7.)

Figure 9.7.

Many ways to use a wave.

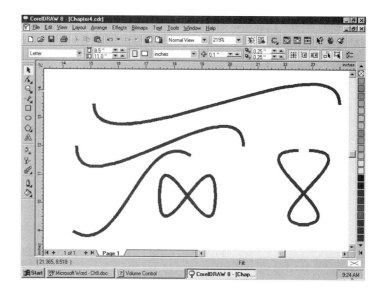

Editing Bézier Curves

You can edit an existing Bézier curve with either the Shape tool or the Pick tool. Resizing a curve with the Pick tool has a different effect than moving nodes with the Shape tool. Experiment with both. Resizing with the Pick tool creates less radical changes in the curve structure. Moving nodes with the Shape tool radically reforms the curve. However, if you create a symmetrical curve (using my "in a rectangle" trick), that symmetry will be maintained as you reshape your curve with either the Pick or the Shape tool. In Figure 9.8, I'm using the Pick tool to compress the curve.

Figure 9.9 shows the more radical change produced by using the Shape tool to compress the curve by dragging in on a node.

You can further expand your wave options by copying waves and organizing them into parallel lines or placing them next to each other to create continuous waves.

Fit Text to Paths

You can use a shape or path that you create as a baseline for text. In Figure 9.10, I've taken the text "Trail's End" and fit it to a path.

There are two options for fitting text to a path. You can type the text directly on a shape or curve or you can take existing text and apply it to a curve.

9

Figure 9.8.

You can preview the changes you make to a curve before you release the mouse button.

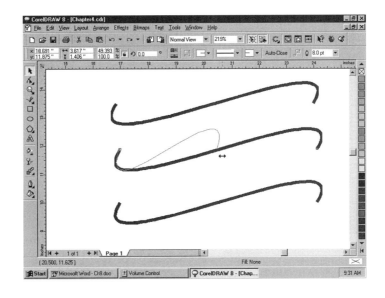

Figure 9.9.

Use the Shape tool to radically revise your curve.

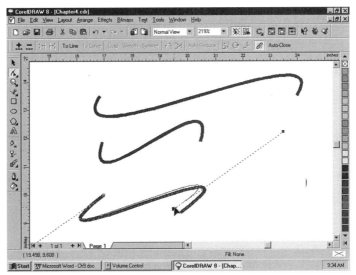

Type Text on a Path

To type text on a path, the first step is to create the shape or curve to which you will be fitting the text. The path can be any shape, but you should size and edit the shape or curve before you apply text to it.

Figure 9.10.

Text fitted to a Bézier curve.

Then, with the shape or curve selected, choose Text | Fit Text to Path from the menu bar. When you do that, the Text Property bar becomes active. Select a text font and size (and other text attributes) from the Text Property bar.

After you assign text properties, start typing. Your cursor automatically attaches to the shape or curve you selected. The text appears centered on top of the shape or curve you selected, as you see in Figure 9.11.

Figure 9.11.

Typing text on a shape.

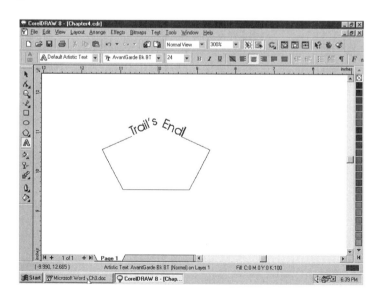

9

Your text might not end up exactly the way you want it to look in relation to the curve or shape. You have many options for changing the position of your text, which you'll learn them in the section "Align Text on Paths," later in this hour.

Attach Text to a Path

You can type text directly on a shape or curve, but you can also attach existing text to a path. All you need is text and a curve or shape.

9.3: Attach Text to a Curve

1. Type some text (a couple words) and draw a curve.
2. Select the text object. Then hold down Shift so that you can select two objects at once, and click to select the curve or shape to which you will be fitting the text. In Figure 9.12, a multisegmented line curve and a text object are selected.

Figure 9.12.

With text and curve objects selected, I am ready to fit the text to the curve.

3. With both the text and path object selected, choose Text | Fit Text to Path in the menu bar.
4. When you attach existing text to a path, you're likely to find an uncomfortable match. The text might not display on the part of the path you want, or it might be too close to the path. You can correct this and other options with the Fit Text to Path Property bar that becomes active after you attach text to a shape or curve.

In Figure 9.13, my text does not fit on the path well, but the Property bar has appeared that will let me fix it. When you select text fitted to a curve, a Property bar appears with buttons that help you adjust the text. In the next section of this hour, I'll show you how to use those tools to adjust your text so it fits better on your curve.

Figure 9.13.

This text needs to be realigned on the path using the Property bar.

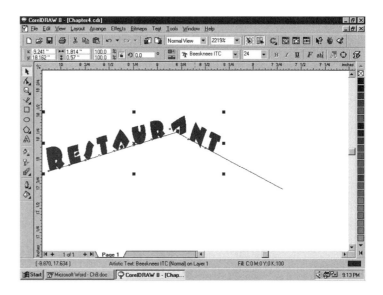

Align Text on Paths

The Property bar that appears when you select text fitted to a path provides several options—such as centering your text on the curve—for controlling the relationship between your text and the path.

When you attach text to shapes or curves, the text sometimes appears upside down or on the wrong side of the path. That's what happened in Figure 9.14.

You can move text from one side of a path to the other by selecting the fitted text and then clicking on the Place Text on Other Side button in the Property bar.

After you place the text on the proper side of the path, you can choose from one of four Text Orientation options from the first pull-down menu in the Property bar.

JUST A MINUTE

Select an Orientation option before you start worrying about the placement and alignment of your text. Different orientation styles will sit differently on your path, and you can determine how you want the text to display before you align it.

9

Figure 9.14.

Don't turn the book upside down! This text needs to be placed on the other side of the path.

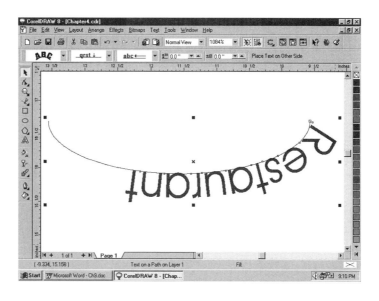

The four Orientation options display when you select your fitted text and pull down the first menu in the Property bar. You can see these options in Figure 9.15.

Figure 9.15.

Text Orientation options require experimenting; you can't tell what they will look like from the drop-down menu.

With your fitted text selected, choose one of the Orientation options. These options have different effects, depending on the text size and font you select and the path to which you apply text. So experiment with all them until you see which one works best for your text.

After you decide on a Text Orientation, you can define the vertical and horizontal alignment of your text in relation to the path. The Vertical Placement drop-down list offers different options depending on the Text Orientation you selected. For simple Text Orientation (the first option in the Text Orientation list), you can align text above or below the path and use "in between" options as well. Other Text Orientation options only enable you to place text on top of a curve. In Figure 9.16, I'm moving text below my curve.

Figure 9.16.

Some text works beneath a path.

With Text Orientation and Vertical Placement selected, you can use the Text Placement drop-down menu to left-align, center, or right-align your text. In Figure 9.17, I'm centering text on a path.

The Distance From Path and Horizontal Offset spin boxes enable you to fine-tune the relationship between your text and the path to achieve just the effect you want. The Distance From Path defines vertical spacing. You can move your text above (with positive values in the box) or below your path.

The Horizontal Offset spin boxes enable you to shift text right or left along your path. In Figure 9.18, I shifted the text to the right of center with a positive value in the Horizontal Offset box, and I increased the space between the text and the path by entering a positive value in the Distance From Path box.

Figure 9.17.
Text centered on a path.

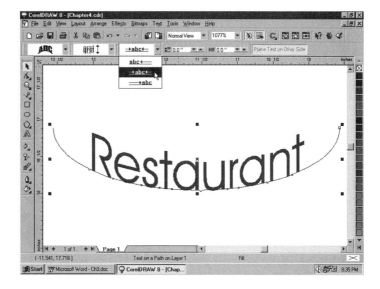

Figure 9.18.
The fun starts when you fine-tune the relationship between fitted text and its path.

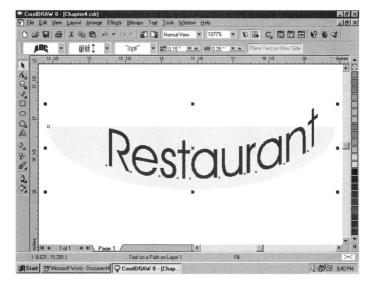

Stretching and Shaping Curved Text

As if the Property bar didn't offer options enough for fitted text, you can transform the look of your fitted text by editing the resulting objects. The following list provides you with some techniques to experiment with. Begin by deleting the path, leaving just the text, as I've done in Figure 9.l9.

Figure 9.19.

After you fit text to a path, you can delete the curve or shape to which the text was fitted.

☐ Select the text with the Shape tool, and use the shape-sizing handle to adjust the spacing of the text. In Figure 9.20, I'm stretching the spacing between characters.

Figure 9.20.

Just because you have fitted text to a path doesn't mean you can't apply the shaping techniques you learned in Lesson 8.

☐ You can also use the Shape tool to select the node for single characters and move them on or off the path to which you have fixed the text. (See Figure 9.21.)

Summary

You can use the Bézier tool for drawings that the Freehand tool doesn't handle well—including outlining objects and drawing waves. Drawing curves with the Bézier tool is not intuitive. Instead of drawing the curve itself, you generate calculated curves by placing nodes and drawing control lines that determine the height of the curve.

You can fit text to curves you design with the Bézier tool or to any shape. Fine-tune fitted text to create interesting effects.

9

Figure 9.21.

*When you kern indi-
vidual characters with
the Shape tool, you can
move apostrophes (')to
spaces above characters
and off the fitted path.*

Workshop

In this workshop, you add Bézier curves to the background of the restaurant logo you designed in Hour 8.

1. Create one wave using the Bézier tool. (You can use the trick you learned in the "Draw a Curve" To Do exercise in this lesson.) Assign a thick line style to the wave and a light outline color.

2. Take the text from the logo and fit it to a circle. Use the centering option in the Text Placement drop-down list in the Property bar to center the text on the curve. Experiment with other Property bar options to fit the text to the curve.

3. Create a lizard for the logo, if you don't have one from the previous hour, by selecting #77 from Animals font symbols. Rotate the lizard so that it is horizontal with the head facing to right. Assign an appropriate (light colored) fill.

4. Create a contour around the lizard using the Bézier tool. With the Bézier tool selected, click around the lizard to form the contour. Assign a thick, light-colored outline to the contour.

5. Move objects to the front or back as necessary. Paul's logo, in Figure 9.22, will provide you with some inspiration as you fine-tune and finish your logo.

Figure 9.22.

Paul's restaurant illustration uses Bézier curves and text fitted to a shape.

Quiz

1. Where do you find the Bézier tool?
2. What are two main drawing tools in CorelDRAW?
3. How do you draw a straight line with the Bézier tool?
4. How do you move text from one side of a path to the other?
5. How do you center text on a path? Or right- or left-align it?

Quiz Answers

1. Select the Bézier tool from the Freehand flyout—the second tool in the flyout.
2. There are two main drawing tools in CorelDRAW: the Freehand tool and the Bézier tool.
3. You can draw straight lines with the Bézier tool by clicking once and then clicking a second time. The result is a straight line between the two nodes.
4. You can move text from one side of a path to the other by selecting the fitted text, and then clicking on the Place Text on Other Side button in the Property bar.
5. With Text Orientation and Vertical Placement selected, you can use the Text Placement drop-down menu to left-align, center or right-align your text.

Hour 10

Working with Shapes and Curves

Many CorelDRAW illustrators start by creating rough sketches of their drawings with shapes and then refining them to create the exact image they want to produce. For example, the sailboat and waves in Figure 10.1 were created by starting with simple triangles.

You've already seen that you can resize shapes using sizing handles. But you can also edit shapes by moving nodes or by using the Knife or Erase tools.

You can do much more with shapes by converting them into curves. You can edit curve nodes in minute detail and define different types of curves to produce any shape you want.

Editing Shapes

When you click on a shape (an ellipse, a rectangle, or a polygon) with the Shape tool, nodes appear. Rectangles have four nodes, one for each corner. Polygons have a node for each side, and one for each point as you can see in Figure 10.2.

Figure 10.1.
The triangle converted into a curve and edited to define the curve.

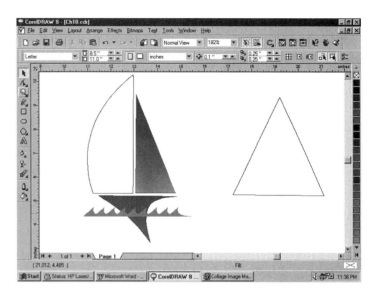

Figure 10.2.
Pentagons have five nodes.

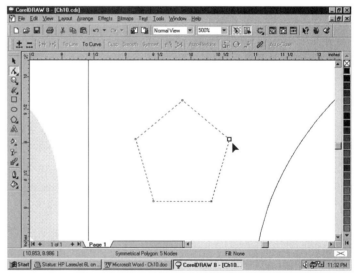

Editing Ellipse Nodes

You started to explore editing shape nodes in Hour 3. Rectangle and polygon nodes are used to edit the appearance of the shape. Ellipses, however, are a special case. Ellipses have an infinite number of sides (theoretically, an ellipse is just points). Ellipses have just one node. You can move this node to create an arc. To do that, drag clockwise or counter-clockwise on the node, as shown in Figure 10.3.

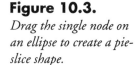

Figure 10.3.

Drag the single node on an ellipse to create a pie-slice shape.

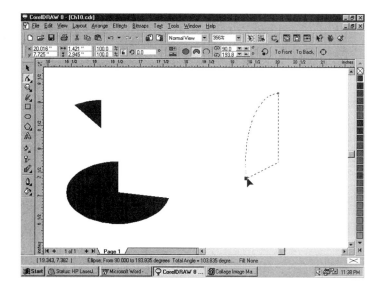

Moving Shape Nodes

You can move the nodes on rectangles and polygons to change the shape of the polygon. Dragging down on the corner handles of a rectangle "rounds" the corners, as you can see in Figure 10.4. Or you can drag up on a bottom corner node to round a rectangle.

Of course, if you can settle for the amount of rounding that comes automatically with a rounded rectangle shape, that's quicker. But by moving corner nodes, you can assign the exact amount of rounding you want to a corner.

Figure 10.4.

Use the Shape tool to drag down and round nodes on the corners of a rectangle.

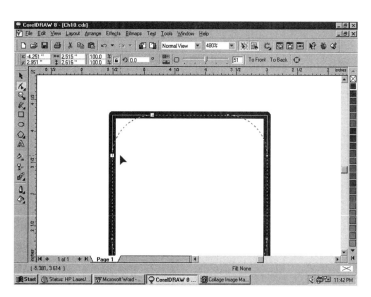

You can custom-transform polygons into stars by dragging on the side or corner nodes. In Figure 10.5, I'm transforming a pentagon into a kind of warped star by dragging on one of the side handles.

Figure 10.5.
When you drag on a side node in a shape, all side nodes move symmetrically—this is true for point nodes as well.

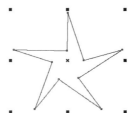

Editing with the Knife Tool

The Knife tool is one of the more descriptively named weapons in the toolbar. It can cut objects in two! The basic routine is that you click twice on an object to make "incision points," and those points become a line that divides your object into two, new objects.

The Knife and Eraser tools are on the Shape tool flyout. You select them by clicking on the Shape tool and holding down the mouse button while you click on either the Knife (the second tool) or the Eraser (the third tool).

JUST A MINUTE

The fourth tool on the Shape tool flyout is the Free Transform tool. This tool (new to CorelDRAW 8) is outside the scope of this lesson, but it enables you to rotate selected objects. The Free Transform tool works like Rotation handles (that you get when you click twice on an object), but you can assign a center of rotation by clicking on any node or point on the screen. To experiment with the Free Transform tool, click on an object with the Pick tool, click somewhere outside the object on your screen, and drag the rotation bar to rotate the object.

10.1: Cutting Shapes with the Knife Tool

As usual with CorelDRAW, you can accomplish a task in many ways. Any shape you create with the Knife tool can also be designed by editing a shape. But sometimes, the Knife tool is easier to use. For example, cutting off the top of a triangle is an easy way to create a trapezoid. Or if you want two shapes to "fit together" and be complementary, you can use the Knife tool to cut one shape in half.

To use the Knife tool to cut a shape into two or more parts:

1. Select Knife tool from the Shape tool flyout.
2. Click at a point on a shape that you want to cut.

10

3. Click a second time at the endpoint of the cut. In Figure 10.6, I am cutting a triangle in half, vertically.

4. After you cut your shape, use the Pick tool to select either of the two new shapes you created. You can drag to move either of the two objects, or delete one of them.

Figure 10.6.

Dissecting a triangle with the Knife tool.

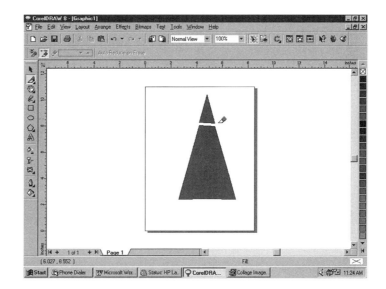

JUST A MINUTE

When you select the Knife tool, the Auto-Close on Cut button is automatically selected in the Property bar. This is the button you want if you are cutting up shapes. The (also available) Leave as One Object button is not that useful if you want to cut up objects with the Knife tool. With the Auto-Close on Cut button selected, you create two shapes from one with the Knife tool. Turning this button off changes the Knife tool so that it cuts the object but creates a nonclosed curve (a line) instead of a new shape.

Erasing Pixels

The Eraser tool is also located on the Shapes flyout and works like an eraser on a pencil. You can erase any pixel within an object, down to the smallest dot. The Eraser Property bar has a spin box that you can use to change the width of the eraser.

After you select the Eraser tool, you can delete pixels you don't want. In Figure 10.7, I'm deleting lines in the middle of a polygon/star.

Figure 10.7.

The Eraser tool is often handy when you want to clean up the middle of a polygon/star.

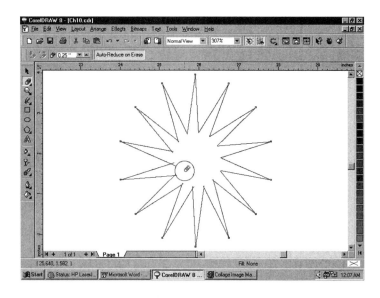

If you accidentally erase more than you want to, click on the Undo button in the toolbar.

JUST A MINUTE

Transforming Shapes to Curves

As you have seen, you can edit shapes by moving shape nodes, by using the Knife tool, or by erasing with the Eraser tool. To have total control over a shape, however, you need to convert it into a curve.

To Curve   When you select a shape node with the Shape tool, a To Curve button appears on the Property bar. Click on that button to transform your shape into a curve. You can convert all the nodes in a shape to a curve by selecting the shape with the Pick tool and then choosing Arrange | Convert to Curves from the menu bar.

Why convert shape nodes to curves? You have seen that when you edit a node in a shape, you also affect other nodes in the shape. That can be handy when you convert a pentagon into a starfish. But what if you want to edit a single node and only have your editing affect that one node? For this, you need to convert the shape into a curve.

Curve nodes can also be edited much more powerfully than Shape nodes. Curve nodes can be of different types and can be fine-tuned to create complex shapes, as you will see in the next section of this hour.

10

Editing Curves

Before you can edit curves, you select nodes. Earlier you learned to select nodes using the Shape tool. With the Shape tool selected, you can click on individual nodes to select them. If you hold down Shift while you click, you can select more than one node at a time.

You can also select all nodes in an object. This is handy when you want to convert every node in a shape to a curve.

10.2: Converting Object Nodes to Curves

To Do

1. Select the shape using the Shape tool (not the Pick tool).
2. Draw a marquee around the shape using the Shape tool.
3. Click on the To Curve button in the Property bar as in Figure 10.8.

Figure 10.8.

After I convert all nodes in this shape to curves; I can fine-tune curve radii and shapes.

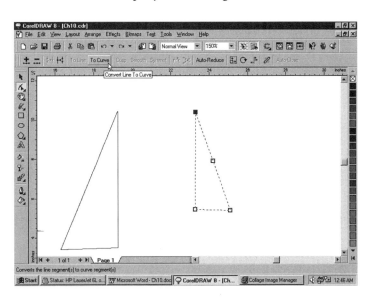

JUST A MINUTE

If you created your object as a shape, you don't have to convert it to a curve; the nodes are already all set to edit.

Add and Delete Nodes

When you select an object with the Shape tool, you can add nodes by clicking anywhere on the shape and then clicking on the + (plus) symbol in the Property bar. You can delete nodes by clicking on a node and then clicking on the - (minus) symbol in the Property bar.

You can delete extraneous nodes in a curve (ones that don't contribute anything to the curve's shape) by selecting all nodes in the curve and clicking on the Auto-Reduce button in the Property bar.

After you learn to edit individual nodes, you'll appreciate the usefulness of getting rid of unnecessary nodes that clutter up your drawing. In Figure 10.9, I've converted a star to a curve, and I'm using Auto-Delete to get ride of unneeded nodes.

Figure 10.9.

Deleting unneeded nodes with Auto-Delete will not affect the shape of a curve. Here Auto-Delete will get rid of five of the nodes cluttering up my drawing.

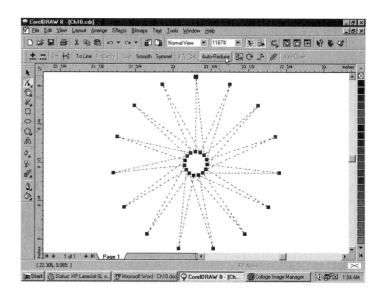

Defining Node Types

CorelDRAW offers three types of curve nodes: Cusp nodes, Smooth nodes, and Symmetrical nodes, which are illustrated in Figure 10.10.

Use Symmetrical nodes to create curves that are equal on each side. Smooth nodes are best for creating rounded curves that are not symmetrical. And Cusp nodes are best for creating pointed curves. All this will make more sense as you experiment with curves and learn to edit control points.

Bending Curves with Control Points

When you select a single curve node with the Shape tool, you see two control points. Node curves are determined by the type of curve (Cusp, Smooth, or Symmetrical) and by the distance and location of the control points. When you pull away from a node on a control point, you increase the effect of the curve. In Figure 10.11, I'm stretching one of the two control points on a Cusp node to increase the intensity or sharpness of the curve.

10

Figure 10.10.

Cusp and Smooth nodes enable you to edit line segments on either side independently.

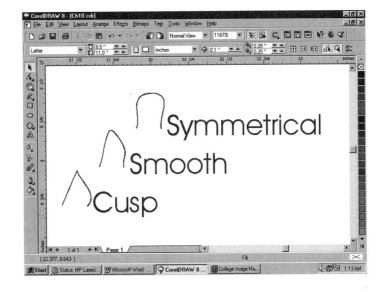

Figure 10.11.

Pulling out on a control point increases the effect of a curve.

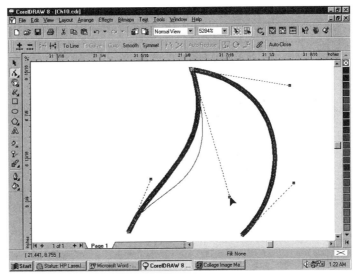

Similarly, dragging in on a control point lessens the impact of a defined curve.

Curves themselves are also regulated by the location of control points. In Figure 10.12, I am sharpening the angle of a curve by dragging on a control point.

Adjust curve angles by dragging control points along a circular radius.

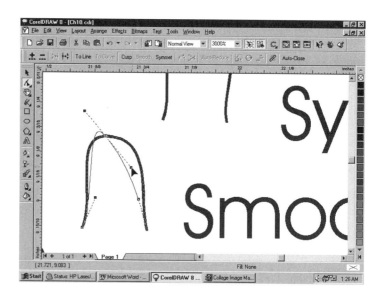

10.3: Transform a Triangle into a Sail

1. Draw a triangle.

2. Cut the triangle in half vertically using the Knife tool. Do this by selecting the Knife tool from the Shape flyout and clicking first at the top of the triangle. Then click on the center of the bottom leg of the triangle. Use the Pick tool to select the right half of the triangle and delete it. Make the triangle about three times as high as it is wide, so you end up with a triangle like the one in Figure 10.13.

Figure 10.13.
A couple clicks with the Knife tool and an Isosceles triangle becomes a right-angle triangle.

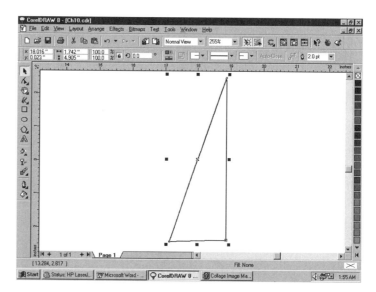

10

3. Use the Shape tool to select the lower-left node on the triangle. Convert the line above the node into a curve by clicking on the To Curve button in the Property bar. Use the control handles to shape the sail, as shown in Figure 10.14.

4. Manipulate the control handles at either end of the curve to create something like a billowing sail.

Figure 10.14.
Control handles become active on either end of a line when you convert the line into a curve.

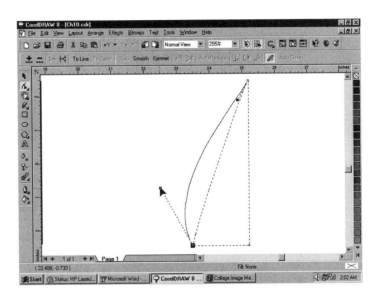

Sculpting Curves with Advanced Node Properties

You need to experiment with node editing. The sail exercise you just completed introduced you to curving lines. You can edit any line on any curve by manipulating nodes and control points.

Don't start with editing control points. Normally, you create a rough shape for your object using the Shape tool or the Freehand Drawing tool. Next, you can further edit the curve by moving nodes with the Shape tool. Finally, fine-tune your illustration by manipulating control points to shape your curves.

Some buttons on the Node Property bar are beyond the scope of this book, but here is a brief description of them:

☐ The Stretch and Scale Nodes button enables you to resize only those curves in an object attached to selected nodes.

☐ The Rotate and Skew nodes enable you to rotate only selected nodes in an object. Nodes that are not selected will not rotate.

☐ The Align Nodes button enables you to align selected nodes horizontally or vertically.

☐ The Elastic Mode button changes the way selected nodes behave when one of the nodes is moved. With Elastic Mode on (the button pressed in), all selected nodes will move when you drag on any one of them.

Summary

CorelDRAW provides almost unlimited control over the appearance of a curve. So don't start with the most detailed tools; start by drawing rough shapes and curves. If you were building a skyscraper, you wouldn't start with sandpaper. Similarly, don't start a drawing by editing control points.

If you create a rough drawing using Shape tools (for example, a 12-pointed star), you can convert that shape to a curve by selecting the shape and choosing Arrange | Convert to Curves from the menu bar.

After you rough out your drawing with shapes or freehand tools, then touch up your illustration by selecting a type of curve (Cusp, Smooth, or Symmetrical) and adjusting control points to shape those curves.

Workshop

Use your newly acquired ability to edit shapes, as well as some techniques you picked up in previous lessons to create the sailing lessons illustration Paul prepared for this workshop. Paul's drawing is shown in Figure 10.15, but feel free to modify it to fit your own skill level.

Figure 10.15.

Paul's illustration transforms a polygon into the sun and another polygon into sun rays, and uses the knife and erase tools to transform polygons into the sail.

10

Here are the basic steps to create the illustration:

1. Open a new document and Create a 12-point polygon/star. Set the sharpness of the star at 4 (using the Sharpness slider on the Property bar). Then use the Shape tool to drag one of the leftmost internal nodes to the right until the star turns inside out. Figure 10.16 shows how this should look.

Figure 10.16.

Dragging an internal node can turn a star inside out.

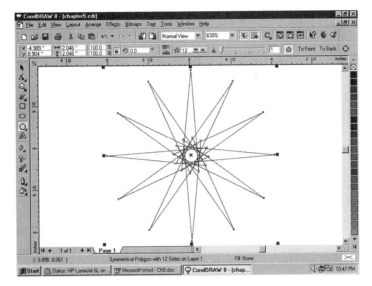

2. Add a node to the line segment connected to the node you just moved. Or to make this easier, just click anywhere with the Shape tool and add a node by clicking on the plus sign (+) in the Shapes Property bar. If the To Curve button in the Property bar is not grayed out, convert the new node to a curve by clicking on the To Curve button in the Property bar. Then drag the node's lowest node handle to the center of the polygon.

3. Add a yellow to white fountain fill to the star. Touch up the star with the eraser to delete some of the extra lines in the middle. Then place a yellow circle behind the star to create the sun. Add the sun rays by creating a 12-point polygon/star. Delete seven of the rays leaving five, and fill them with a yellow to white fountain fill. Your sun should look something like the one in Figure 10.17.

4. Use symbols for objects in the illustration: Add a blue background with a large rectangle, filled with blue. Throw in some clouds using the Webdings font symbol, character #217. Resize and touch up the clouds by editing nodes on the cloud symbols. Add trees using Plant Symbol font, character #34. Use the same symbol

you used for the clouds to create the island, just enlarge it. Add the Arrows2 symbol, character #34 and enlarge it to create the arrow in the illustrations. If you don't have this font installed, you'll find arrows on the Symbol font list.

Figure 10.17.

The five sun rays are the result of creating a 12-point polygon/star and deleting seven of the star nodes.

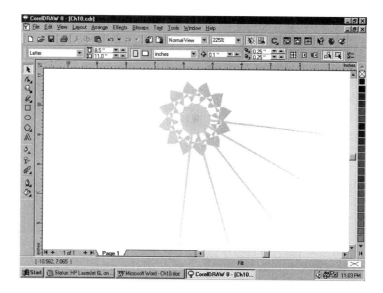

5. Add text: Sailing Lessons.
6. The boat and sails are composed of three triangles. Create three three-pointed polygons, and edit the nodes to produce the three elements of the boat, as shown in Figure 10.18.
7. You can create waves by duplicating the bottom of the boat, flipping it upside down, and duplicating that curve across the screen.

Quiz

1. How do you round the corners on a rectangle?
2. Which tool can cut a shape in two?
3. How do you transform a selected line or shape into a curve?
4. How do you add nodes to a curve?
5. How can you fine-tune the appearance of a curve?

10

Figure 10.18.

The triangle converted into a curve with extra nodes auto-deleted and a cusp node control point edited to define the curve.

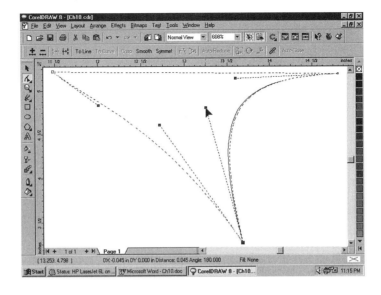

Quiz Answers

1. Round the corners on a rectangle by clicking and dragging on a corner node, and pulling in toward the middle.

2. The Knife tool can cut a shape into two or more parts. Click twice on edges of the object to create a dissection line. Then select either of the two new objects and edit (or delete) either one of them.

3. When you select a shape node with the Shape tool, a To Curve button appears on the Property bar. Click on that button to transform your shape into a curve. You can convert all the nodes in a shape to a curve by selecting the shape with the Pick tool and then choosing Arrange|Convert to Curves from the menu bar.

4. When you select an object with the Shape tool, you can add nodes by clicking anywhere on the shape and then clicking on the + symbol in the Property bar. You can delete nodes by clicking on a node and then clicking on the - in the Property bar.

5. Node curves are determined by the type of curve (Cusp, Smooth, or Symmetrical), and by the distance and location of the control points.

Hour **11**

Working with Bitmap Images in CorelDRAW 8

In Hour 1 of this book, you learned the difference between CorelDRAW's vector-based graphic images and bitmap images. Vector-based images consist of curves and nodes, which are stored on file as mathematical formulas, generated as you draw. Because of this, CorelDRAW gives you unmatched power to draw complex and smooth curves.

Furthermore, because objects in CorelDRAW are saved as formulas, these images can be reproduced at any size, from a postage stamp to a billboard. You will start to notice the difference between bitmap- and vector-based graphics when you attempt to edit them. Bitmaps cannot have outlines and fills defined with the same detail that vector-based images can. When vector-based images are enlarged, they maintain the same outline and fill characteristics. In Figure 11.1, the vector-based dinosaur has the same outline width even when enlarged five times, whereas its bitmap-based cousin does not maintain the same outline characteristics.

Figure 11.1.

The vector-based dinosaur on top keeps its outline width even when enlarged five times; the outline on the bitmap dinosaur on the bottom gets thicker when the object is enlarged.

The advantages to using bitmap images include:

☐ For objects that will *not* be enlarged, bitmap files can be much more efficient than vector-based images. Because files are saved as bitmap dots, not curves, an object made up of a hundred curves is simpler to save if it is saved only as dots.

☐ Many effects and distortion tools are available for bitmap images and are not available for vector-based objects.

☐ Graphic images used on most World Wide Web sites must be bitmapped in order to be recognized by web browsers.

For these reasons, it is important that you become "bilingual" as far as graphic image formats and that you learn to work with bitmap images as well as vector images. In this lesson, you learn to incorporate bitmap images in your CorelDRAW illustrations.

What Are Bitmap Images?

When you start working with Corel PHOTO-PAINT 8, in Hour 20, "PHOTO-PAINT Basics," you'll be introduced to bitmap images in detail. PHOTO-PAINT is exclusively a bitmap image editing program. But here's the "short course" on what bitmaps images are and how they work.

Simply put, bitmaps are images that store a location and description of pixels. Pixels are nothing but dots. So rather than defining images in terms of curves and lines, bitmap images are defined as dots.

11

Bitmap properties are defined mainly by the *resolution* of the image and the *number of colors* that compose the image. These two properties determine the quality of the image and the size of the file. As you might guess, higher-quality images take up more disk space.

Frequently used bitmap resolutions include 300 dots per inch (which is what older laser printers use to reproduce images), 600dpi (which is what newer laser printers support), and 72dpi (which is what most computer screens use). If, for example, you are creating an image for a web site, don't assign a resolution higher than 72dpi because the final output (a computer screen) will not support the additional pixels. When you work with bitmap images in CorelDRAW, you assign resolutions to them.

Bitmap images can also have different numbers of colors. Those include black and white images, 8-bit grayscale (256 shades of gray), and 8-bit paletted (256 colors). Other color modes exist as well, but these are sufficient to use with most bitmap images that you will work with in CorelDRAW. When you explore PHOTO-PAINT 8, you'll learn to use bitmap color modes that support even larger numbers of colors.

Why Edit Bitmap Images in CorelDRAW?

CorelDRAW is not really a full-features bitmap editor. PHOTO-PAINT is. And with every copy of CorelDRAW 8, you get PHOTO-PAINT 8 free. So what's the point of editing bitmaps in CorelDRAW 8? If you work *exclusively* with bitmap images, you should work in Photo-Paint instead of CorelDRAW. But if you combine both vector and bitmap images, CorelDRAW supports this much better than PHOTO-PAINT or any bitmap editor.

At this point, you might be asking yourself, "Can't we all just get along? Why can't *somebody* come up with a program that will edit both bitmap- and vector-based graphics?" Well, somebody has, and you're using the program. CorelDRAW 8 includes a Bitmap menu that lets you create, edit, and save bitmap images in CorelDRAW. So, in effect, you can work in a mixed environment.

The one thing that you cannot do is transform bitmap images to vector-based images. Programs exist that attempt to trace the lines in bitmap images and convert them into vector-based curves, but these programs are basically trying to guess at which dots should be converted to which lines, and the results are usually not satisfactory.

Where to Get Bitmap Images

Several ways to get bitmap images in CorelDRAW include:

- ☐ Scan images into CorelDRAW with your scanner.
- ☐ Import bitmap images created with other programs such as PHOTO-PAINT.

☐ Copy and paste bitmap images into CorelDRAW from the web or from other sources.

☐ Convert objects created in CorelDRAW to bitmap images.

In this section of Hour 11, you learn to obtain bitmap images in CorelDRAW using all four of these techniques.

Scanning Images into CorelDRAW

Scanning has become much more accessible over the last year or two. The price of scanners has been plummeting, and quality flatbed scanners can be bought for not much more than a hundred dollars if you watch for rebates and sales.

Scanning has also gotten easier to do. CorelDRAW 8 comes with CorelSCAN, a program that walks you through the process of scanning photos or other images into CorelDRAW.

After connecting your scanner (which is beyond the scope of this book, but most scanners come with easy-to-follow instructions), CorelSCAN helps you decide what bitmap format you want to assign to your imported image.

11.1: Scanning Images into CorelDRAW

1. Place your image (face down—but you knew that!) on your scanner.
2. Select File | Acquire from CorelSCAN from the menu bar.
3. The first CorelSCAN 8 dialog box lists your installed scanners. Click on one (if you have more than one installed) and click on the Next > button.
4. The next step varies depending on your scanner, but in most cases, you see a Preview screen and a dialog box associated with your scanner. If you have a Prescan button in your dialog box, click on it. An image of your scanned object appears in your Preview window. Draw a marquee in your preview window to define the section of your image you want to scan. Then click on the Scan button in your scanner dialog box.

JUST A MINUTE

> Your scanner dialog box prompts you to tell it what type of bitmap image you want to create from your scanned image. Ignore these settings for now, as CorelSCAN soon takes over to help you make these decisions.

5. After your scanner loads the image, the CorelSCAN dialog box will ask, "What type of image(s) are you processing?" Choose from the list. In Figure 11.2, I'm selecting a color photograph. After choosing, click on the Next > button.

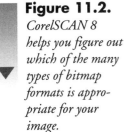

Figure 11.2.
CorelSCAN 8 helps you figure out which of the many types of bitmap formats is appropriate for your image.

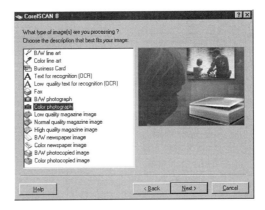

6. Based on the type of image you scan, CorelSCAN suggests a color mode. I'm choosing a paletted (256 color) mode in Figure 11.3. This 256-color palette works well for display on monitors or web sites. The great thing about Corel Photo-Scan is it does not require you to worry about this. You get prompted to describe the kind of illustration you are creating, and CorelDRAW figures out the right number of colors and other options.

Figure 11.3.
The paletted (256 color) color mode is perfect for creating bitmap images that will be used in a web site.

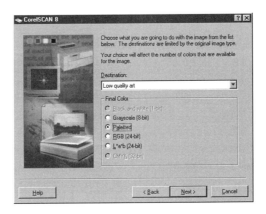

7. At this point, the options available to you depend on what kind of image you import. In most cases, the dialog boxes are self-explanatory. In Figure 11.4, I'm choosing from a list of 256-color modes.

8. Based on the type of image you scan, CorelSCAN suggests a resolution for your bitmap image. In Figure 11.5, I'm accepting the recommended resolution of 72dpi (dots per inch).

Figure 11.4.

Because I'm designing an image that I expect to be viewed on a web site by Internet Explorer, I'm choosing that color palette.

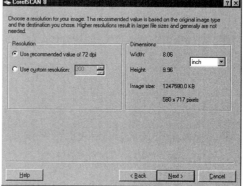

Figure 11.5.

CorelSCAN knows that my web image should have 72 dots per inch.

9. Finally, you have the opportunity to touch up your scanned images. CorelSCAN provides three filters: Image Enhancement, Red-Eye Removal, and Dust and Scratch Removal. These filters alter the pixels (dots) in your scanned image. Each of these filter dialog boxes has two preview screens: Before and After. The After screen shows your image with the filter applied, so you can experiment before you decide if you want to apply the effect.

These filter dialog boxes also have sliders that enable you to determine how much of the various effect(s) you want to apply to your scanned image.

Each of the filter dialog boxes has three buttons underneath the preview area: the Navigator, Preview, and Reset buttons. These dialog boxes have check boxes that enable you to apply the effect to your scanned image.

11

You can control what part of your image is visible in the Preview window. When you click on the Navigator button, a thumbnail image appears, and you can select the portion of your image that you want to appear in the Preview window. You can also move the section of your image that is visible by dragging directly on the left side of the Preview window. In Figure 11.6, I am dragging the image using the grabber hand that appears when I move my cursor over the left Preview window.

If you don't like the effect that you applied, click on the Reset button (it looks like an Undo button).

Figure 11.6.

CorelSCAN comes with filters that are controlled and applied with sliders.

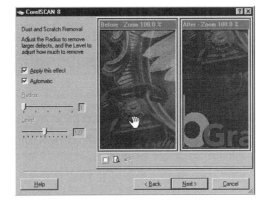

10. When you finish importing your scanned bitmap image, click on the Finish button in the dialog box. Then choose the Exit CorelSCAN? Radio button, and click on OK in the final dialog box.

Importing Bitmap Images

Another way to place a bitmap image in the CorelDRAW Drawing window is to import an exiting image. This is a cinch. Simply select File | Import from the menu bar, and use the Look In drop-down list to navigate to the folder on your system in which your graphic files are stored. Or if you are opening one of the thousands of bitmap clip art images that come with CorelDRAW from your CD-ROM, navigate to your CD drive.

If you click on the Preview check box in the Import dialog box, you can see a thumbnail of your image before you elect to import it. In Figure 11.7, I've found the graphic image I want, and I'm looking at it in the Preview window.

Figure 11.7.
*The Preview check box
turns the Import dialog
box into a graphic index
of your saved images.*

When you find your image, double-click on it to import it into your open CorelDRAW drawing.

Copy and Paste Bitmap Images

The easiest way to bring bitmap images into CorelDRAW is to copy and paste them. Any image that you can see on your computer screen can be copied and pasted into CorelDRAW as a bitmap object. That includes images that you see on the World Wide Web (provided of course that you have permission to copy them).

11.2: Copying a Bitmap Image into CorelDRAW

1. Open a program in which you can view the bitmap image you want to import into CorelDRAW. This can be another graphics program or a web browser.

2. Open the file or view the web site containing the image you want to copy into CorelDRAW.

3. Right-click on the image you want to copy, and select Copy from the shortcut menu. In Figure 11.8, I'm copying an image from a web site.

JUST A MINUTE

> If your program does not support this method of copying an image using the right-click shortcut menu, you can select the image and choose Edit | Copy from your menu bar. Or if neither of those options are available, click on the image and press Ctrl+C on the keyboard.

4. With your image copied to the Clipboard, close the program from which you copied it and return to, or open, a new CorelDRAW 8 drawing.

5. Right-click in the Drawing window and select Paste from the shortcut menu. The bitmap image will be copied into your drawing.

Figure 11.8.
I checked to make sure it was okay to copy images from this web site before pulling a graphic into CorelDRAW 8.

Most of the time when you work with bitmap objects within CorelDRAW it will be because you brought a bitmap image from somewhere else into CorelDRAW. However, sometimes you'll want to convert a vector image into a bitmap so that you can apply effects only available in bitmap images. To learn how to do that, read on.

Converting Objects to Bitmaps

You can create bitmap images from CorelDRAW by first designing a drawing. To do that, just create a drawing in CorelDRAW. Select the objects that you want to convert into a single bitmap image, and then choose Bitmaps | Convert to Bitmaps from the menu bar.

The Convert to Bitmap dialog box offers you options similar to those you chose from when you scanned an image. The Color drop-down menu offers different color modes. Paletted is best for images that will be placed on web sites. One color is best for black-and-white drawings. RGB or CMYK color is best for images that will appear on a high-resolution monitor or printed using a color printing process.

The Dithered check box enables a feature (*dithering*) that compensates for colors that are not on your color palette by mixing colored dots. The Transparent Background check box can eliminate a colored background from your image. The Resolution drop-down list enables you to choose how many dots per inch (dpi) you want to assign to your image. More dots make a higher quality image but take more disk space. The projected file size is shown on the bottom of the dialog box and changes as you select color and resolution settings.

Antialiasing is discussed in some detail in the hours in this book devoted to PHOTO-PAINT. The short explanation is that it eliminates jagged edges in bitmap objects, but the downside is that it makes them blurrier. The Convert to Bitmap dialog box gives you three Antialiasing options: None, Normal, or (the max) Super-sampling.

After you define settings for your selected object(s), click on OK.

Applying Effects to Bitmaps

After you create a bitmap image in CorelDRAW 8, you can apply some useful effects that are not available for vector-based objects.

Those effects include using a color mask to strip any unwanted color out of an image, assigning transparency to bitmap images so that they appear to have no background when displayed on web sites, and applying a fun range of distortion effects to your image.

Other effects include transformations with names such as Solarize, Impressionist, Psyche-delic, Glass Block, and Vignette.

Using a Color Mask on Bitmap Images

You can use bitmap color masks to eliminate any color from any bitmap image. This is especially useful with scanned or imported photos. Color masking can be, in effect, a recoloring tool. Too much red or blue in a photo? You can correct that with color masking.

You can also use color masking to transform the fills of any bitmap images.

11.3: Stripping a Color from a Bitmap Image

1. Create a bitmap image by scanning a photo, converting a drawing, or importing or copying a bitmap image into CorelDRAW.

2. Select the bitmap image. Handles appear, just as they do when you select any object in CorelDRAW.

3. Select Bitmap | Bitmap Color Mask from the menu bar.

4. Click on the first bar in the Bitmap Color Mask rollup.

5. Click on the Color Selector, as I am doing in Figure 11.9. (It looks like an eyedropper.)

6. Move your cursor, in the bitmap image, over the color you want to remove. That color appears in the first bar of the Bitmap Color Mask rollup. When the color in the rollup matches the color you want to delete, click with the Color Selector cursor. In Figure 11.10, I'm selecting one color from my scanned image to delete.

11

Figure 11.9.
Use the color selector to create a perfect match for a color you want to remove from a bitmap image.

Figure 11.10.
Moving your eyedropper-cursor even one pixel can change the selected color.

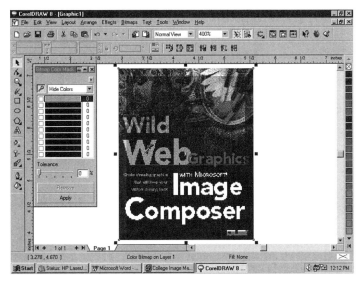

7. To delete only the exact color you selected, leave the Tolerance slider set at or near zero. To blast away at any color that even remotely resembles the one you chose, push the slider up to 100. Settings in between determine how close a color match you are defining.

8. If you need to delete additional colors from your bitmap image, use the remaining bars in the Bitmap Color Mask rollup and assign additional colors to as many of them as you need.

9. Before you apply the color mask, you can click on the check boxes next to any of the color bars to exclude that color from the list of those that will be removed.

10. When you've fine-tuned your Color Mask criteria, click on the Apply button to transform your bitmap. In Figure 11.11, I stripped all the dark colors out of a copy of my book cover.

Figure 11.11.

The Bitmap Color Mask rollup is basically a "decolorizer."

Assigning Transparency to Bitmap Images

Transparency is like color masking, but a bit simpler. When you assign transparency to a bitmap image, you strip away a single background color.

You can use the Convert to Bitmap dialog box to transform existing bitmap images. If you copy or import an image with a background that you want to remove, select it, choose Bitmap | Convert to Bitmap from the menu bar, and use the Transparent Background check box to strip the background from the image.

Assigning Effects to Bitmap Images

CorelDRAW's Bitmap menu includes a number of fun distortion effects that you can apply to bitmaps. These effects are culled from the arsenal that you will learn to use in the hours on Corel PHOTO-PAINT. You'll investigate these effects more in those hours (20–22), but you can try 3D effects now.

Not all Bitmap effects can be applied to every bitmap. The available effects depend on the color mode and type of the bitmap image.

When you select a bitmap image and choose an effect from the Bitmap menu, you can see the changes you are applying in two different ways. In the effect dialog box, shown in Figure 11.12, you can click on the Preview button to display changes you make with the sliders before they are applied to the image in the Drawing window.

Figure 11.12.

You can preview bitmap effects in a dialog box.

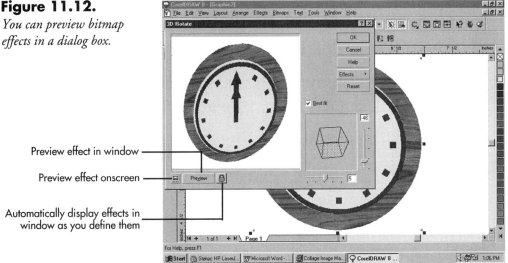

Preview effect in window

Preview effect onscreen

Automatically display effects in window as you define them

The three buttons in the effect dialog box enable you to add your effect to the display in the Preview window, to display the effects in the Drawing window, or to automatically transform the image in the Preview window as you experiment with changes in effect settings.

If you choose the left-most button in the Preview dialog box, your effects dialog box no longer includes a Preview window, and effects appear on the screen, as shown in Figure 11.13.

When you toggle to the effect dialog box without a Preview screen, the button on the left toggles back to the Preview dialog box, and the button on the right displays the effect you are defining in the Drawing area.

When you have defined and previewed a bitmap effect, click on OK in the dialog box to apply that effect to the selected bitmap object.

Figure 11.13.
*You can also preview
bitmap effects in the
Drawing area.*

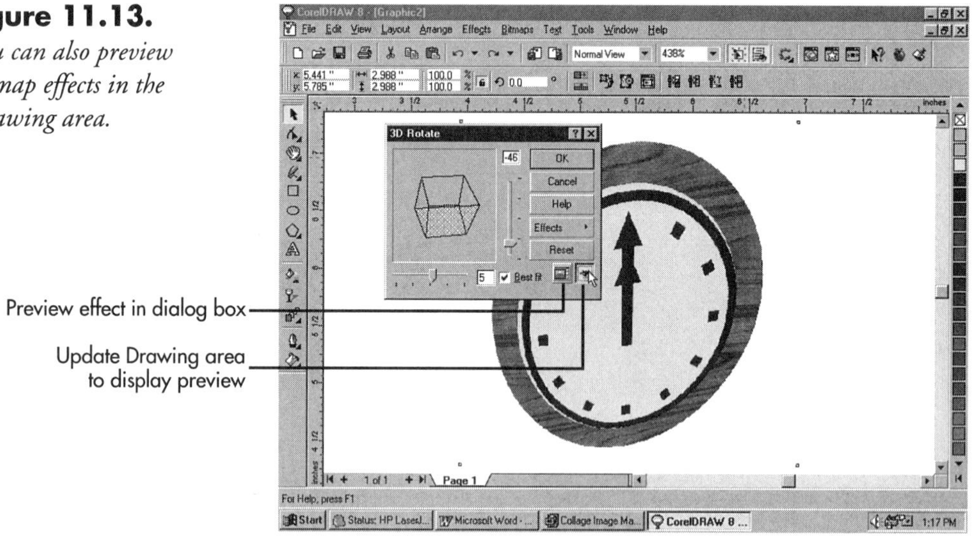

Preview effect in dialog box

Update Drawing area
to display preview

Summary

You have many reasons to work with objects as bitmap images. You might want to import images in bitmap file formats. And many effects and distortion tools are available for bitmap images and not available for vector-based objects.

You can edit bitmap images in CorelDRAW, but many of the editing techniques you've learned so far do not apply to bitmaps. You cannot edit nodes or curves in bitmap images. But you can apply a sample selection of bitmap effects to these images.

Workshop

In this workshop, you create a fun clock or compass by combining bitmap objects with vector objects and applying bitmap effects to the bitmaps. Feel free to skip steps that seem a bit over your level. You can still have fun applying bitmap effects even if you skip steps 2, 3, 4, or 5.

1. Drag one of the clock face symbols from the Wingding font set into the Drawing area. Fill the symbol with a dark color fill, and convert it to a transparent bitmap by selecting the symbol, choosing Bitmap | Convert to Bitmap from the menu bar, and clicking on the Transparent Background check box in the dialog box.

2. Create a circle. Assign one of the wood-panel bitmap fills. To assign this fill, open the Pattern Fill dialog box on the Fill flyout.

3. Create a round, yellow circle. Your three objects should look like the ones in Figure 11.14.

Figure 11.14.

Converting the clock symbol to a bitmap enables you to assign bitmap effects to it.

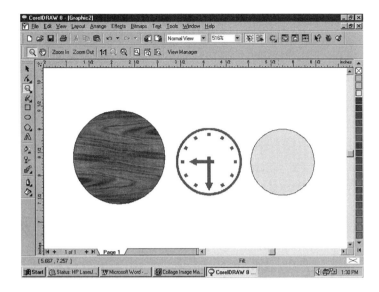

4. Place the yellow circle on top of the wood-panel circle, and put the clock face symbol on top of both of them. Size the three so that they look like the set in Figure 11.15. Bring the clock face back to the top (right-click and select Order | to Front from the shortcut menu).

5. Select all three objects and convert them to a single 300dpi, transparent, paletted bitmap with Normal aliasing.

Figure 11.15.

You can convert more than one selected object to a single bitmap.

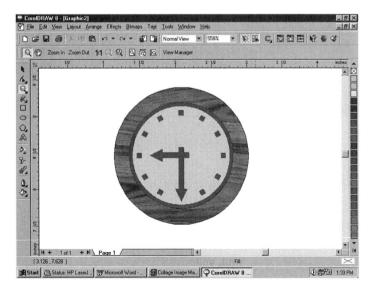

6. Select the bitmap object, choose Bitmap | 3D Effects | 3D Rotate from the menu bar, and set the vertical effect slider at about -10 and the horizontal slider at about 50.

7. Click on OK to assign the effect to your bitmap image.

8. Save your illustration.

Nice work! Even if you didn't exactly follow my steps, you experimented with combining bitmap and vector objects.

Quiz

1. What are bitmaps?

2. How do you remove a background from an imported bitmap?

3. How do you bring bitmaps into CorelDRAW?

4. How do you strip several undesired colors from a scanned photo?

Quiz Answers

1. Simply put, bitmaps are images that store a location and description of pixels. Pixels are nothing but dots. So rather than defining images in terms of curves and lines, bitmap images are defined as dots.

2. Select the image with the background you want to remove, choose Bitmap | Convert to Bitmap from the menu bar, and use the Transparent Background check box to strip the background from the image.

3. You can bring bitmaps into CorelDRAW by importing files, copying images from any program, scanning images, or converting existing drawings to bitmaps.

4. You can strip undesired colors from a scanned photo by using the Bitmap Color Mask rollup.

11

Hour 12

Lenses and PowerClips

For the first eleven hours of this book, you've put in some hard work learning how CorelDRAW works. You've explored the process of generating curves, editing curve nodes, and working with bitmap images within CorelDRAW. Congratulations! Now it's show time!

Starting with this hour, you begin to explore some of the fun effects available in CorelDRAW. This is where you get to play with the almost magical array of special effects such as fisheye lenses, magnifying lenses, and filling objects with other objects. These effects are built into CorelDRAW's Lens and PowerClip tools.

In this hour, you learn to create lenses such as the one in Figure 12.1. Lenses can apply many different effects; the one in Figure 12.1 has a magnifying effect attached to it.

You will also explore using PowerClips to insert bitmap fills into objects. In Figure 12.2, I've taken a fill and "injected" it into some artistic text.

In this hour, you will also explore the Interactive Transparency tool, which enables you to assign varying degrees of transparency to different parts of a single object. In Figure 12.3, I'm tweaking the transparency assigned to the lens covering some of my artistic text.

Figure 12.1.
*Looking at artistic text
through a lens effect.*

Figure 12.2.
*Filling artistic text with
a bitmap PowerClip.*

Figure 12.3.
*Interactive Transparency
enables you to assign
varying degrees of
transparency to an object.*

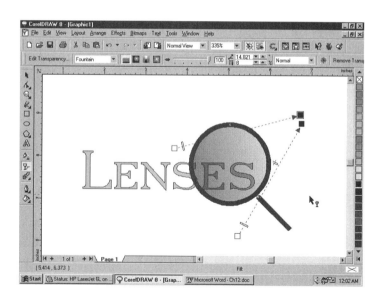

So, if you're ready to have some fun, read on!

Creating Lenses

CorelDRAW's lens effect works just like a glass lens. But just like a glass lens can have many different effects, so can a CorelDRAW lens. For example, a glass lens can be dark like sunglasses, magnify, like my glasses, or even warp an image. In the same way, lenses in CorelDRAW 8 can have different attributes (effects).

Applying a lens effect to an object (often a circle) allows that object to act as a lens—darkening, magnifying, or in some other way distorting any object it is placed on top of.

Lens effects are used in connection with an object below the lens. That object can be artistic text, a drawn object, or even a bitmap object in the Drawing window. The only objects not affected by placing lenses over them are objects that have extrude, contour, or blend effects applied to them.

The key thing to keep in mind is that lens effects do not change the appearance of the object to which they are applied. A circle with a magnify lens effect applied to it does not change its own appearance. The effect takes place when that circle is moved over another object.

You can group objects that have lens effects applied. For example, to create the magnifying glass in Figure 12.1, I attached a line to the circle with a lens effect applied to it and grouped them. The lens effect will not apply to the line because there's no open area inside the line to act as a lens.

Types of Lenses

The Lens rollup offers 12 different lenses. Those lens effects are No Lens, Brighten, Color Add, Color Limit, Custom Color Map, Fish Eye, Heat Map, Invert, Magnify, Tinted Grayscale, Transparency, and Wireframe.

I've illustrated all twelve of these effects (eleven, if you don't count "No Lens") in Figure 12.4.

Lens Options

Many lenses come with these options: Frozen, Viewpoint, and/or Remove Face. A frozen lens applies the effect of the lens permanently (more or less), in that you can move or delete the lens and the distortion remains. Clicking on the Viewpoint check box produces an Edit button, which in turn lets you move the center of the lens effect through x- and y-axis spin boxes.

The Remove Face check box is available for lenses that distort colors. This option enables you to turn off the section of a lens that doesn't cover any other objects.

12

Figure 12.4.

*Each of the lens effects
has its own distortion
affect.*

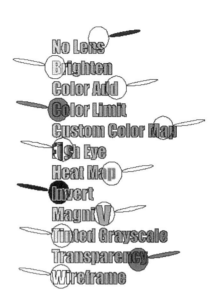

How to Apply Lenses

Different lenses have different effects, but the process for applying them is basically the same. First, create an object over which you will place your lens. Then, create another object to be used as a lens. Often lenses are composed of circles, but you can use any closed curve (a rectangle, polygon, or closed curve you drew yourself).

Finally, select the object that is to act as the lens, and choose Effects | Lens from the menu bar. Select a type of lens from the drop-down list, edit the lens options, and then click on the Apply button to apply your effect to your lens. Move the lens over your object to create the lens effect.

12.1: Assign a Magnification Lens Effect to Artistic Text

1. Type some artistic text. If you're not poetically inspired this hour, just type Lens Effect.
2. Draw a circle.
3. Select Effects | Lens from the menu bar.
4. Click with the Pick tool to select your circle if it isn't selected.
5. Pull down the drop-down list in the Lens rollup, and choose Magnify.
6. Change the degree of magnification by entering 2.5 in the Amount spin box, as I'm doing in Figure 12.5.
8. When you have defined your lens effect, click on the Apply button.
9. Drag your circle, with its attached lens property, over another object to apply the effect.

12

Figure 12.5.

You can adjust most lenses; for example, you can change the amount of magnification of the Magnify lens.

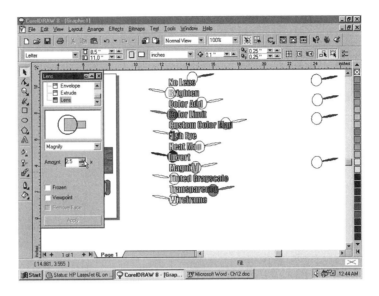

JUST A MINUTE

You can apply more than one lens at a time to an object. Or you can use many lenses in an illustration. However, you'll quickly notice that the calculations CorelDRAW has to perform to achieve these awesome effects are an awesome drain on your computer memory. You might want to switch to Wireframe mode while you edit other parts of your illustration to speed CorelDRAW up a bit. However, you'll have to switch back to Normal view to see your lens effects on your screen.

Applying PowerClips

PowerClips place a selected object inside another object. The object that is inserted into another object is placed in what CorelDRAW calls a *container*. The source for the container can be a closed path, a shape, or artistic text (but not paragraph text).

PowerClips do not change the size of either the container object or the target object. So if you copy a large object into a small one, it will get cropped to fit the size of the target object. If you copy a small object into a large object, it will not fill the target object completely.

You apply a PowerClip by first creating the container object. Fill that object. Edit it. Touch it up, keeping in mind that you're about to use it to fill another object. Then create the object into which you will inject the PowerClip.

With both the container and target objects created, select the container object with the Pick tool. Choose Effects | PowerClip | Place Inside Container. As soon as you do, a large black arrow appears on your screen. Point that arrow at the target for the PowerClip and click. The container object gets injected into the target object.

12

12.2: Insert a PowerClip into Artistic Text

1. Use your artistic skills to create something that looks like an igloo. Make the igloo wider than your Drawing page (the shaded page area in the Drawing window).
2. Type the word IGLOO in artistic text. Select Ice Age font, and stretch the text so that it is the width of the page. Your page should look something like Figure 12.6.

Figure 12.6.

By making my container object (the igloo) wider than the text, I'm ensuring that the entire text object will be filled when I use the igloo as a container.

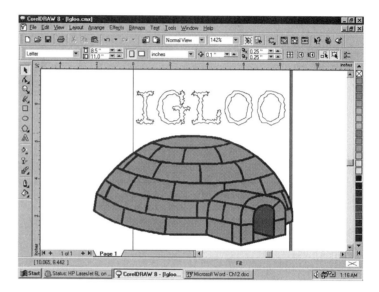

3. Use the Pick tool to select the igloo.
4. Select Effects | PowerClip | Place Inside Container from the menu bar.

5. Point the new, thick black arrow cursor at the text, as I am doing in Figure 12.7.

You can edit the contents of a PowerClip by clicking on the (combined) object and selecting Effects | PowerClip | Edit Contents. After you edit the PowerClip container contents, choose Effects | PowerClip | Finish Editing This Level to place the container object back into the target object.

Defining Interactive Transparency

The last effect you learn this hour is interactive transparency. This effect works a bit like lens effects in that it is applied to one object that is then placed on top of another object. What's unique about the Interactive Transparency tool is that you can define a graded degree of transparency within the "lens" object.

Interactive transparency is assigned by using the Interactive Transparency tool on the toolbox.

In Figure 12.8, I used the Graph Paper tool (on the Polygon flyout) to create an object that I placed over artistic text. I applied a dark fill to the Graph Paper and used interactive transparency to assign almost complete transparency to the left side of the Graph Paper, and much less transparency to the right side of the object.

12

Figure 12.7.

After you load an image into a PowerClip container, just point and click to insert that image into another object. On top the Lion is about to be "injected" into the text. The bottom image shows the resulting image.

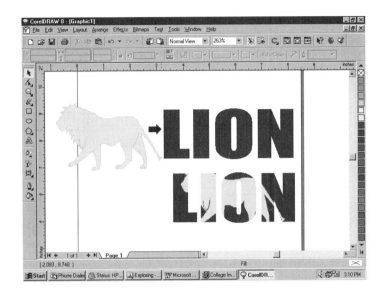

12.3: Assign Interactive Transparency to an Object

To Do

1. Type a word in artistic text.
2. Create a closed object—a circle will do fine.
3. Select the circle, and click on the Interactive Transparency tool. Click and draw across the circle, starting at the less transparent end of the circle. In Figure 12.9, I'm defining more transparency in the upper-left of the circle and less in the lower-right.

Figure 12.8.

Any closed object can have interactive transparency assigned to it.

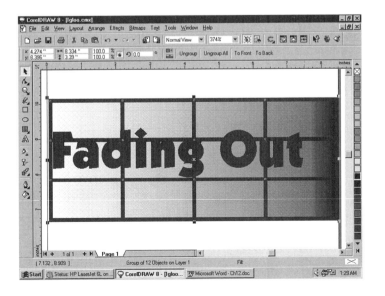

12

Figure 12.9.

The light square in the Interactive Transparency line indicates the more transparent end of the spectrum.

4. Adjust the bar in the middle of the Interactive Transparency line to move the shift-point for transparency.

5. Click on a fill color in the color palette.

After you assign interactive transparency to an object, you can edit the shift-point by clicking on the Interactive Transparency tool in the toolbox and adjusting the shift-point. You can also move either end of the Interactive Transparency line to adjust the direction of the applied transparency. In Figure 12.10, I'm moving the end points to redefine the direction of the transparency gradient.

Figure 12.10.

After you apply interactive transparency, you can select the Interactive Transparency tool and move either endpoint to edit the direction of the transparency gradient.

12

Summary

CorelDRAW 8 comes loaded with special effects that you can apply to objects. In this hour, you examined three effects that are applied by combining two different objects. Both Lenses and Interactive Transparency involve one object acting as a lens and being placed over another object.

PowerClips use more than one object to achieve their effect as well. A first object is loaded into a Container and then "injected" into a second object.

Workshop

1. Type some artistic text.
2. Create a rectangle, larger than the artistic text, and choose a good fill from the Pattern Fill dialog box.
3. Place the Pattern fill in a container, and use it as a PowerClip fill for the text.
4. Create a circle and a thin oval. Fill the thin oval, and group them together to form a lens, as shown in Figure 12.11.

Figure 12.11

You can use this object as a lens.

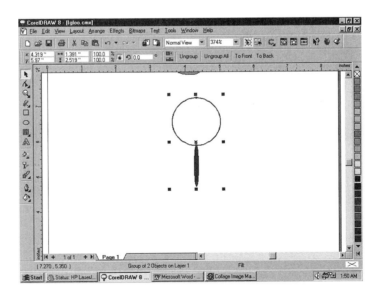

5. Assign a 1.5 magnification lens effect to your new drawing, and move it over the text.
6. Remove the lens effect by choosing No Lens from the Lens rollup. Assign interactive transparency to the lens, as shown in Figure 12.12.

Figure 12.12.

You cannot mix lens effects with interactive transparency, but you can change your lens from one to the other.

Quiz

1. How are lens effects different from fills?
2. Do PowerClips enlarge (or shrink) to fit the object into which they are injected?
3. What is so special about the Interactive Transparency tool?
4. Can you apply more than one lens at a time to an object?
5. How do you edit the contents of a PowerClip?

Quiz Answers

1. Lens effects do not change the appearance of the object to which they are applied. A circle with a magnify lens effect applied to it does not change its own appearance. The effect takes place when that circle is moved over another object.

2. Neither. PowerClips do not change the size of either the container object or the target object. So, if you copy a large object into a small one, it will get cropped to fit the size of the target object. If you copy a small object into a large object, it will not fill the target object completely.

3. What's unique about the Interactive Transparency tool is that you can define a graded degree of transparency within the "lens" object.

4. Yes. As well, you can use many lenses in an illustration. However, you'll quickly notice that the intense calculations necessary to create this effect slow down your system.

5. You can edit the contents of a PowerClip by clicking on the (combined) object and selecting Effects | PowerClip | Edit Contents. After you edit the PowerClip container contents, choose Effects | PowerClip | Finish Editing This Level to place the container object back into the target object.

12

Hour 13

Blends and Contours

In the previous hour, you started to experiment with the PowerClip, Lens, and Interactive Transparency effects that distort objects to which they are applied.

In this hour, you explore a couple effects that change objects based on duplicating them and distorting the clones.

The blend effect enables you to fill the space between two different objects with a set of new objects that change, step-by-step, from the first object to the second. Not only do the size and shape of blended images evolve from one object to another, but the color as well. Figure 13.1 shows artistic text blending from one size, rotation, and color to another.

Figure 13.1

Blends convert one object to another, step-by-step.

The contour effect enables you to create concentric lines inside or outside of a selected object. This is a quick, easy way to draw concentric circles. Figure 13.2 shows the three ways you can apply contours: a defined number of lines inside the original object, a defined number of lines outside the original object, or as many lines as it takes to get to the center of the entire selected object.

The contour effect also has a feature that enables you to transform colors from an inside to an outside color, as you create contours. The concentric circles in Figure 13.2 transform from a dark color to a light color.

Figure 13.2

Use contours to draw concentric circles.

13

Working with Blends

Blends are an amazingly intelligent effect, and as such it's often hard to predict the exact effect you will create using them. If you are blending one object into another with a similar size and shape, the results are fairly straight-forward. In Figure 13.3, I'm blending one oval into another, with slight color differences between the two objects. The results are a smooth, almost gradient evolution from one color to the other.

Figure 13.3
Blends between similar objects are smooth and gradient.

However, blends between objects that are very different in size, shape, and color produce some wild transitional shapes, as you can see in Figure 13.4.

Figure 13.4
Blending a bright square and a dark star produces some unusual transitional shapes.

Defining Blends

Aside from the shapes that you blend into each other, you can control the effect of a blend by defining the number of steps (transformations) to take place, and assigning rotation to the intermediate objects created by the blend effect.

13

13.1: Blend a Circle into a Square in Three Steps

1. Draw a circle and draw a square. Select both objects.
2. Select Effects | Blend from the menu bar and enter 3 in the Number of Steps spin box in the Blend rollup.

JUST A MINUTE

When you select Effects | Blend from the menu bar, the Blend rollup appears in your CorelDRAW window. You can also make the rollup appear by pressing Ctrl+B.

The more "steps" in a blend, the more transitional effects you create. A three-step blend has relatively dramatic changes between each intermediate object in the blend, whereas a 30-step blend has relatively imperceptible changes between intermediate objects.

▲ 3. Click on the Apply button in the Blend rollup.

JUST A MINUTE

After you create a blend, you can edit the effect by changing the settings in the Blend rollup or by editing either the starting or ending object. For example, when you edit the fill color of the square you used in the previous To Do exercise, the whole blend will change. Or you can edit (or remove) outlines from either the start or finish objects, or both. Resizing either the starting or ending object changes all the intermediate objects generated by the blend.

Blending Along a Path

The blend effect can generate intermediate objects along a defined path. To do this, you first draw a line and then blend two objects from the start to the finish of that line.

If you have two objects you want to blend into each other and a drawn path, you're ready to blend along that path.

13.2: Blend Circles Along a Path

1. Draw one circle. Duplicate it. To make things easier to keep track of, separate the circles a bit.
2. Draw a Bézier curve. Any curve will do nicely.
3. Select both circles, and press Ctrl+B if the Blend rollup is not visible.
4. Select 20 in the Number of Steps spin box in the rollup, and click on the Apply button to create the blend.

13

5. Click on the Path button, the curved line button on the bottom of the Blend rollup. Choose New Path from the shortcut menu that appears.

6. Point the curved line cursor that appears at the Bézier curve you defined in step 2. I'm doing that in Figure 13.5.

Figure 13.5

Blends can travel along custom-defined paths.

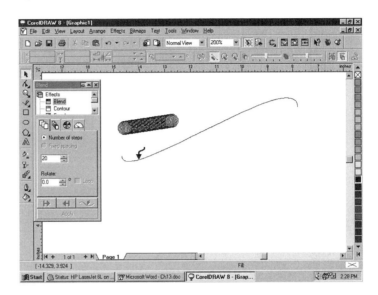

7. Click on the Apply button in the rollup. Then click on the Blend Along Full Path check box to stretch the intermediate circles along the full path. Click on Apply again in the Blend rollup.

You can hide the line that forms the blend path by simply assigning no outline to it. In Figure 13.6, I've assigned different colors to the first and last circles, and made the last circle larger.

The Blend rollup has three other tabs and more features than will fit in this hour. But one effect that you can experiment with easily is acceleration, found in the second tab from the left in the rollup. This effect changes the effect of a blend from a smooth, gradual, equal transition to a distorted transition so that most of the changes happen either toward the beginning or the end of the blend.

The blend options available in the rollup are pretty much duplicated by the Blend Property bar that appears when you define a blend. Blends are so flexible and have so many options that this book could be filled with nothing but blending! But a good way to experiment is to just take the blend you created in the two To Do exercises so far and try applying the different effects in the Property bar or rollup.

13

Figure 13.6

When you change one of the two blended objects in a blend, the intermediate objects react and transform interactively.

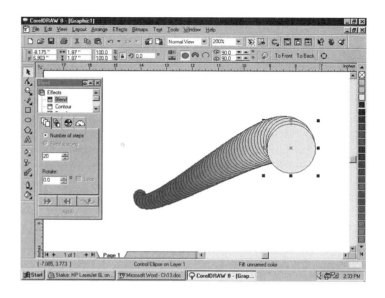

Defining Contours

At the beginning of this hour, you saw how you can use contours to create concentric circles. That's one quick, handy use of the Contour tool.

You can also use contours to create 3D and beveled effects. In Figure 13.7, contours around the edges of a rectangle create a picture frame effect.

Figure 13.7

Contours can create a variety of outline effects, including a 3D beveled look.

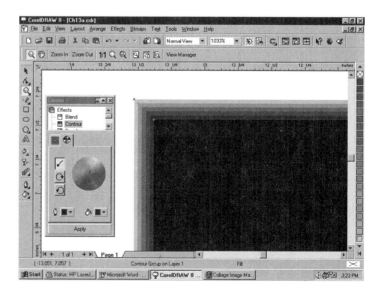

13

Defining Contour Lines

The most basic application of contours is to create lines around or inside a selected object. You can define how many lines and what distance they should be from each other.

The thickness and color of the generated contour lines is determined by the thickness and color of the original lines. You can define line properties the same way you define any outline color and thickness: right-click on the color palette to assign outline color and select outline color from the Outline flyout.

You can define a set number of contour lines inside or outside your selected object. Or you can define contours that completely fill your object (if your object is a closed curve).

13.3: Create Inside, Outside, and Centered Concentric Circles

To Do

1. Draw a circle, about an inch in diameter, and duplicate it twice. Move the circles so that they are spaced a couple inches apart.

2. Select the first circle, and choose Effects | Contour.

3. Select the first (left) tab of the Contour rollup, and click on the Inside radio button.

4. Set the Steps spin box at 2 and the Offset spin box at .1 inch. Your rollup should look like the one in Figure 13.8. Click on the Apply button.

JUST A MINUTE

The number of steps in a contour means the number of new spirals to be created. The Offset spin box regulates the spacing between the contours.

The functions of the Contour rollup are duplicated by a Property bar that appears when you assign a contour effect. The Steps spin box in the Property Bar is shown in Figure 3.8.

5. Select the second circle. Click on the Outside radio button and leave the Steps and Offset spin box settings the same. Click on the Apply button in the rollup.

6. Select the third circle, and click on the To Center radio button. The Steps spin box appears grayed out because CorelDRAW is going to compute how many steps are necessary to fill the circle. Leave the Offset spin boxes unchanged and click on the Apply button.

Your contours should look similar to the ones in Figure 13.2, that you looked at near the beginning of this hour.

13

Figure 13.8

Contour Offset and Steps can be defined in the Contour rollup. The settings also appear in the Property bar as soon as the effect is applied.

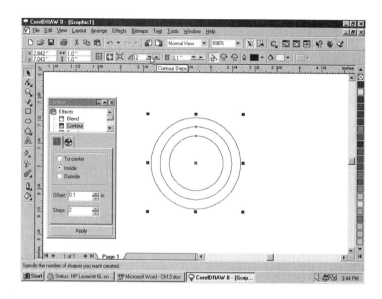

Coloring Contour Lines

After you create contours, you can define color gradation between your original outline (or fill) color, and a contour outline (or fill) color. In this way, contours act a bit like blends—the color blends from the original to the contour color.

Contour color changes are defined in the Color Wheel tab in the Contours rollup. You can also select these colors from drop-down lists in the Property bar.

13.4: Assign Color Changes to a Contour Outline

1. Draw a rectangle about 7" wide and about 4" high . Assign a black fill and a black outline to the rectangle.

2. Define a five-step, inside contour with an offset of .05 inches in the Contour rollup.

3. Click on the color wheel in the rollup to switch to the color wheel tab of the Contour rollup. Choose gray from the outline color palette in either the rollup or the Property bar. In Figure 13.9, I'm selecting a color from the Property bar.

4. Click on the Apply button to assign the changes to your object.

The transition between object outlines and contour outlines functions interactively. In other words, you can change either an object outline color or the contour color, and the contours will evolve from the assigned outline color to the assigned contour.

13

Figure 13.9

Contours can transform from the original outline (or fill) color to a new color.

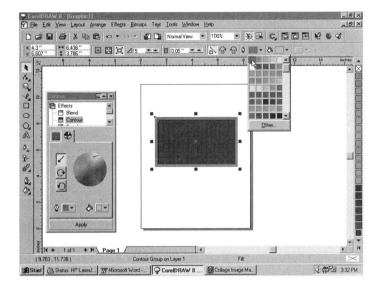

In Figure 13.10, I changed the outline color for my framed rectangle to a light color and my contour outline color to black. The intermediate, generated contour lines transform gradually from my light color to black.

Figure 13.10

Contour outlines can transform from one color to another.

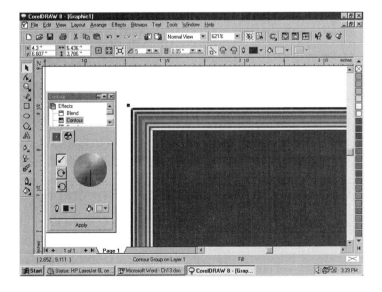

Summary

Both the blend and contour effects apply gradual changes to selected objects. The blend effect requires two different objects that are "blended" into each other by generating a series of intermediate objects.

The contour effect is useful for creating 3D type outlines as well as concentric circles. It is applied by defining a number of steps, as well as the distance between steps.

Workshop

In this workshop, you review some of the techniques you learned in Hours 11, 12, and 13. Some of the effects in this workshop are a bit of a challenge, but please feel free to modify them to fit your current skill level. As long as you use the effects listed in each step, you'll reinforce your effects skills. The goal is to create something similar to the model illustration that our resident artist Paul Mikulecky cooked up. Paul combined bitmap images, PowerClips, lenses, and contours to create the compass in Figure 13.11.

Figure 13.11

Paul's illustration combines PowerClips, bitmap images, contours, transparency and lenses.

1. Draw a rectangle to create a background, about 7" wide and 4" high. Duplicate the rectangle and fill with a tile pattern of your choice. Fill the original rectangle with gray, and add an inside contour offset .03 and five steps. Make the duplicate (tile pattern filled) rectangle slightly smaller than the original (gray, contoured) rectangle, and center them on each other. In Figure 13.12, you can see the beveled effect created by the contour applied to the background rectangle.

13

Figure 13.12

The five-step contour applied to the background rectangle creates a beveled-looking frame from the illustration.

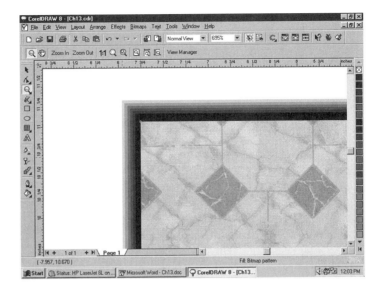

2. Create the compass face by loading a bitmap image of a compass from the CorelDRAW clip-art collection found on the CD. In my case, I simplified this by loading a clock face from the Wingding symbol font set. I filled my clock face symbol with black and converted it to a 300dpi bitmap without transparency. Frame the compass (or in my case clock face) with a larger circle, and apply a one step, outside contour to the framing (larger) circle. Create a third circle and transform it into a lens. Your clock or compass face can look something like the one in Figure 13.13.

Figure 13.13

The clock face combines a symbol converted to a bitmap, a contoured circle, and a lens.

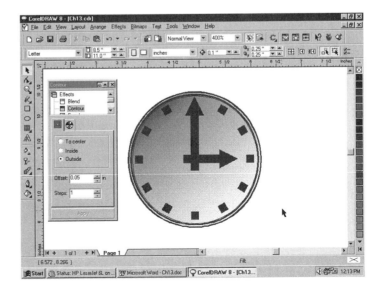

3. Create a shadowed, wood background for the watch or compass by filling a circle with a wood bitmap fill. Create a second circle over the first (filled) one, and fill it with black. Apply Interactive Transparency, with the most opaque (black) handle in the upper-left corner. Group these two circles and duplicate. Select the duplicate and expand it to be slightly wider than the original. Change the Interactive Transparency of the second black circle to go the other direction, and put the larger wood circle behind the smaller one. Your effect can look something like the one in Figure 13.14.

Figure 13.14

The beveling effect in the wood background is created by duplicating and rotating filled circles filtered with interactive transparency.

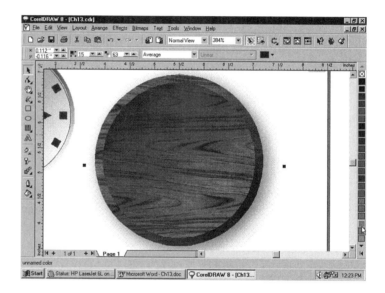

4. You can add a "gold" hinge to your compass or watch by first creating a small circle and duplicating it. Fill one circle with yellow, one with orange or gold, and blend the two. Delete outlines from both the first and last circles. Figure 13.15 shows the resulting blended image. I've copied it and moved it next to the watch/compass setting.

5. Add a lens to the compass or watch face: Create a circle and size it to the size of the watch or compass face. Contour using 1, .125-inch contour. Reshape the circle so that it is more of an oval. Add a new oval over the existing one and assign the Tinted Grayscale Lens effect to it. You can add a gold handle such as you created in step 4 to connect the lens and the watch or compass, as you see in Figure 13.16.

13

Figure 13.15

A yellow circle blended into a gold or orange one creates a gold handle for the watch or compass.

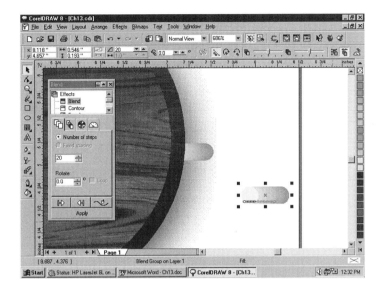

Figure 13.16

The watch/compass lens is created with a Tinted Grayscale Lens effect.

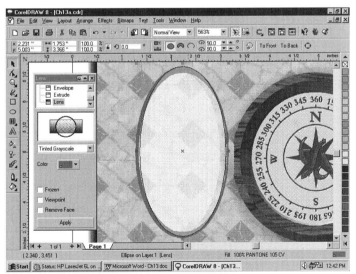

6. Touch up your illustration by moving objects front and back.

Quiz

1. What does the Blend tool do?
2. What are the two main ways to define the appearance of a blend after the objects have been selected?
3. How do you define the line thickness of the lines generated by the contour effect?
4. What happens when you edit one of the two objects used to generate a blend?

Quiz Answers

1. The blend effect fills the area between two different objects with a set of new objects that transform attributes such as shape and color, step-by-step, from the first object to the second.
2. You can control the effect of a blend by defining the number of steps and assigning rotation to the intermediate objects created by the blend effect.
3. The thickness and color of the generated contour lines is determined by the thickness and color of the original lines.
4. Blended objects affect the generated transitional objects interactively. In other words, if you change one of the two blended objects, all the generated intermediate objects change as well.

13

Hour **14**

Working with Perspective

Adding perspective allows you to transform objects to create a three-dimensional look. The artistic text in Figure 14.1 appears to be coming off the page and toward the viewer. You can apply perspective with three different effects: Extrusion, Envelopes, and the Perspective effect itself. In this hour, you learn to work with vanishing points, which make any object appear to display three dimensions; such objects have *perspective*.

Figure 14.1

*Perspective applies a
different point of view to
your objects.*

Applying Perspective

You apply perspective by moving specially empowered handles that appear when you apply the Perspective effect. These perspective handles enable you to stretch your selected object as if it were enclosed in a rubber band.

As you drag the perspective handles, a vanishing point is created. This vanishing point represents the spot at which your object would hypothetically disappear into a point if it extended that far. In Figure 14.2, you can see the vanishing point for the artistic text. That vanishing point is quite a distance from the object on the Drawing window but off the Drawing page.

You can move the vanishing point for an object to change the degree of perspective. Moving the vanishing point closer to the object increases the degree of the effect. After you apply perspective to an object, you can edit the vanishing point by selecting the object with the Shape tool.

If you drag the vanishing point very close to the object, the degree of perspective will be quite extreme, as you can see in Figure 14.3. Dragging the vanishing point far from the object creates a subtle effect.

JUST A MINUTE

> You can clear perspective from an object by selecting that object and then selecting Effects | Clear Perspective from the menu bar.

14.1: Apply Perspective to an Artistic Object

TO DO

1. Create a text object using artistic text; your name, my name, you'll figure something out. Size the object so it is about 4" wide, and 2" high.

2. With the text object selected, choose Effects | Apply Perspective from the menu bar.

14

Figure 14.2

The location of the vanishing point determines the degree of perspective.

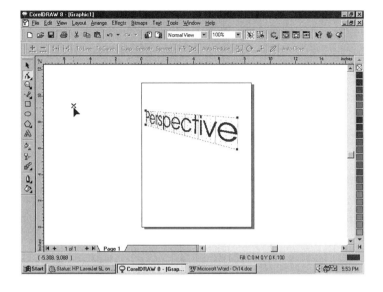

Figure 14.3

Moving the vanishing point close to an object creates an extreme effect.

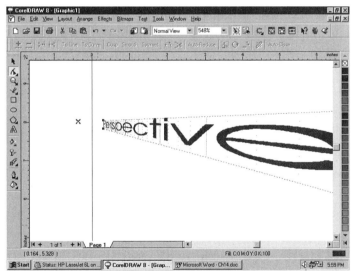

14

3. Hold down Ctrl and drag the bottom Perspective handle down as I'm doing in Figure 14.4.

Figure 14.4
The perspective handles move the vanishing point.

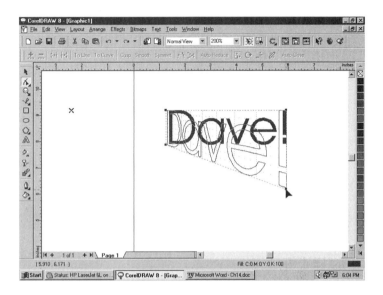

By holding Ctrl down as you drag on a perspective handle, you are constricted to pulling straight down.

JUST A MINUTE

 4. Release the cursor and examine the effect of adding perspective.

Editing Perspective

After you have assigned perspective to an object, you can edit that perspective by moving the vanishing point. If you deselect your object, you can reselect it with the Shape tool to see the vanishing point.

14.2: Edit Perspective

1. Choose the Shape tool and click on the object to which you just applied perspective.

2. Drag the vanishing point in toward the artistic text to intensify the degree of perspective.

3. Drag the vanishing point out to moderate the degree of perspective.

14

4. Pull the vanishing point all the way across the object so that the vanishing point moves to the other direction.

5. Experiment with moving the perspective handles on your object. As you can see in Figure 14.5, the vanishing point moves as you adjust the handles.

Figure 14.5

You can create 3D vanishing points by moving perspective handles.

If you make an insane mess of your object, you can always select Effects | Clear Perspective from the menu bar.

Enclosing Objects in Envelopes

The Envelope effect allows you even more control over vanishing points and perspective. Envelopes provide a frame for whatever object is inside of them. So, for example, you can take artistic text, put it in a triangular-shaped envelope, and squish the text to fit the triangle. You can apply four different types of envelopes to an object: Straight Line, Single Arc, Double Arc, and Unconstrained. Examples of all four are on display in Figure 14.6.

Display the Envelope rollup by selecting View | Rollup | Envelope from the menu bar. Figure 14.7 identifies the buttons on the Envelope rollup and the Envelope Property bar that select the different types of envelopes.

14

Figure 14.6
The Envelope effect comes with four ways to apply perspective.

Straight Line

Single Arc

Double Arc

Unconstrained

Figure 14.7
You can assign envelope effects from either the rollup or the Property bar.

Property bar

Straight line
Single arc
Double arc

Unconstrained

Creating Straight Line Envelopes

When you apply a straight line envelope, you are restricted to straight lines between each perspective handle. When you apply a single arc envelope, you can have a curved line serve as an envelope. Double arc envelopes allow complex curves in between handles. And unconstrained envelopes are just what they sound like; they can be reshaped in any form.

14

14.3: Apply a Straight Line Envelope to Artistic Text

1. Type your name in artistic text and enlarge the object to four inches wide and about two inches high.

2. Select Effects | Envelope from the menu bar.

3. With the Single Line mode selected in the rollup (or the Property bar), click on Add New in the rollup.

4. Hold down Shift and drag in on the top-right handle.

5. After you experiment with your envelope, select Effects | Clear envelope from the menu bar to restore your object to its pre-envelope state.

> By holding Shift down as you drag on a perspective handle, you force your envelope to be symmetrical.

JUST A MINUTE

Creating Arc Envelopes

The single and double arc modes enable you to assign curved lines to the envelope shape. They work in a similar way, except that the double arc mode enables you to create more complex shapes. The really interesting stuff happens when you use the unconstrained mode or you use an existing object as an envelope.

14.4: Apply a Single Arc Envelope to Artistic Text

1. Your name or some other artistic text should still be in your CorelDRAW drawing. If not, type your name in artistic text.

2. If the Envelopes rollup is not on your screen, select Effects | Envelope from the menu bar.

3. With the Single Arc mode selected in the rollup (or the Property bar), click on Add New in the rollup.

4. Hold down Shift and drag up on the bottom (center) handle.

5. After you experiment with this effect, select Effects | Clear Envelope from the menu bar.

Molding Objects with Envelopes

You can use the Envelope effect to mold an object to a preset shape. This can be a shape from a nice list of geometric shapes and popular symbols available from the Envelope rollup, or you can define your own shape and use that to enclose your object. These techniques are often used to shape artistic text.

14

14.5: Place Artistic Text in a Shaped Envelope

1. Select artistic text.
2. Select Unconstrained mode in the Envelope rollup.
3. Click on Add Preset in the rollup, and click on the waving banner shape in the list of available shapes. Figure 14.8 shows this selection.

Figure 14.8

The Envelope rollup comes stocked with popular shapes that you can use to envelop text.

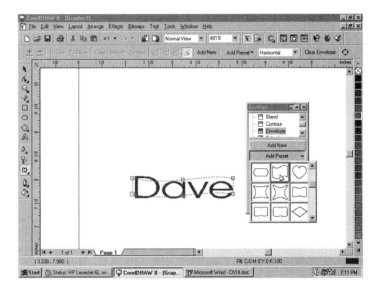

4. Click on the Apply button in the rollup.
5. After you place your text in a shape, you can edit the shape handles to reform your text.

Envelopes and Artistic Text

Not every envelope looks good with every text object. Sometimes placing artistic text in an envelope distorts it so badly that it is unreadable. It is often hard to predict whether your artistic text will look good in a defined envelope, so some trial and error is usually necessary.

To get rid of an envelope, select the object that has been placed in an envelope, and then select Effects | Clear Envelope. You can apply more than one envelope to a single object. Each time you choose Effects | Clear Envelope, you delete one envelope, but you can delete more than one by repeating that process.

You can also use an object that you create from a shape or closed curve as a mold for an envelope.

14

14.6: Place Artistic Text in a Hexagon

1. You have artistic text in your Drawing window, so create a hexagon shape. Stretch it out so it's about twice as wide as it is high.

2. Select your text.

3. Click on the Unconstrained mode button in the Envelope rollup, and then click on the eyedropper in the rollup. A large black arrow appears, as you can see in Figure 14.9.

Figure 14.9

You can select existing shapes to create envelopes.

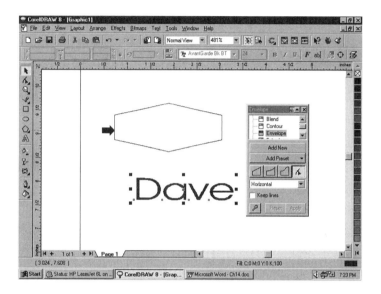

 4. Click on the Apply button to apply the envelope to your text object.

JUST A MINUTE

Even after you apply an envelope effect to text, you can edit the text content by pressing Ctrl+Shift+T with the text selected.

Wild Effects with Extrusion

Extrusion is another way of adding perspective to a selected object. Extrusion effects give text, curves, or shapes a 3D look.

Extrusion combines 3D effects with shading to create a whole range of wild effects. These are ideal for flashy, colorful, attention-getting text. Extrusion is a form of adding perspective.

14

Extruded effects have vanishing points that you can edit, just like objects to which you apply perspective.

Although extrusion can be applied to any vector object in CorelDRAW, it's usually used on text to add flair to a message, such as the text in Figure 14.10.

Figure 14.10

Extruded text.

The Extrusion effect is potentially one of the most complex things you can work with in CorelDRAW. However, you can have a lot of fun with this effect without applying every single element available in the rollup.

When you select text and then apply the Extrusion effect, you can define a vanishing point for the effect, rotate the extruded object, apply lighting from various angles, edit colors, and add beveling. This is done through four different tabs in the Extrude rollup.

14.7: Extrude Text

1. Type some text. Your first name will work well for this. Then select the text and choose Effects | Extrude from the menu.

2. Click on the first tab in the Extrude rollup, and change the setting in the Extrusion Depth spin box to 15. You might see the vanishing point on your Drawing window move as you change the spin box settings. Click on the Apply button in the rollup.

3. Click on the second tab in the rollup, the Rotation icon. Click and drag on the "C" to rotate your extruded object, as shown in Figure 14.11. Click on Apply. Press Ctrl+Z to undo this or any extrusion effect you don't like.

4. Click on the third tab, the Lighting icon. Click on light source 1 from the set of three on the left side of the rollup. Click to place that light source in the upper-left corner of the object, as shown in Figure 14.12. Click on Apply.

14

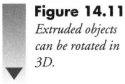

Figure 14.11
Extruded objects can be rotated in 3D.

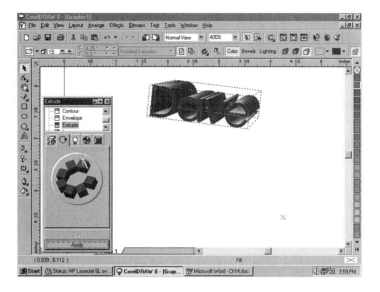

Figure 14.12
Moving the light source defines shading in the extruded object.

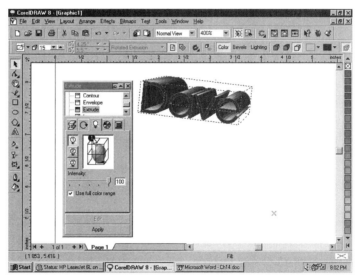

5. Click on the fourth icon (from the left) in the rollup, and select the Shade radio button. Select white in the From color palette and black in the To palette. This creates a gradient fill that is applied to the Extrusion effect. Click on Apply to observe the effect of the Shade effect.

6. Click on the last tab in the Extrusion rollup, and click on the Use Bevel check box. Click on Apply to add beveled edges to your extruded effect.

As you can see, you have almost unlimited effects that you can apply with extrusion, and not all of them look great. In the previous exercise, you applied five different effects through the Extrusion rollup, but normally you will want to be a bit more restrained. A little extrusion goes a long way.

Summary

Perspective, Envelopes, and Extrusion are three ways to apply 3D effects to objects in CorelDRAW 8. Perspective is relatively restrained and subtle. Envelopes provide more dramatic effects, and extrusion is over the top.

Both perspective and extrusion are defined by the location of a vanishing point, an imaginary spot where your object would disappear if it extended all the way to that point. You can change the impact of these effects by moving the vanishing point.

Workshop

The poster in Figure 14.13 includes an envelope effect applied to a musical symbol, and extruded text. Give it a try.

1. Create an artistic text object, "Shining Stars The Musical." You can press Enter after the first two words to create a two-line text object.

2. Apply an extrusion effect to the text.

3. Get musical note symbols from the Symbols Docker window. You can find these symbols in the Webdings font set.

4. Apply envelopes to distort the musical notes. Add extrusion effects to the notes.

5. Create a five-star polygon and rotate it 45 degrees. Edit the nodes to distort the star. Use a fountain fill in the star. Duplicate (Ctrl+D) the star to fill the background.

6. Type "shining star", and then use Copy and Paste to copy the text about a hundred times.

7. Use a PowerClip to fill a large star with the text you created in step 6.

8. Move objects front and back as necessary and touch up the poster.

14

Figure 14.13

This poster includes extruded text and envelope effects.

Quiz

1. How do you move the vanishing point when you apply extrusion?

2. What does a straight line envelope allow you to do?

3. How do you remove perspective from an object?

4. How do you mold artistic text to a shape?

Quiz Answers

1. You can move the vanishing point in the first tab of the Extrusion tab of the Extrusion rollup (the first one) by using the Depth spin box.

2. When you apply a straight line envelope, you create a shape in which you can place other objects. Straight line envelopes are constricted to straight lines between each handle.

3. You can clear perspective from an object by selecting that object and then selecting Effects | Clear Perspective from the menu bar.

4. You can use the Envelope effect to mold any object including an artistic text object to a preset shape.

14

Hour **15**

Designing with Paragraph Text

CorelDRAW's paragraph text features provide all the power of a modern word processor. A built-in, automatic spell checker flags words not found in the dictionary with a wavy red underline and can even change DAve to Dave for you automatically.

You might be saying to yourself, "Yes, but I have all that with my word processing program." Okay, but can your word processing program take that text and shape it into a warped star, like I'm doing in Figure 15.1?

Figure 15.1

Can your word processor do this?

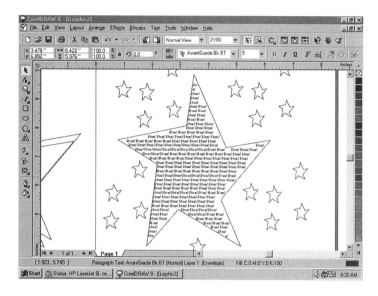

You can also apply other graphic features to paragraph text in CorelDRAW 8. For example, in Figure 15.2, I've applied a fountain fill to a block of paragraph text, and then placed a black background behind the light-colored text.

Figure 15.2

Fountain fills and background objects can be added to paragraph text for effects not available in a word processor.

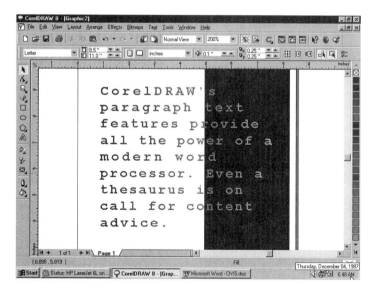

Figure 15.3 shows a cover page for a newsletter designed by Paul. It includes paragraph text, shapes, fountain fills, a bitmap image, and artistic text.

15

Figure 15.3

CorelDRAW 8 enables you to combine artistic and paragraph text along with graphic objects.

You use the same tool to create paragraph text that you used to create artistic text, the Text tool in the toolbox. What is different is that when you create paragraph text, you start by clicking and drawing a rectangle in the Drawing window (as opposed to just clicking with the Text tool, which creates artistic text).

In this hour, you create paragraph text frames and learn to check spelling and adjust word and line spacing for frames of paragraph text. You also learn to shape paragraph text with envelopes and flow text from one frame into another.

Create Paragraph Text and Check Spelling

CorelDRAW 8 has a spelling checker that flags words not found in the dictionary as you type. It even automatically corrects common spelling or capitalization mistakes.

15.1: Create a Paragraph Text Frame and Correct Spelling Automatically

To Do

1. Click on the Text tool.

2. In the Drawing window, drag to create a rectangle.

3. Type "DAve is teh man," with those spelling and capitalization mistakes. Note that the spelling and capitalization are corrected automatically.

4. Type "nott," and note the red, wavy line under the misspelled text. Right-click on the text and click on the correct spelling for "not" in the shortcut menu.

5. Right-click on the word "man" that you just typed, and choose Thesaurus from the shortcut menu. Use the Thesaurus to select a synonym for "man."

6. Click on the Pick tool, and use the Pick tool to select the text frame you just created. Press Delete on your keyboard to delete the text frame.

That was easy, huh? Just like your word processor. Now let's see what CorelDRAW 8 can do with text that your word processor cannot do.

Assigning Effects to Paragraph Text

Most effects that you can assign to other objects can be assigned to paragraph text. For example, you can assign fill colors, outline colors, or fountain fills to paragraph text.

You can also assign special effects to paragraph text that are not available for other objects in CorelDRAW 8. The most useful of these special features is drop caps, extra large letters that you can place at the beginning of any paragraph.

Assign Drop Caps

You can assign a drop cap to the first word in a selected paragraph. Drop caps are available from the Effects tab of the Format Text dialog box.

15.2: Assign a Drop Cap to a Paragraph

1. Draw a paragraph text frame at least 4" wide and 4" high.

2. Type "CorelDRAW's paragraph text features provide all the power of a modern word processor. Even a thesaurus is on call for content advice."

3. Select Text | Format Text from the menu bar, and click on the Effects tab in the dialog box.

4. Select Drop Cap from the Effect drop-down list.

5. Click on OK in the dialog box. Your drop cap will look something like the one in Figure 15.4.

6. Save this document so that you can use it in the next To Do exercise.

Assigning Effects to Text

You can assign different effects that you've learned in earlier hours to paragraph text. Because you already learned these techniques and applied them to other objects, you can try them out on paragraph text.

Figure 15.4

Easily assign a drop cap to any paragraph.

Try these effects on paragraph text:

☐ Assign a fountain fill to the paragraph text (use the same fill techniques you learned in Hour 7).

☐ Create a colored shape, and move it behind the text.

☐ Drag with the Text tool to select some of your text (not all), and assign a color to that text from the color palette.

Adjust Line and Word Spacing

When you select a frame of paragraph text using the shape-sizing handles, you can adjust letter, line, word, or paragraph spacing interactively.

Dragging up on the bottom shape handle makes line spacing tighter (less). Dragging down increases line spacing.

When you drag to the right with the right side shape-sizing handle, you stretch out spacing between letters. When you drag to the left, you compress letter spacing.

Holding down Ctrl while you drag on the shape-sizing handles changes the effect. If you hold down Ctrl while you drag on the right side shape-sizing handle, you increase *word* spacing. And if you hold down Ctrl while you drag on the down shape-sizing handle, you increase spacing between *paragraphs* instead of between lines.

15.3: Increase Line and Letter Spacing

1. Use the Pick tool to select the paragraph text frame you typed in the previous To Do exercise, and note the two shape-sizing handles in the lower-right corner. You can see them in Figure 15.5.

Figure 15.5

You can adjust character and line spacing interactively.

2. Drag down on the bottom shape-sizing handle. Note that line spacing increases.
3. Drag to the right on the right shape-sizing handle to increase letter spacing.
4. Hold down Ctrl and drag to the right on the right shape-sizing handle to increase word spacing.

Shape Text with Envelopes

In Hour 10, you learned to edit shapes and curves around objects. When you edit the shape of artistic text, the shape of the letters changes, and you create cool but strange effects with distorted text. However, when you place paragraph text in an envelope shape, the text flows in the shape without changing the look of the letters. Figure 15.6 shows paragraph text in a shape. Notice that whereas the text conforms to the shape of the envelope, the letters are not misformed.

15

Figure 15.6

You can shape paragraph text with envelopes.

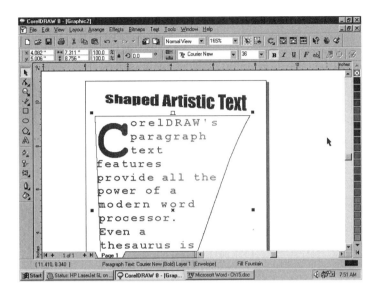

To shape text to an envelope, use the Pick tool to select the paragraph text frame, and then shape the envelope with the Interactive Envelope tool.

15.4: Shape Text with the Interactive Envelope Tool

1. Click with the Pick tool to select the paragraph text frame you've been working with.
2. Select the Interactive Envelope tool from the Interactive Blend tool rollup, as I'm doing in Figure 15.7.

Figure 15.7

The Interactive Envelope tool lets you shape text frames.

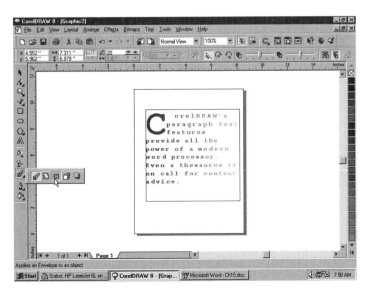

3. Click on the To Line button in the Property bar.
4. Drag in on the lower-right corner shape handle, as I'm doing in Figure 15.8.

Figure 15.8
Shape text with line nodes.

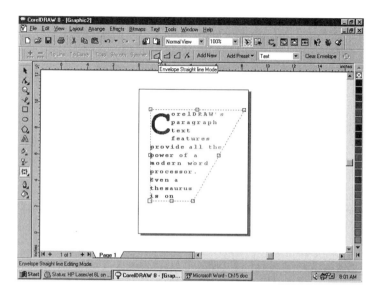

5. Click on the To Curve button in the Property bar, and reshape the text envelope using the bottom-right node again. All the techniques you learned for shaping envelope nodes in Hour 10 can be applied to paragraph text frames.

Figure 15.9
Shape text with complex curves.

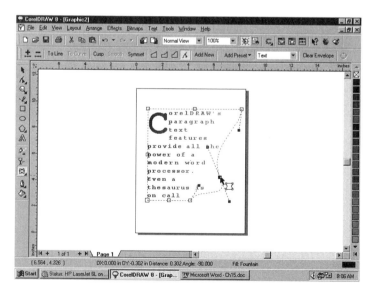

15

Flow Text Between Frames

If all your text does not fit in a single frame, you can flow it from one frame to another.

15.5: Flow Text from One Frame into Another

To Do

1. Select the text frame you've been working with using the Pick tool.

2. Drag up on the bottom handle (not the shape-sizing handle, but the regular bottom sizing handle). Keep making your text frame smaller until the text you typed does not fit into the frame.

3. When text does not fit in the frame, the bottom sizing handle changes from an open square to one with a triangle in it. Click on that triangle to "load" the cursor with the text that didn't fit in the frame.

4. Drag with the text-loaded cursor to draw a new text frame into which you will continue the text. I'm doing this in Figure 15.10.

Figure 15.10

Flowing text into a new frame.

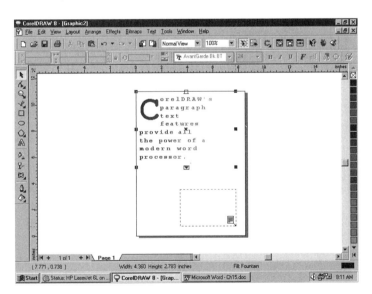

5. After you continue text, the bottom handle of the first text frame displays a box with lines, meaning the text is continued. A line appears connecting the original frame to the "continued to" frame, as you can see in Figure 5.11.

6. Enlarge your second text frame until all the continued text fits, like I'm doing in Figure 15.12. When there is no more text to display, the bottom handle of the final frame displays as an open square.

Figure 15.11

Flowed text is marked with lines.

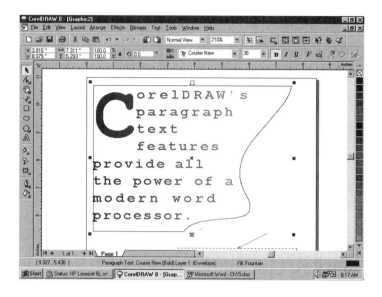

Figure 15.12

An open box indicates all the continued text fits in the "continued to" frame.

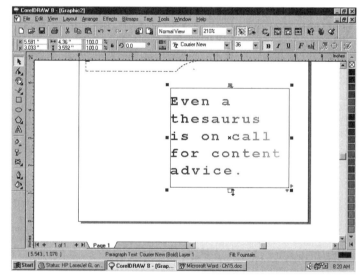

Summary

Paragraph text combines the features of a word processor with CorelDRAW's graphic features. You can create, edit, and spell check text in the Text Edit window. After you create paragraph text in CorelDRAW, you can apply effects to the text frame, including color fills and shaping.

15

If your text does not fit in your text frame, you can continue that text into other text frames. This is especially helpful if you lay out a brochure that mixes graphics with text.

Workshop

In this workshop, you sharpen your paragraph text skills. You create some paragraph text, add a drop cap, shape the text, and flow it from one frame to another.

1. Open a new drawing. Use the Pick tool to drag from the vertical ruler to create guidelines at 1", 4", 4 $^1/_2$ ", and 7". Draw horizontal lines (by dragging down the horizontal ruler) at 3" and 9". The guidelines are shown in Figure 15.13. Select Layout | Snap to Guidelines from the menu bar.

Figure 15.13

Guidelines make it easy to create two matching text frames.

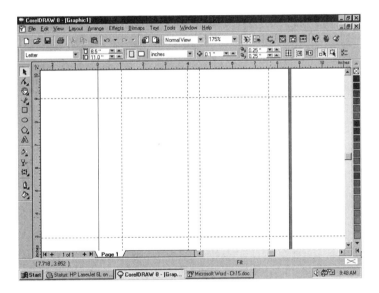

2. Drag with the Text tool to create a marquee. Select Text | Edit Text from the menu bar to open the Text Edit window.

3. Type: This is sample txt.

4. Right-click on "txt" and select "text" from the pop-up list of spellings.

5. Drag to select the entire sentence. Press Ctrl+C to copy the text. Click to place your insertion point at the end of the sentence, and press Ctrl+V ten times. Press Enter and press Ctrl+V ten times again. Create five more of these repetitive paragraphs.

6. Drag to select all the text, and apply 12-point Arial font.

7. Click on OK to close the Text Edit window.

8. Resize the text frame so it fits on the left side of the page, as shown in Figure 15.14.

Figure 15.14

The black triangle at the bottom of the text frame indicates more text than will fit in the frame.

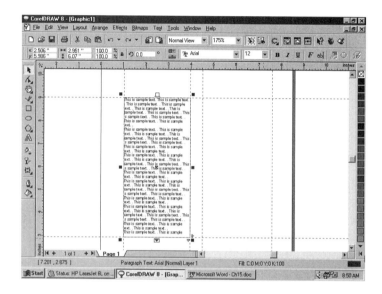

9. Click on the icon at the bottom of the text frame, and draw a new marquee on the right side of the page, as shown in Figure 15.15.

Figure 15.15

Flowing text into a new frame.

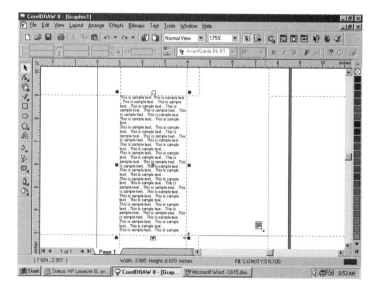

15

10. Drag a symbol from the Symbol Docker window into the middle of the page. You can use one of the symbols from the Animals1 font set. Enlarge the symbol by about 400%.

11. Click on the Interactive Shape tool in the toolbox, and shape the two text frames so they don't cover the symbol, as shown in Figure 15.16.

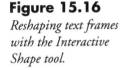

Figure 15.16

Reshaping text frames with the Interactive Shape tool.

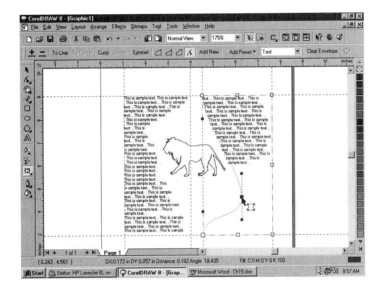

12. Select the first (left) text frame, and choose Text | Edit Text from the menu bar. Drag to select the first paragraph of the text frame, and then click on the Format Text button in the Text Edit window. Click in the Effects tab of the Format Text dialog box, and assign a 3 line drop cap to the selected paragraph. Click on OK in the dialog box.

13. Select Text | Fit Text to Frame to resize your text so it fits perfectly in your frames.

14. Save your file; you'll use it in the next hour.

Quiz

1. How do you enter paragraph text, as opposed to artistic text?

2. How do you assign font type and size to paragraph text?

3. How do you shape paragraph text?

4. If you want to resize your text to fit in a text frame, what's the quick, easy way to do that automatically?

Quiz Answers

1. To type paragraph text in the Drawing window, start by selecting the Text tool in the toolbox and drawing a marquee to frame your text.

2. You can format the font type and size for selected paragraph text in the Edit Text dialog box or in the Drawing window. In either case, use the cursor to select the text (in the Drawing window, you have to select the Text tool first). Then choose font type and size from the drop-down menus in the toolbars.

3. When you select a frame of paragraph text with the Text tool, you can shape it with the Interactive Shape Tool—the third one on the Interactive Blend flyout.

4. You can resize text to fit a frame by selecting the text frame and then selecting Text | Fit Text to Frame from the menu bar.

15

Hour 16

Managing Layers and Pages

You can add, delete, and navigate between pages in CorelDRAW 8. This is useful for creating multipage brochures or newsletters, or working with longer documents that you want to publish with CorelDRAW.

The Object Manager Docker window works as an organizing tool to help you arrange and edit objects in complex illustrations. Even at this point, in working with one page, you might have noticed that keeping track of the wide variety of objects you create in an illustration can get crazy. Some of the illustrations our resident artist Paul designs involve hundreds of objects. You can often find objects more easily using Wireframe view than you can in Normal view, but when you have stacked a dozen objects on top of each other, even Wireframe view isn't much help in sorting through or finding objects.

With CorelDRAW 8, Corel has beefed up the Object Manager. If you're used to the old Layers rollup in earlier versions of CorelDRAW, it's gone. But that's okay because all its features have been incorporated into the new and improved Object Manager. The Object Manager makes it easy to find objects. You can even assign unique names to each object you create, such as "Dave's big ol' red rectangle" or something more creative.

Finally, in this hour you'll explore the process of creating a master page using the Object Manager. Objects on a master page appear on every page in your drawing. This is handy, for example, if you want to place a logo or text such as "Zoo News" on every page in your drawing.

Working with Multiple Pages

You can add pages to your publication, delete them, and even name them. After you create several pages, you can navigate between them using the navigation bar and tabs at the bottom of the Drawing window (just above the status bar).

To Add pages, select Layout | Insert Page from the menu bar. You'll see the Insert Page dialog box, shown in Figure 16.1. This dialog box lets you define how many pages you want to insert and whether you want those pages before or after the current page.

Figure 16.1.

You can insert pages before or after the current (selected) page.

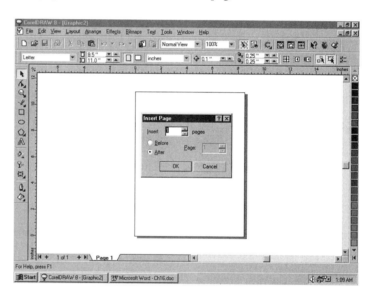

16.1: Add Three Pages to a Drawing, Name Your Pages, and Delete Pages

1. Open a new CorelDRAW file.
2. Select Layout | Insert Page from the menu bar and enter 3 in the Insert Pages spin box.
3. Leave the After radio button selected.

4. Click on OK.

5. Note that you now have four page tabs on the bottom of your Drawing window.

You can view all four Drawing window tabs at once by dragging on the divider between the page tabs and the scrollbar. In Figure 16.2, I'm enlarging the page tabs area so I can see all four tabs.

Figure 16.2.

You can resize the area dedicated to page tabs.

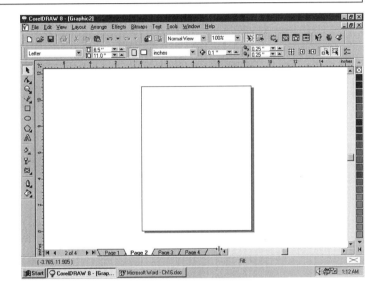

6. Right-click on the Page 1 tab, and select Rename Page from the shortcut menu.

7. Enter a new name, "Cover," in the Rename Page dialog box, as I'm doing in Figure 16.3.

Figure 16.3.

You can name pages.

8. Name the last page (page 4) "Back" on your own.

9. Right-click on Page 3 and select Delete Page from the shortcut menu. Delete Page 2 as well, so only the Front and Back pages remain.

After you create a couple different pages, you can navigate between them by clicking on a page tab or by using the arrow navigation buttons to the left of the page tabs. These arrows differ depending on how many pages are in your publication, and which page you have selected. But the ones on the left move you to the front of the publication, and the ones on the right move you toward the end. If two arrows point in one direction, the one on the outside takes you to the beginning or end of the publication.

Navigating with the Object Manager

The Object Manager enables you to navigate from one page to another and from one object to another. You view the Object Manager Docker window by selecting Layout|Object Manager from the menu bar.

The Object Manager has three icons on top, as shown in Figure 16.4.

Figure 16.4.

The three icons on top of the Object Manager let you add layers, control how much you see about each page, and control your editing.

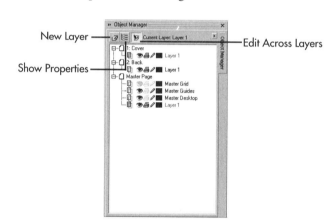

For now, just be aware of these three icons, and refer back to Figure 16.4 if I ask you to click on one of them.

The Object Manager displays all the pages you have created and an extra page as well called the Master Page. Objects on the Master Page apply to *all* pages in your publication.

Navigating Layers

You can have more than one layer on a page. Why would you want to do that? There are a number of uses for multilayered pages:

☐ You can view one layer at a time so that you can see only part of your illustration. Sometimes that makes it easier to work with a complex drawing.

☐ You can print only one (or selected) layers on a page. That way you can use one layer for nonprinting objects, such as shapes you use to help design your page.

☐ You can make one (or more) layers "uneditable." So, for example, if you have a number of objects on a page that you don't want disturbed, you can place them on a noneditable layer. You won't accidentally delete or change these objects while you work with objects you do want to edit.

The examples I just listed illustrate the three properties on every layer that you can control: View/Not View, Print/Not Print, and Edit/Not Edit. These properties are set by selecting or unselecting the Eyeball (View/Not View), Printer (Print/Not Print), and Pencil (Edit/Not Editable) icons next to each layer.

16.2: Create a Nonprinting Layer to Mark a Photo

1. Open the two-page CorelDRAW file you created in the previous To Do exercise. Open the Object Manager Docker window if it is not visible (Layout | Object Manager).

2. Click on the small - (minus) sign next to each page to display only the page. In Figure 16.5, I've compressed the Cover and Back pages, and I'm compressing the Master Page.

Figure 16.5.

Page display can be shrunk so only the Page title appears in the Object Manager.

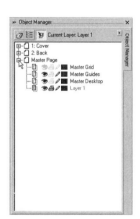

3. Switch to the Back (or 2) page by clicking on the Back (2) page in the Object Manager. Note in the page tab of the Drawing window that you are now looking at Page 2.

4. Switch back to page one and click on the + (plus) symbol to see all layers and objects on that page. Click on the New Layer icon at the top of the Docker window. Name the new layer "Non-Printing," as shown in Figure 16.6.

5. Click on the small printer icon next to the new, nonprinting layer. The little printer should turn gray, indicating that this layer will not print.

6. Draw a 3" by 3" rectangle in the upper-right corner of the page in the Drawing page.

Figure 16.6.

Creating a new,
nonprinting layer.

7. Click on the + next to the nonprinting layer in the Object Manager Docker window. You see your new rectangle listed as the (so far, only) object on this layer.

8. Click twice (slowly, don't double-click) on the new rectangle name in the Object Manager. Enter a new name for this object, "Paste-up photo goes here," as I am doing in Figure 16.7.

Figure 16.7.

Naming an object
in the Object
Manager.

9. Look at the properties of your selected object by clicking on the Show Properties icon at the top of the Object Manager Docker window. After you see your object properties, click on the Show Properties icon again to unclutter the window.

10. Switch back to Layer 1 on the Cover page in the Object Manager by clicking on the small page icon next to Layer 1. Create a couple text frames and fill them with a word or two of copied text. Make sure the text frames do not overlap with the rectangle you created to mark the spot where a photo will be pasted (see Figure 16.8).

16

Figure 16.8.

Combining a printing layer with a nonprinting layer on the same page.

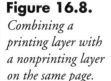

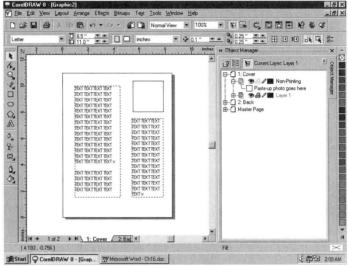

11. Select the Pick tool. Then click on the Eyeball icon next to the nonprinting layer to hide the nonprinting rectangle.

12. Click on the Pencil icon next to the nonprinting layer so that this layer cannot be edited. The nonprinting layer will not be visible, as in Figure 16.9, nor can it be edited. The object on the nonprinting layer looks grayed out in the Object Manager because it cannot be edited.

Figure 16.9.

Any layer can be hidden onscreen or declared off-limits to editing.

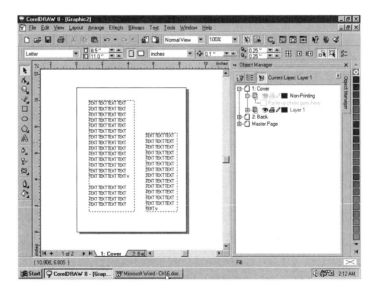

13. If you have access to a printer, print the page and note that objects on the nonprinting layer will not print. (For more information about how to print your CorelDRAW files, see Hour 18, "Printing.")

Another handy thing you can do with the Object Manager is select objects in cluttered, hard-to-edit illustrations. In Figure 16.10, I right-clicked on an ellipse in the Object Manager (not the Drawing window), and I'm choosing delete from the shortcut menu to cut it. This is easier than clicking over and over again trying to find that object in the Drawing window.

Figure 16.10.

Selecting objects is often easier in the Object Manager than in the Drawing window.

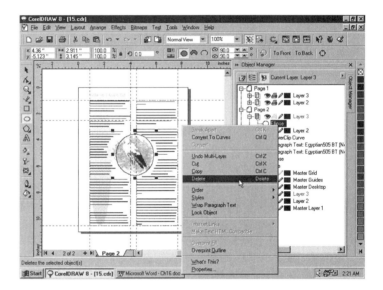

Creating a Master Layer

Objects on Master Layers appear on every page. The default Master Layer generated with each new drawing includes nonprinting Master Guides, Master Grid, and Desktop Layers. These layers simply support the CorelDRAW Drawing window. The Desktop Layer is the area outside the Drawing page in the Drawing window, and normally it does not print.

You can also include printing objects on Master Layers. The best way to do this is to create a new layer on one of your pages and define it as a Master Layer. Place objects on that layer that you want to print on each page. Master Layers are defined by right-clicking on any existing layer and choosing Master Layer from the shortcut menu.

16

16.3: Create a Master Page with an Icon

1. Click on any page in the Object Manager, and click on the New Layer icon.
2. Name the new layer "Every Page" as I am doing in Figure 16.11.

Figure 16.11.

Creating a new layer that will be a Master Layer.

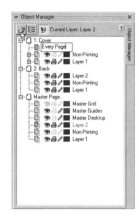

Because CorelDRAW already includes a Master Page, I'm avoiding calling my new layer Master Page to avoid confusion.

JUST A MINUTE

3. Right-click on the new "Every Page" layer and choose Master from the shortcut menu. As soon as you do, this layer will jump down to the Master Page in the Object Manager.

4. Make every level on every page invisible, except for the new Master Every Page layer. Click on that layer in the Object Manager to select it, and enter some text on the page like I'm doing in Figure 16.12.

5. Make every layer on both pages in your drawing visible, and examine pages 1 and 2.

Because the Master Layer text is visible (and will print) on both pages, you should see it in the same place on both the Cover and the Back Page of your drawing.

You can edit the Master Layer text from any layer on any page. So if the Master Layer text is not located right, you can simply move it while you edit your regular pages. If you want to restrict yourself from editing the Master Layer while you're working on other layers, click on the Edit Across Layers icon on top of the Object Manager (the icon on the right). With Edit Across Layers deselected, you can edit only the layer that you have currently selected in the Object Manager.

Figure 16.12.

Master Layer objects will appear on every page.

Summary

By adding more than one page to your drawing, you can use CorelDRAW as a desktop publishing tool to design publications. You can easily navigate from one page to another or rename pages.

The Object Manager Docker window is a powerful way to locate and work with objects in your drawing. It's useful to find objects in crowded illustrations. The Object Manager can also be used to create layers and assign layer properties. Those properties can include nonprinting layers, layers that cannot be edited, or layers that are not visible on the screen.

Workshop

In this workshop, you practice working with multiple pages and layers. You will create a two-page flyer, with a nonprinting layer and a Master Layer.

1. Open a new drawing and add a second page. Name the two pages Front (1) and Back (2).

2. Use the Object Manager to create a second, nonprinting layer on page 2.

3. Working on the nonprinting layer, draw a 4" by 4" square in the lower-right corner of the page, and a 2" by 2" square in the upper-left corner.

4. Give these squares names that remind you that they are saving space for photos that will be pasted up later.

16

5. Create a Master Layer with text on the bottom of the page, as you see in Figure 16.13.

Figure 16.13.

Master Layer text will appear on all pages.

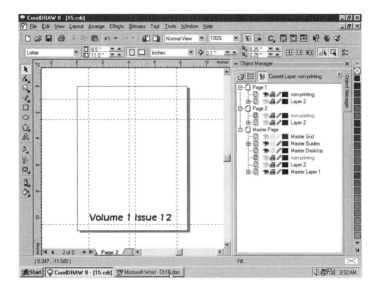

6. View all layers of your drawing.

7. Get creative. Add some text and images to create a two-page edition of *Zoo News*. The front can look like Figure 16.14. Add some text (copy a few words over and over to create practice text) to page 2.

Figure 16.14.

Master Layer text shows up on the front page of the newsletter.

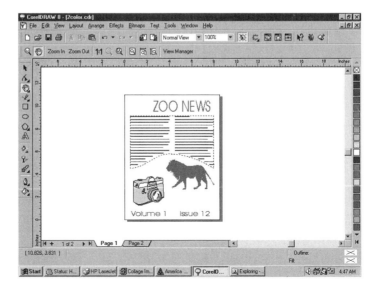

Quiz

1. How do you make the Object Manager Docker window appear?
2. How do you add pages to a drawing?
3. How do you make a layer nonprinting?
4. Can you rename pages?

Quiz Answers

1. You can work with the Object Manager Docker window by selecting Layout | Object Manager from the menu bar.
2. To add pages, select Layout | Insert Page from the menu bar. The Insert Page dialog box enables you to define how many pages you want to insert and whether you want those pages before or after the current page.
3. You can make a layer nonprinting by clicking to deselect the Printer icon in the Object Manager next to the layer.
4. Yes, you can rename pages. Just right-click on the Page tab, and select Rename Page from the shortcut menu.

Hour 17

Importing and Exporting Objects

If you plan to use CorelDRAW objects in a web page, a Word document, a PageMaker publication, or a PowerPoint slide show, for example, you need to export them to a file format other than CorelDRAW (.cdr). Try opening a CorelDRAW file in PowerPoint, for example, and you see a disappointing dialog box such as the one in Figure 17.1.

It hasn't always been easy to move CorelDRAW's vector-based images into desktop publishing, or bitmap graphic or word processing programs. But that was then; this is now. In most cases, transferring graphic images between CorelDRAW 8 and other programs is a smooth process. Usually you can handle the process by copying objects from CorelDRAW into other applications and choosing from various Paste options in the target application.

Moving objects from other programs into CorelDRAW is a bit different. Copied bitmap images enter CorelDRAW as bitmap images, not as vector-based objects. But when you get those bitmap images into CorelDRAW, you can edit them just like you would any other bitmap object in CorelDRAW. You explored that process in Hour 11.

Figure 17.1.
Not all applications like CorelDRAW files but you can get around that and bring your CorelDRAW objects into any program.

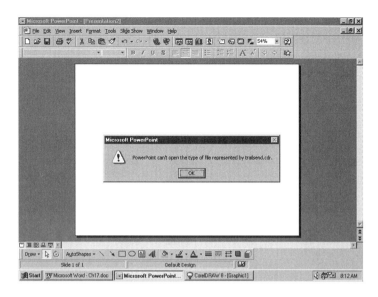

Finally, if you bring your CorelDRAW illustration to a printing service bureau, you might need to provide a file that its software and printers can recognize. Almost every printing service bureau can handle files saved to EPS (Encapsulated PostScript Format). And Corel handles that just fine.

Many Ways to Transfer Objects

Before you walk through some specific examples of importing and exporting different types of other files, it will be helpful to understand the different ways you can move objects in and out of CorelDRAW. Importing, opening files, exporting, copying, pasting—you can use all these techniques to transfer objects in and out of CorelDRAW.

Importing Versus Opening

You can bring files from other programs into a CorelDRAW file either by importing them or by opening them. Opening a foreign format file create a *new* CorelDRAW file. Importing files from other programs brings those objects into *already open* CorelDRAW files. The only difference is that opening foreign files creates a new drawing, whereas importing brings the file contents into your drawing. What happens if you import a file from Adobe Illustrator, for example, into a blank, new document? You get the same result as if you opened that Illustrator file using the CorelDRAW open menu.

You can open the Import and Open dialog boxes using the toolbar, as shown in Figure 17.2. Figure 17.2 also shows the Export button.

17

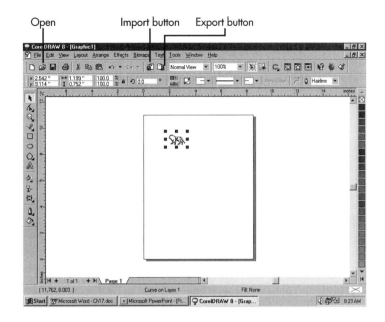

Figure 17.2.

You can bring files from other formats into CorelDRAW using either the Import or the Open buttons.

Exporting Versus Saving As

Although there is a subtle difference between opening foreign format files and importing them, there is no substantial difference between exporting files or using the Save As dialog box to save them to other formats. Okay, one exception to that rule exists. When you learn to export files to EPS format at the end of this hour, you will use the Export dialog box. Whether you export your CorelDRAW drawing or save it as another format, you have the option of saving the entire drawing or just selected objects as another file format.

In short, there's not much difference between exporting objects from CorelDRAW into other file formats and using the Save As dialog box to save them in other file formats.

Copying and Pasting

Most of your transfer problems between CorelDRAW and other programs can be handled by copying and pasting objects. When you select an object, or objects, you can copy them into the Windows Clipboard and then paste them into other applications. In this hour, you explore those options and when to use which one.

In other words, the Windows operating system manages many, if not most, of your importing and exporting problems.

Exporting Paragraph Text

Text frames can be exported to word processing files. The text that you create in CorelDRAW can be saved as a WordPerfect, Word, or generic RTF file.

17.1: Export Text to a Word Processor

1. Create a paragraph text frame by dragging with the Text tool from the toolbox.
2. Type some text in your frame.
3. With the text frame selected, click on the Export button in the Standard toolbar.
4. Click on the Selected Only check box in the Export dialog box.
5. Pull down the Save File as Type drop-down menu in the Export dialog box and choose MS Word or your favorite word processor. Enter a filename in the File name field of the dialog box.
6. Click on the Export button to save the selected text in your word processor format.
7. If you have a word processor installed, you can open the file to see that this worked. If you do this, make some editing changes and save your file again.

Importing Paragraph Text

You are more likely to import word processing documents into CorelDRAW than you are to export them. When you import text into CorelDRAW from a supported word processing format, that text automatically gets poured into a new paragraph text frame. You cannot open word processing documents as new CorelDRAW files. But you can always open a new, blank CorelDRAW file and import the text into it. Your options are to let CorelDRAW figure out the size of that frame or to define your own frame as you import.

17.2: Import a Text File into CorelDRAW

1. If you saved a publication drawing in Hours 15 or 16, you can open that file, or you can open a new, blank CorelDRAW file. If you open an existing file with paragraph text, delete the existing text file(s).
2. Click on the Import button in the toolbar. Select All Files in the Files of Type drop-down menu, and navigate to an existing word processing document.
3. Click on the word processing document file, and then click on the Import button in the Import dialog box.
4. Your cursor will become a paragraph text cursor, with the name of the imported text file, as you see in Figure 17.3.
5. Drag with your imported text cursor to define a frame for the imported text. If your text does not fit in the paragraph text frame, you can enlarge the frame or use the flowing text techniques you learned in Hour 15 to continue the text into other frames.

Your other option is to simply click with the import text cursor. If you do that, CorelDRAW will create a text frame large enough to hold the entire text file.

17

Figure 17.3.

*The imported text cursor
enables you to define a
paragraph text frame to
pour your text into.*

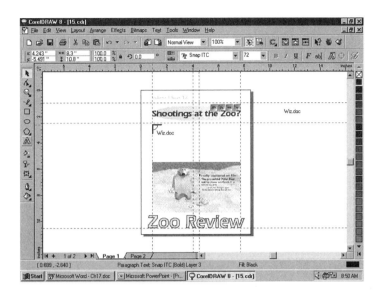

Importing Graphic Objects into CorelDRAW

As you learned earlier in this hour, importing and opening files from other formats is very similar. The difference is that importing brings the file into an open CorelDRAW drawing, whereas opening the file creates a brand new CorelDRAW file.

To import a file from another format, open an existing drawing or create a new one in CorelDRAW. Then click on the Import button in the toolbar and select All Files in the Files of Type drop-down menu in the dialog box. This way, CorelDRAW figures out the type of file.

When you click on the Preview check box in the Import dialog box, you see a thumbnail of supported images in the Preview area of the dialog box.

If your imported image is a bitmap format, the drop-down menu with Full Image showing becomes active. You can select Crop from this drop-down list to crop the file before you import it. If you select the Crop option and click on the Import button, you can crop your image in the Crop Image dialog box before you bring it in. In Figure 17.4, I'm cropping a bitmap image before I import it.

The other option in this drop-down menu enables you to resample a bitmap image before you import it. If you select this option and click on the Import menu, you see the Resample Image dialog box shown in Figure 17.5.

Figure 17.4.

You can crop bitmap images as you import them.

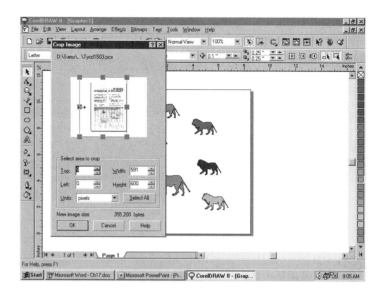

Figure 17.5.

Resampling enables you to change the size and resolution of imported images.

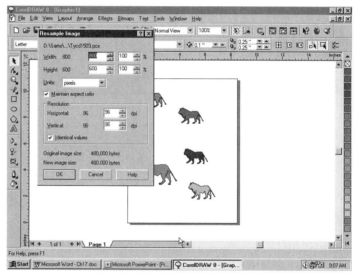

Imported vector-based images from Adobe Illustrator cannot be resampled or cropped as they are imported. However, they can be edited using all the vector-based editing options in CorelDRAW.

17

Copying Objects from CorelDRAW

You can copy files from CorelDRAW into any Windows application. Most applications provide several options for pasting the CorelDRAW file. They include Bitmap File, CorelDRAW Object, and Picture (vector-based) Image.

These are the three main options: If you paste your objects from CorelDRAW as bitmap objects, that are converted into bitmap format and pasted into the target application. If you select CorelDRAW objects, your objects will be pasted into the target application as vector-based images, and you can then edit them in CorelDRAW from within the target application. If you choose Picture format, your graphic will be placed in the target application as a vector-based image format, usually Windows Metafile (*.wmf), but it will not be linked to CorelDRAW.

17.3: Copy a Graphic from CorelDRAW into Another Application

1. Create a graphic image (or several) in CorelDRAW. Select the images you want to copy to another application.

2. Open another application into which you want to paste your selected objects.

3. Select Edit Paste from the target application menu bar.

CAUTION

Don't right-click and choose Paste from a shortcut menu. In most cases, this doesn't provide you with as many Paste options. The Paste option on the Edit menu provides you with more control over the format in which you import your object, as you will see in the next step.

4. Choose one of the radio button file format options. These differ from application to application but, in general, will fit into three categories: copy as bitmap, copy as CorelDRAW object, or copy as a vector format.

JUST A MINUTE

In Figure 17.6, I've opened PowerPoint 97 and am attempting to import a CorelDRAW object. I'm presented with five options in PowerPoint 97. The first option imports the copied graphic as an object that can be edited in CorelDRAW. The two different Picture options import the graphic as vector-based graphics. The two bitmap choices import the image as bitmap graphics. You can experiment when you have more than one vector or bitmap option to see which one looks better when you copy your graphic.

Figure 17.6.

Paste format options break down to three types: CorelDRAW object, (other) vector-based, or bitmap.

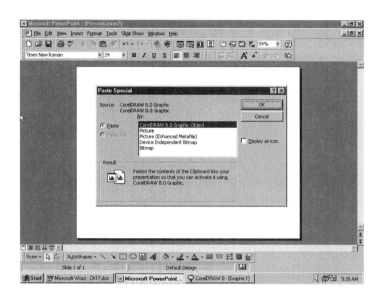

When you select a format, click on OK in the target application Paste Special dialog box.

JUST A MINUTE

Some older applications that still run under Windows 95 do not support Paste Special options. In those cases, you are restricted to pasting in a format defined by the target application.

Most applications to which you copy objects have some way to edit those pasted graphics. If you choose to paste as CorelDRAW objects, they will let you edit those objects in CorelDRAW when you double-click on them.

Exporting Objects from CorelDRAW

You might have situations where copying and pasting, even using Paste Special options, is not enough. One of those options is when you have to convert a CorelDRAW file to a file format that a printing service bureau can handle.

Try calling your favorite printing service bureau or find one in the yellow pages. Ask what kinds of output they can create and they'll impress you with a list of brochures, billboards, posters, and so on. But ask if they have a lot of experience printing CorelDRAW 8 files and they'll probably put you on hold, ask around, and tell you no, not really. However, almost every printing service bureau is comfortable working with EPS files, and CorelDRAW files can be saved to PostScript format.

17

You export drawings to PostScript files using the Export dialog box.

17.4: Export a Drawing to a PostScript File

1. Create a drawing in CorelDRAW or open an existing one.
2. Click on the Export button in the Standard toolbar, and choose Encapsulated PostScript (EPS) from the Save As Type drop-down list.
3. Navigate to a folder if necessary in the Save In drop-down list.
4. Enter a filename in the File name box.
5. Click on the Export button.
6. In the EPS dialog box, you can choose to export text as curves or text. Consult with your printing service bureau to find out how they want you to set this and other options in the dialog box. Or leave the options in the default setting.
7. Click on OK in the dialog box.

JUST A MINUTE

> CorelDRAW can open EPS files, but you will find that the objects in them do not edit well; many effects cannot be applied to objects in these imported files. EPS is not a good format to use for files that you intend to edit. If you save a file as an EPS file for a printer, save the drawing as a CorelDRAW file as well.

Summary

Much of the work of moving objects, either text or graphics, in and out of CorelDRAW can be handled by copying objects. When you copy objects, you can usually paste them into other Windows applications as CorelDRAW objects, other vector-based (Picture) formats, or bitmap images.

When you copy graphic images in or out of CorelDRAW 8, the Paste Special option on the Edit menu gives you control over the format of the graphic image.

The Import button in the CorelDRAW toolbar enables you to bring objects or even entire files into CorelDRAW. When you use the Import dialog box, you can bring objects into CorelDRAW even if you don't have the software in which those imported objects were created.

You can also export images from CorelDRAW to other file formats. You can export either selected objects or entire files. One useful export application is to export CorelDRAW files in Encapsulated PostScript format, which is recognized by almost every printing service bureau.

Workshop

In this workshop, you experiment with exporting and importing graphic objects and text.

1. Create a paragraph text frame and enter a paragraph of text. Apply text formatting including text size, font type, italics, boldface, and text colors.

2. Select the paragraph text frame, and click on the Export button. Export the selected text frame as a document file for your favorite word processor through the options in the Export dialog box.

3. Open the exported file in your word processor. How did CorelDRAW do in exporting your formatting? Don't close your word processing file.

4. Create a drawing in CorelDRAW. Keep it simple, such as a shape or a symbol. Copy the drawing to the Clipboard, and switch to your word processing program.

5. Select Edit | Paste in your word processor menu, and if available, check the CorelDRAW Object radio button in the Paste Special dialog box.

6. Click on OK in the Paste Special dialog box, and note the look of your object in your word processor.

7. Double-click on the pasted object, and, if prompted, choose Open CorelDRAW from the dialog box that appears.

8. Edit your graphic object in CorelDRAW by changing the fill color. Exit CorelDRAW and save your changes.

9. Note the updated appearance of your object in your word processor.

Quiz

1. What's the difference between importing objects from other file formats and opening files of other formats?

2. What features are available to filter imported bitmap images?

3. What do you do when your printing service bureau cannot handle CorelDRAW files?

4. What's the quick, easy way to transfer CorelDRAW objects into other Windows applications?

Quiz Answers

1. Importing files from other programs brings those objects into *already open* CorelDRAW files whereas opening foreign files creates a new drawing.

2. You can crop or resample imported bitmap images.

3. Almost every printing service bureau is comfortable working with EPS files, and CorelDRAW files can be saved to PostScript format.

4. Most of your transfer problems between CorelDRAW and other programs can be handled by copying and pasting objects. When you select an object, or objects, you can copy them into the Windows Clipboard and then paste them into other applications.

Hour 18

Printing

In the hours that you put into learning CorelDRAW, you learned to create some complex illustrations. How do you share those graphic images with the world? You can print them or you can display them onscreen, for example, in a web site. In this hour, you learn to print your CorelDRAW illustrations. You learn to move your CorelDRAW 8 objects into a web page in the next hour in this book.

Printing can be easy or complex. If you print your CorelDRAW illustrations with your own laser printer, the process is basically governed by Windows 95 (or Windows NT). This is true for both color and black-and-white printing. If you've looked at the displays at your local copy shop, you've seen some spectacular color printer output, including full-color posters with near-photographic quality.

CorelDRAW also comes with a full set of printer options that make it easy to print business cards, labels, and other odd-sized output. You learn to print cards and labels in this hour.

Where things get tricky is when you want to translate your CorelDRAW illustration into a mass-produced printed publication. That requires bringing something, a file or printed layout, to your printer. You learn to manage that process in this hour as well.

Printing with Your Printer

If you are preparing a limited number of copies of your illustrations, you can get excellent quality from a color printer. Home-quality color printers are extremely low-cost, and office-quality color printers are more accessible as well.

For the next step in quality, your local Kinko's, Copymat, or the equivalent has color printers with output quality that will create impressive posters and displays. If you need 100,000 copies of your illustration, this isn't a viable option. But if you need one or two copies, or even a hundred copies, the new technology in color printers is your best option.

In the previous hour, you learned how to deal with printing your CorelDRAW illustration on machines that don't support CorelDRAW. You can export your illustration to a program that is supported by the computer connected to a quality color printer. Or if CorelDRAW is on your laptop, take your laptop to your local printer and have them print from your computer.

A Look at Printing Options

If you print the final output for your illustration on your own printer, your print options are basically those available to all Windows applications. You can print selected objects, select pages when you have a multipage document, and print multiple copies. If you have multiple copies of a multipage document, you can click on the Collate check box.

JUST A MINUTE

> The Collate check box organizes your copies so that your documents print out in sets. For example, if you have a four-page document and you want to print two copies, collating prints pages 1, 2, 3, and 4, and then print pages 1, 2, 3, and 4 in that order again. If you do not select the Collate check box, your two copies print in the order of two copies of page 1, followed by two copies of page 2, two copies of page 3, and then two copies of page 4. Collating makes it easier to organize your work, but it slows down the printing process by up to 40%.

To access printer options, don't click on the Print button in the Standard toolbar; instead select File | Print from the menu bar. You see the General tab in the Print dialog box, shown in Figure 18.1

In the General tab of the Print dialog box, you can select an installed printer from the Name drop-down menu, and choose which pages to print in the Print Range area. If you print more than one copy of your file, you can click on the Collate check box in the Copies area to place your copies in order. If, for example, you print 20 uncollated copies of a four-page publication, you'll get 20 page ones, 20 page twos, and so on. If you collate your copies, you'll get 20 sets of the complete document.

18

Figure 18.1.

The General tab of the Print dialog box has the basic controls for printing your illustration.

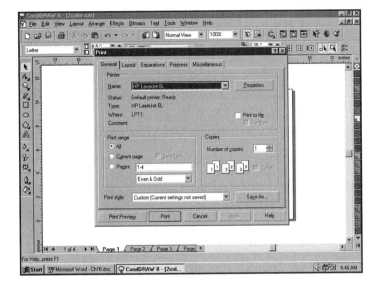

One interesting option is the Even or Odd selections available from the drop-down list in the Print Range area. You can use this to create two-sided copies with a single-side printer. Do this by first printing odd pages, then even pages. Double-sided printing is handy for creating small numbers of pamphlets or two-sided handouts. You can also use double-sided printing to create models of publication that a printer will publish.

There's an easier way to print duplex (double-sided) pages using printers that print on only one side of the page. The Layout tab of the Print dialog box has an option that walks you through the process of printing double-sided pages, and helps you avoid printing twice on one side of the page and not at all on the other. To access that option, select the Layout tab and pull down the Signature Layout drop-down list. Choose Double Sided Full Page. You can then click on the Print Preview button to see how your publication will look when it's printed back to back on pages. Figure 18.2 shows the Preview screen illustrating double-sided pages.

After you preview your double-sided document, you can click on the Close button in the Preview window toolbar to return to the Print dialog box. Then, after you click on the Print button in the Print dialog box, CorelDRAW patiently walks you through the process of double-sided printing. Be prepared to waste a few sheets of paper while CorelDRAW tests your printer and asks you some questions. You supply the answers to a wizard, which determines how your printer works. After that, you get explicit directions on how and when to load sheets of paper to achieve double-sided printing.

Figure 18.2.

Even if your printer doesn't print duplex, you can print double-sided pages with CorelDRAW.

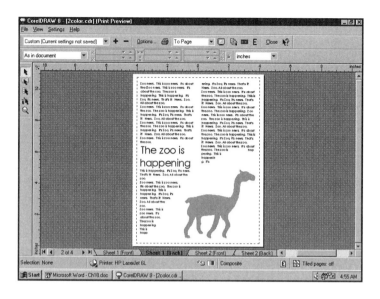

Printing Business Cards or Labels

Business cards and labels are created a bit differently than they are in some other desktop publishing programs or word processors. Rather than duplicating a full sheet of cards or labels, you simply choose an appropriate Page Layout, and then create a single card or label.

CorelDRAW's Page Layout options dialog box supports hundreds of label and card layouts from several major publishers. Your local office supplies store has standardized size labels for everything from video cassettes to CDs. They also sell full-sheet business card paper that separates into individual business cards.

18.1: Design and Print a Business Card

It's not necessary to purchase laser business card sheets to try this; you can experiment with a regular sheet of paper.

1. Open a new drawing in CorelDRAW.
2. Select Layout | Page Setup from the menu bar.
3. Double-click on Label in the Options window.
4. In the Label area of the window, click on the label size that matches the business card size on the sheets of business cards you bought. If you're experimenting with a plain sheet of paper, you can choose Avery 5371, as I have in Figure 18.3.
5. Click on OK in the Options window, and design a business card. In Figure 18.4, I've made myself an editor of Zoo News.
6. Select File | Print, and click on the Preview button in the Print dialog box. You see a page full of business cards.

18

Figure 18.3.
CorelDRAW comes with hundreds of preset card and label sizes.

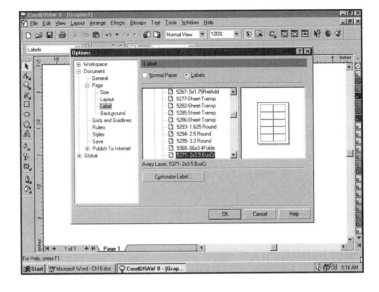

Figure 18.4.
Designing business cards or labels is as easy as creating any other CorelDRAW illustration.

Bringing Your Publication to a Commercial Printer

If all you need is professional black-and-white printing, you can take your CorelDRAW file to a commercial printer and let them print it. Or export your CorelDRAW file to a file format your printer can work with. In Hour 17, you learned to export your CorelDRAW objects to other file formats, including the universally recognized EPS file format.

If you need to prepare your CorelDRAW pages for commercial color printing, you have many different qualities of output available to you. Commercial, large-quantity printing requires separate plates for different colors. Two ways that colors can be separated for color printing are spot color or process color. Spot color is typically used for two-color printing. For example, if you have a brochure you want to print in red and black, you can arrange with your printer to provide him with a black master and a red master page. Both the black and red masters will be converted to printing plates and printed over each other to produce two-color output.

Process color involves combining four color plates, usually Cyan, Magenta, Yellow, and Black (abbreviated as CMYK). With process color, you provide your printer with four different color masters used to create four color plates.

Reproducing complex or spectacular color-mix fountain fills is beyond the capability of spot color separations. You can use one-color fountain fills, such as from black to white, with spot coloring. But even with process color printing, fountain fills sometimes appear as bars of color. Fine-tuning very complex color mixes for process color printing is a complex art that requires a lot of experimenting and experience.

JUST A MINUTE | Although transferring coloring from monitor to paper is very complex, your color images translate into web graphics much more easily, as you'll see in the next hour on web graphics.

Preparing Spot Color Separations

Scenario: The next issue of your newsletter or brochure is going to be printed in color. In a quick call to your printer, you learn he will accept your 600dpi output to create printing plates with. Your printer also informs you that he can duplicate PANTONE colors.

JUST A MINUTE | To see exactly what colors you'll get from your printed output, do not rely on what you see on your monitor. Instead, ask your printer for a sample book showing the way PANTONE colors will look when printed.

The first step in preparing your publication for two-color spot color printing is to make sure that all the fills and outlines in your publication are confined to two colors. If you've created a publication already, you can use the Object Manager (see Hour 16) to determine the fill and outline properties of all your objects. Pick the two PANTONE spot colors that you will assign to objects, and change the assigned colors of every object to those colors.

18

Most printers define two-color spot printing as black, plus a second color. Some allow you to use any two colors, but most pass on some additional charge for washing out black plates. Check with your printer about the policy on charging for two-color printing.

One way to check your publication and see what colors are assigned to every object is to view the Object Manager Docker window. You explored the Object Manager in Hour 16. You can display the Object Manager Docker window by selecting Layout | Object Manager from the menu bar . In Figure 18.5, every object in my publication is either PANTONE Process Black CV or PANTONE Process Red 032 CV.

Figure 18.5.

The Object Manager is a good way to check assigned colors to objects.

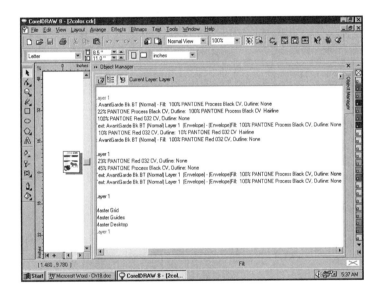

After you assign two (and only two) colors to all the objects in your publication, select File | Print from the menu bar. Normally, if you prepare master pages for a printer, you want to select all pages and one copy in the General tab of the Print dialog box.

Click on the Separations tab in the Print dialog box. In the Separations tab, click on the Print Separations check box. If you have restricted your publication to two colors, you see those two colors in the list at the bottom of the dialog box, as in Figure 18.6.

Most of the other check boxes in the tab are not relevant for spot-color separations. But the Print Empty Plates check box is useful. It prints two master sheets for each page, even if only one color is used on that page. This makes it easier to keep your pages organized.

Figure 18.6.

The Separations tab lists all the colors assigned to your publication.

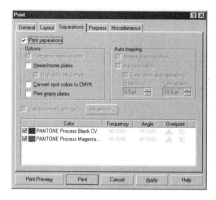

You can print an additional set of your separation masters that have information on them identifying which color goes with that plate. This is helpful in avoiding mixed up colors when plates are printed. You can add this information in the Prepress tab of the Print dialog box. Click on the Position Within Page check box to print color information on each page.

Before you print your two different spot-color separations for each page, you can click on the Preview button in the Print dialog box to see how the separations will come out. Figure 18.7 shows a single-color separation without the reference color information This is the sheet that your printer will use to create a printing plate.

Figure 18.7

Color separations can be previewed.

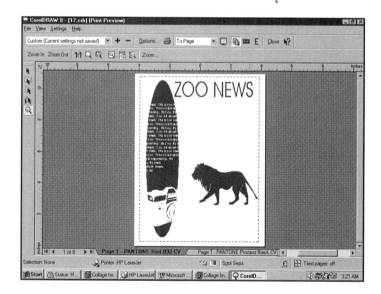

18

Preparing Four-Color Masters

Printing process color separations is similar to creating spot color separation. The results are much less predictable in that all colors and fountain fills are broken down into four colors. CorelDRAW does this automatically for you.

To create four-color CMYK process color separations, select File | Print from the menu bar and click on the Separations tab in the Print dialog box.

If you applied only process colors to objects in your publication, you see four colors listed in the color list: Cyan, Magenta, Yellow, and Black. If you mixed process colors and spot colors, no problem. Click on the Convert Spot Colors to CMYK check box, and the spot colors you assigned will be broken down to mixtures of the four CMYK colors.

When you separate your colors into the CMYK colors, you can follow the same steps you learned for printing spot color separations. The difference is, you get four sheets per page if you click on the Print Empty Plates check box.

For high-quality CMYK color separation, you need to rely on a very high-quality service bureau printer to create your copy-ready masters. You can, of course, print lower-quality copies on your own laser printer to get a basic idea of what your color plates will look like.

PostScripting Your Files

To bring your file to a service bureau, find out what printer output they use and how you can send your printer output in a compatible file. Many times, the printer can provide you with printer drivers for a compatible printer. You don't need the printer, only the software that creates files for that printer. If you already have a postscript printer installed, you can often select that printer.

To create a file for a service bureau, select a compatible printer in the General tab of the Print dialog box. In Figure 18.8, I've selected an Imagesetter printer. I don't have an Imagesetter because I can't afford one! But my service bureau has one. By selecting the Print to File and For Mac check boxes (because my service bureau uses a Macintosh), I can create a file that I can take to my service bureau.

When you click on the Print button in the Print dialog box after selecting the Print to File check box, you'll be prompted to choose a folder and filename for your print file. Take that file to your service bureau. It can use the file to create high-quality output that your printer can use to shoot printing plates for the production process.

18

Figure 18.8.

*Print output can be sent
to a file and taken to a
service bureau for high-
quality copy-ready
output.*

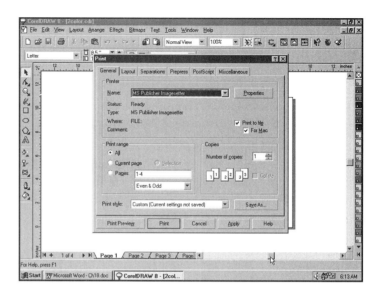

Summary

Printing with CorelDRAW can be as simple or complex as your needs. If all you need is output on your laser printer, CorelDRAW provides you with complete control over pages, and can create back-to-back duplex output.

If you need to take your CorelDRAW file to a commercial printer for color printing, your two options are spot colors or process colors. Spot colors are typically used for two-color printing. Process colors mix four colors to create a full array of colors. You can create color separations in CorelDRAW, and print them, or create a file with print output to take to a commercial service bureau for high-quality copy-ready output.

Workshop

In this workshop, you first print mail labels. Then, you create a two-color publication and print color separations.

1. Open a new CorelDRAW file and define a label output by selecting Layout | Page Setup and double-clicking on Label in the Options dialog box. Click on the Labels radio button. If you have labels, use the appropriate size; if not, choose Avery 5160, as in Figure 18.9. Click on OK.

2. Design a cool-looking return-address label with text and a symbol.

3. Select Print | Print Preview to see how the labels will look when printed.

4. Click on the Close button in the Preview window to return to the dialog box. Then either close the dialog box or click on the Print button to send your labels to the printer.

18

Figure 18.9.
Label and card layouts in the Options dialog box.

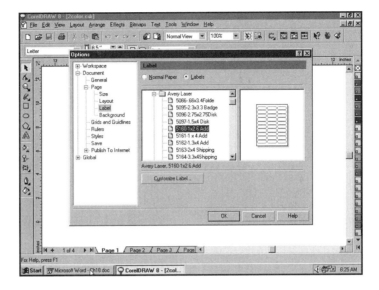

5. Create a four-page newsletter or brochure. You can open and edit the *Zoo News* newsletter you have worked on in previous hours.

6. Assign only PANTONE Process Black CV or PANTONE Process Red 032 CV to each object. You can assign less than 100% of either of these colors to any object.

7. Create color separations by selecting File | Print and clicking on the Print Separations check box in the Separations tab.

8. Click on the Print Preview button to see the two plates for each page that you will print.

9. Close the Preview screen. Either close the Print dialog box or print separations for your publication.

Quiz

1. Where do you define layout for different size paper such as business cards or labels?

2. If you bring a two-color brochure to a commercial print shop, which color separation process works best?

3. When you print color separations, how do you know what color is associated with each plate?

4. Can you print CMYK color separations if you used process color in designing your publication?

18

Quiz Answers

1. To define layout for cards or labels, select Layout | Page Setup from the menu. Then double-click on Label in the Options window.

2. Spot color separation is more economical and dependable, and will work fine for two-color output.

3. You can print an additional set of your separation masters that have information on them identifying which color goes with that plate.

4. Yes. To convert spot colors to process colors, click on the Convert Spot Colors to CMYK check box in the Separations tab of the Print dialog box. The spot colors you assigned break down to mixtures of the four CMYK colors.

18

Hour **19**

From CorelDRAW to the World Wide Web

There's no need for me to tell you how strategic web sites have become. Both sites on the World Wide Web and sites on internal intranets are becoming an important way to share information, and that includes graphics.

In Hour 18, you saw that when you transfer your CorelDRAW illustrations to printed output, it is often difficult to re-create the coloring of your onscreen illustration on the printed page. One of the fun things about transferring your CorelDRAW images to web sites is that viewers see your fountain fills and colors in full living color.

You can place your CorelDRAW illustrations on web sites in two ways: save individual objects as web-compatible graphic images and then import them into a web page you are designing with another web publishing program; create the HTML (HyperText Markup Language) code yourself. That works fine if you already know how to create web pages.

If you don't know HTML from WWW, you can still create full-fledged web pages with text, graphic images, backgrounds, and links to other sites in CorelDRAW. I've written many books about web-design packages and I found the process of generating web pages in CorelDRAW 8 pretty smooth and easy to use. In a half hour, I created the web page you see in Figure 19.1.

Figure 19.1.

You can easily publish a CorelDRAW 8 page as a web page.

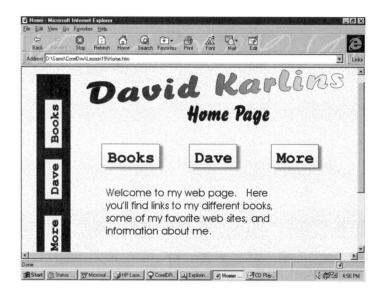

Saving Objects as Web-Compatible Graphics

This short hour can only scratch the surface of web-compatible graphics, but that's okay. You don't need to know a lot of graphic file format theory to transform your CorelDRAW images into graphics for the World Wide Web. Here's the 30-second crash course.

Most web browsers—the programs that folks use to visit web sites—can interpret only images saved in the GIF or JPEG file formats.

☐ GIF files have the advantage of having a transparent color assigned to them so that the backgrounds appear invisible on a web site.

☐ GIF files can be "interlaced" to appear to "fade in" while a viewer waits for a site to completely download. Most people think this reduces boredom while visitors wait to see your images.

☐ The file format of JPEG images mixes colors in such a way that it often reproduces color photographs better than GIF files. So if you have a photo, save it as a JPEG file. Save other graphics as interlaced GIF images.

19

Now that you've been introduced to the two universally recognized web-graphic formats, you can convert your CorelDRAW objects to either one of them.

Saving Objects As GIF Images

Any object (or group of objects) in CorelDRAW can be saved to the GIF file format. Those GIF images can be placed in a web page.

19.1: Save a Graphic As a GIF file

To Do

1. Type your name in artistic text.
2. Add a fountain fill.
3. Click on the image and click on the Export button in the toolbar. You met this button back in Hour 17.
4. Choose the Selected Only check box in the Export dialog box, as I've done in Figure 19.2.

Figure 19.2.

The Selected Only check box is necessary to save only a selected object as a web image.

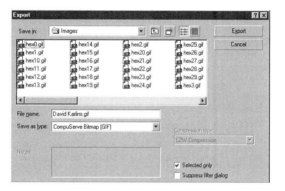

5. Choose CompuServe Bitmap GIF (that's the full, formal name for GIF files) from the Save as Type drop-down menu. Enter a filename. Then click on the Export button.
6. In the Bitmap Export dialog box, choose Paletted (8-bit) from the Color drop-down menu. The Anti-alisasing Normal radio button smoothes out rough edges in your object when it converts to a 72dpi bitmap image.

JUST A MINUTE

All graphic images destined for the web are saved at 72dpi. There's no point in saving the images to a higher resolution because that is the resolution of most monitors. Saving at a resolution other than 72dpi distorts the size of your image when you place it in a web site.

19

7. Click on the Dithered check box to reduce the effect of any color loss when you convert your image to a 256-color graphic. Leave the fountain steps at the default setting for the smoothest possible transitions when your image is transformed into a bitmap web graphic.

8. Click on OK. The next dialog box is the Gif Export dialog box. Click on the Interlace check box to create the "fade in" effect. Leave the Transparency area settings at the default, with the Image Color radio button checked. The Preview screen on the top-right of the dialog box shows how your image will look on a web site, as you can see in Figure 19.3.

Figure 19.3.
CorelDRAW 8's Gif Export dialog box enables you to add interlacing and transparency to your web graphic.

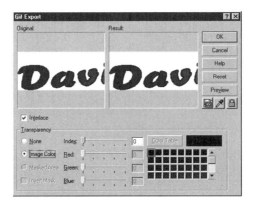

 9. Finally, click on OK. Your image is ready to be placed in a web site.

Saving Objects As JPEG Graphics

Saving an image to JPEG file format is less common than saving images to GIF format. But if you have a scanned photo, JPEG images will probably reproduce the colors better on a web site.

To export an image to JPEG format, start by selecting the object(s) and clicking on the Export button in the toolbar. Click on the Selected Only check box in the dialog box.

Choose JPEG Bitmaps (JPG) from the drop-down menu and enter a name for the file in the File name box. Click on the Export button.

Because you do not have to (or get to) define a background color for JPEG graphics, you can just click on OK in the Bitmap export dialog box to let CorelDRAW make intelligent decisions about how to format your JPEG file.

19

If you want to experiment with the two sliders in the JPEG Export dialog box, you can. Increasing the value setting for the Compression slider makes the file smaller but of poorer quality. It will load faster but look worse. Increasing the Smoothing slider value rounds off rough edges produced when you convert a vector-based image to a bitmap. The downside is that more smoothness also means blurrier images. To see the effect of your slider settings before you assign them, click on OK. The Progressive check box causes your JPEG file to "fade in" like GIF images do, but this feature is not recognized by all browsers. The Standard (4:2:2) setting in the drop-down list in the Encoding Method area is more memory efficient than the other (Optional 4:4:4) setting and the quality difference is usually unnoticeable.

This quick hour gives you enough skills to transfer your graphics to web sites. For expert level web graphic design, check out the many web graphics books entirely devoted to creating graphics for web sites.

Publishing Your Illustration As a Web Page

CorelDRAW 8 comes with all the tools you need to create a web page that can be posted at a web site. You can design a page layout with a tiled background image. You can automatically transform all the objects on your page to web-compatible text and images. And you can even define links from your web page to other web sites.

In this section of the hour, I'll share a few tips to get you through this process without crashing into some of the pitfalls that can make this a bit frustrating. In no time, you'll have a web page designed. Do you have a web browser installed on your computer? If so, get ready to see your own web page in 40 minutes.

19

Designing a Web Page

The best page layout to use for designing web pages in CorelDRAW 8 is a regular size page (8 $\frac{1}{2}$ by 11"), layed out in Landscape orientation. You can select Layout | Page Setup from the menu bar, choose Letter for paper size, and click on the Landscape radio button. Click on OK, and your page is ready to become a web page.

I won't attempt a crash course in the aesthetics of web page design except to give you one piece of advice: keep it simple. That doesn't mean you can't have a sophisticated CorelDRAW illustration on the page. It just means keep your web page to as few objects as possible. The page I shared in Figure 19.1 won't win design awards for flashiness, but it will open quickly and the information is easy to find. Most web pages have a title, a basic explanation of the page, and buttons composed of text and shapes that let visitors navigate to other web pages. Don't worry for now about defining those links, but you will probably want to put some on your page.

19.2: Create a Basic Home Page

1. Open a new CorelDRAW page, letter size, Landscape orientation.

2. Type a title for the page; your name is okay.

3. Assign a fountain fill to your page name.

4. Type a short explanation of your web page in paragraph text.

5. Add two or three buttons composed with a light color-filled shape and dark text. These can let visitors navigate to other sites or to other pages you will create. You can always copy my site in Figure 19.1 if you want a simple model.

6. Save your page.

Creating a Page Background

Web page backgrounds are created by taking a small graphic image and "tiling" it; that is, placing it side to side and top to bottom to fill the whole page. Why take a small image and tile it, instead of creating a background image large enough to fill the whole page? Mainly to keep the file size down and help the page load faster.

CorelDRAW handles this for you. You can save any object as a GIF image, and then use it as a tiled-page background.

19.3: Create a GIF Image to Use As a Background Tile

1. Create a rectangle about 1" square.

2. Fill the rectangle with a subtle fill from the Bitmap Pattern fill list (you can flip back to Hour 7 to refresh your fill skills). In Figure 19.4, I'm selecting a light wood-grain fill. Assign no outline to the filled square. (Right-click on the X at the top of the color palette)

Figure 19.4.

You can define your own, custom web page background tiles in CorelDRAW.

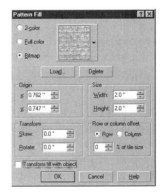

3. Click on the new, filled square, and click on the Export button. Click on the Selected Only check box in the Export dialog box, choose GIF as the file type, and name the file BG1. Click on the Export button.

4. In the Bitmap Export box, leave the default settings and click on OK.

5. Select Layout | Page Setup from the menu bar.

6. Double-click on Background in the left side of the Options window.

7. Click on the Bitmap radio button, and then click on the Browse button. Navigate to the BG1.BMP file you just created, and double-click on it as I'm doing in Figure 19.5.

Figure 19.5.

Once you export an object as a GIF bitmap file, you can use it as a page background for your web page.

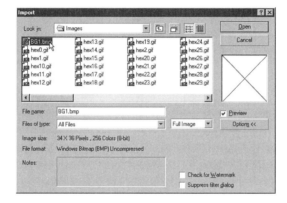

8. Click on OK. Your image will be tiled as a background for your page. When you save your page as a web page, this background will be attached. My wood background is illustrated in Figure 19.6.

Figure 19.6.

Any tiny filled rectangle can be a web page background.

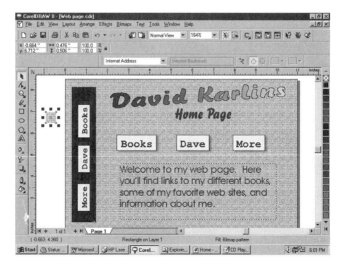

19

Creating Web Compatible Text

You can make text web-compatible two ways. You can convert artistic text to curved objects or assign attributes to paragraph text that make it display well on web sites.

19.4: Convert Artistic Text to a Curve

1. Click on some of the artistic text you're using in your site. Make sure your spelling is correct, because you're about to lose your ability to edit the text.

2. Choose Arrange | Convert to Curves from the menu bar.

3. Convert any additional artistic text to curves.

CorelDRAW 8 comes with an automatic feature that ensures that your paragraph text will be interpreted more or less as you format it when it's viewed in a web browser. You can still edit paragraph text after you make it web compatible.

19.5: Make Paragraph Text Web Compatible

1. Select your paragraph text frame with the Pick tool.

2. Choose Text | Make Text HTML compatible from the menu bar.

3. The text Property bar changes. The formatting features available from the new Property bar assign formatting that can be interpreted by web browsers. A third drop-down menu, to the right of the Font List and Font Size List, is the HTML Font Size List shown in Figure 19.7. When you choose a font size from this list, you are pretty much guaranteed that all web browsers can interpret it.

Figure 19.7.

The HTML Text Property bar comes with preset font sizes that are interpreted by all web browsers.

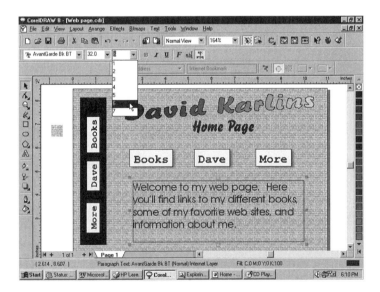

You can edit HTML (web site) compatible text the same way you edited regular paragraph text. But when you assign format features, choose attributes from the HTML Text Property bar.

Defining Links to Other Web Sites

Links to other web sites are most easily defined using the Internet Objects toolbar. To view this toolbar, choose View | Toolbars from the menu bar, and then click on the check box next to Internet Objects in the Options window. Click on OK to see this toolbar in your Drawing window.

The Internet Objects toolbar can be moved or docked. You can refresh your docking skills by checking back to Hour 4 in this book.

19.6: Assign a Link to an Object on Your Page

To Do

1. Click on an object on your page to which you want to assign link properties. Visitors to your web page who click on this object will jump to the assigned web page.

2. Click in the Internet Address drop-down list in the Internet Objects toolbar, and type the URL to which you want to assign a link. If you don't have any good links in mind, share mine: http://www.ppinet.com. In Figure 19.8, I'm assigning a link to that site from the "Dave" button on my web page.

Figure 19.8.

Links to other web sites can be assigned to any object.

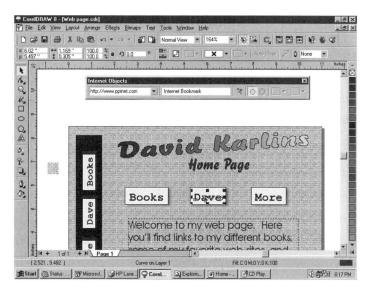

3. Assign links to additional objects on your page.

Publishing Your Page As an HTML File

The web page you have defined needs to be converted to an HTML file before it can be published on a web site. To do that, select File | Publish to Internet from the menu bar.

The first Publish to Internet Wizard dialog box gives you three choices for HTML style types. The first radio button, HTML, is much more reliable. Click on it and click on the Next > button.

In the second wizard box, leave the HTML tables radio button checked for the most reliable conversion to HTML. If you need to save your HTML page in a folder other than the selected one, use the Browse button to locate that folder. Then click on the Next > button.

The third wizard box asks what kind of graphic image files you want to use. Click on the GIF radio button and the Interlaced check box to convert your images to GIF files that will "fade in" when visitors go to your web page. If, as in the exercises you did earlier in this hour, you already made your text web compatible, you don't have to check the Render All Text as Images check box. Click on the Next> button one last time.

In the final wizard box, enter a filename for your web page by clicking in the File Name column and typing a filename. In Figure 19.9, I'm saving my page as Dave.htm. Most browsers require the *.htm filename extension.

Saving your file as an HTML file will not place your page on the World Wide Web or on an intranet site. Transferring HTML files to web servers, computers that are accessible to web browsers, is beyond the scope of this book. Many Internet service providers, such as AOL, give you access to free web page space, and you can find out from them how to transfer your HTML-compatible files to their server. You can assign any name to your web page, but you should check the rules of the server to which you will publish your web site to find out what filenames are acceptable.

Just a Minute

If you plan to create and manage a web site that includes web pages, input forms, and sophisticated page design, you might want to check out the wide assortment of good books on web page publishing. I happen to have one out called *Teach Yourself Microsoft FrontPage 98 in a Week* (Sams.net, 1997, ISBN # 157521-350-8). That book covers the entire process of bringing together pages, input forms, other web page components (such as sound and video), and working with web servers to make your site available on the World Wide Web or your intranet.

Whatever route you take to publish your web pages, you'll find that the graphics and pages you create in CorelDRAW 8 will mesh smoothly as you put together a site for the web.

19

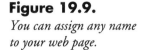

Figure 19.9.

You can assign any name to your web page.

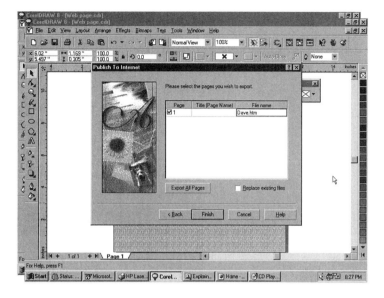

After you name your web page, click on the Finish button in the final wizard page. After you do, CorelDRAW 8 checks your page for any problems that will prevent it from being published. You can elect to see those errors in the HTML Conflict Analyzer Docker window. The most common conflicts are:

- [ ] You didn't make your paragraph text HTML compatible. Check each frame of paragraph text and make sure you used the Text | Make Text HTML Compatible menu option.

- [ ] You didn't convert your artistic text to curves. Make sure you choose each artistic text object and select Arrange | Convert to Curves from the menu bar.

- [ ] You have objects in the Drawing area that are not in the Page area, and those objects won't make it onto your web page. You can delete objects off your Drawing area, or move them onto the Drawing area so that they become part of the web page.

After you fix your HTML errors, if any, run the wizard again to save your illustration as an HTML page.

Even if you haven't made arrangements to publish your HTML page to a server, you can still use the File | Open option in any web browsing software to open your file. You might get a warning message from CorelDRAW stating that it is unable to find your URL (Uniform Resource Locator, or web site address). Just click on OK and don't worry about that warning if you haven't transferred your page to the World Wide Web. This just means that your site isn't online yet.

In Figure 19.10, I'm viewing the web page I created in CorelDRAW 8 using Internet Explorer. IE recognizes the link to another web site and displays the target of the link in the IE status bar.

19

Figure 19.10.

Web browsers will interpret the links you assign to objects in CorelDRAW 8.

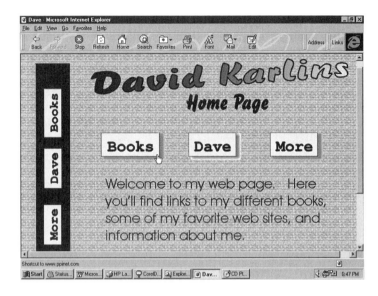

Final Advice on CorelDRAW 8

This is the last hour in this book concerned with CorelDRAW. The next hours introduce you to PHOTO-PAINT and 3-D Dream. At this point, you've been introduced to enough of CorelDRAW 8 to have a lot of fun and create some impressive illustrations. You've also seen that CorelDRAW 8 is an extremely powerful software package, and a full investigation of its features is beyond what can be covered in 24 quick hours.

You have several resources to help you move up to the expert class of CorelDRAW illustrators. Corel's site for DRAW 8 was at `http://www.corel.com/products/graphicsandpublishing/draw8/main.htm` at this writing. If it gets moved, you can find it by going to Corel's home page at `www.corel.com` and following links for DRAW 8.

You'll also find several other CorelDRAW associated sites on the web where you can get advice and inspiration. The best of these is Rick Altman's CorelDRAW site at `http://www.altman.com`. Rick conducts entertaining, irreverent, high-energy seminars around the world, and his web site is at the center of the CorelDRAW design community.

Finally, let me close this section of the book by inviting you to share your CorelDRAW illustrations. When you create something you have to show off, email it to me at `dkarlins@aol.com`. Stay in touch with me via my website: `http://www.ppinet.com`.

19

Summary

You can convert CorelDRAW illustrations to web pages two ways: You can export individual objects as GIF or JPEG files, or you can use CorelDRAW 8's Internet Publishing Wizard to convert an entire drawing to a web page.

When you convert an illustration to a web page, text, graphics, and page background are converted to web-compatible file formats.

Workshop

In this workshop, you publish a web page as an HTML file that can be placed on a web server and visited by web browsers.

1. Start by designing a simple page that can be a home page for your web site. Use a letter-sized page oriented in Landscape. Include artistic text and paragraph text.

2. Create a 1" square and fill it with a bitmap fill. You can find these fills in the Pattern Fill dialog box that is opened from the Fill flyout.

JUST A MINUTE

> The image you use to create a background fill will be saved and then deleted from your web page. Use the saved file version of the image as a page background.

3. Delete the outline for this square by right-clicking on the X at the top of the color palette. Export this object as a GIF file by clicking on the Export button and choosing GIF from the Files of Type drop-down menu. Click on the Selected Object check box in the Export dialog box. Name the file BGX.GIF and accept all defaults to save the file. After you save this object as a GIF file, delete it. The image is saved on your disk and can be used as a page Background tile fill.

4. Select all the paragraph text in your drawing, and choose Text | Make Text HTML Compatible from the menu bar.

5. Select each artistic text object and select Arrange | Convert to Curves from the menu bar.

6. Select Layout | Page Setup and double-click on Background.

7. Click on the Bitmap radio button, and use the Browse button to navigate to the BGX.GIF file you created in step 3. Double-click on that file in the Import dialog box; then click on OK in the Options window.

19

8. Select File | Publish to Internet from the menu bar. In the first Publish to Internet Wizard dialog box, click on the HTML radio button and click on the Next > button. In the next window, leave the HTML tables radio button checked and click on the Next > button again. In the third wizard box, click on the GIF radio button and the Interlaced check box to convert your images to interlaced GIF files. Click on the Next> button for the last time. Enter a filename for your web page and click on Finish.

If you have a web browser installed on your computer, open the *.htm file you just created and test it in the browser.

Quiz

1. How do you prepare a single object you created in CorelDRAW to be embedded in a web page you are defining in HTML code or with a web page layout program?
2. What does transparency do to GIF images?
3. How do you assign links to CorelDRAW objects?
4. What should you watch out for when you convert text objects to HTML?

Quiz Answers

1. To send CorelDRAW objects to web publishing programs, export them to GIF or JPEG file format.
2. By making a single color in a GIF image transparent, you can get rid of any one color (usually the rectangular background associated with the image). Transparency allows the background of a web page to show through a part of the GIF image. In most cases, this is the rectangular background, but any one color in a GIF image can be made transparent.
3. Links can be assigned from the Internet List drop-down menu in the Internet Objects toolbar.
4. Check to make sure you converted all paragraph text to HTML-compatible paragraph text and that you converted artistic text to curves.

19

Hour 20

PHOTO-PAINT Basics

CorelDRAW is an excellent tool for creating fine-looking illustrations and graphics, so why does Corel offer another program to deal with graphic images? PHOTO-PAINT works in a different realm. Unlike CorelDRAW, Corel PHOTO-PAINT is a tool that works exclusively and expertly with bitmap images. The world of bitmap images is the world of photographic quality images, and the best way to modify these images is to use PHOTO-PAINT 8.

PHOTO-PAINT 8 includes some new effects, tools, and techniques that make image manipulation easier. And anytime that a tool becomes easier to use, it inevitably enables you to be more productive and creative, and to have more fun.

Taking a Look Around

PHOTO-PAINT's environment (Figure 20.1) is similar to the CorelDRAW environment. Some main differences exist, but they have to do mainly with functionality and the type of tools that are specific to PHOTO-PAINT.

By default, you see a tool box on the left, a color palette on the right, a status bar on the bottom, a standard toolbar on the top and, like Draw, a floating Property bar. Like CorelDRAW, you can customize the interface of PHOTO-PAINT to suit your needs. Each toolbar can detach to become a floating toolbar; conversely the toolbar can dock just about anywhere.

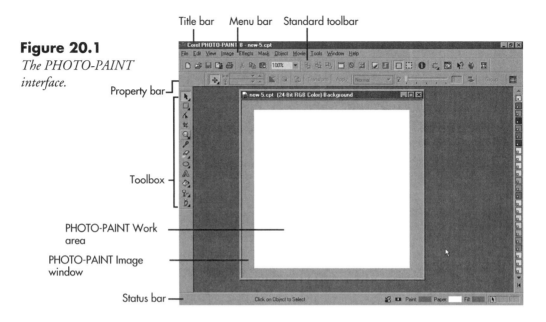

Figure 20.1
The PHOTO-PAINT interface.

Setting Up the Environment

Once you begin to work in PHOTO-PAINT, you see that desktop space becomes limited when the rollups, toolbars, and Docker windows start to appear. If you are like me, you want as much room on the screen as you can get. To maximize PHOTO-PAINT, press the square at the top-right of the PHOTO-PAINT window or double-click in the PHOTO-PAINT title bar located at the top of the window.

JUST A MINUTE

You can make most customizations to the PHOTO-PAINT interface from one place. To customize the interface, select Tools | Options. Spend some time browsing the Tools | Options hierarchy to see the different customizable features.

Creating a New Bitmap Image

To create a bitmap image in PHOTO-PAINT, simply click the New icon from the Standard toolbar at the top of the screen (located just below the menu items) or choose File | New. PHOTO-PAINT opens a dialog box asking for the type of bitmap image you want to create (see Figure 20.2).

20

Figure 20.2

Create a New Image
dialog box.

The first thing that PHOTO-PAINT needs to know is the color mode for your new bitmap. To create an image that displays on the monitor, select the 24-bit RGB Color Mode.

Next select the paper color. This determines the color of the background of the image. Notice that the white paper color has an RGB value of 255,255,255; that is, all colors are turned on at full intensity to create white. You can also select the No Background check box to tell PHOTO-PAINT that you want a transparent background.

JUST A MINUTE

If you select No Background, the background displays a checkerboard pattern. The checkerboard pattern serves only as a visual cue when working with transparent objects and it does not print. You will learn about objects and their transparency later in this lesson.

The next section in the Create a New Image dialog box asks questions dealing with image size and resolution. The Image Size list box offers predefined sizes or you may select Custom and set a specific height and width for your new image.

In order to ensure that the image size reflects a real size that is not affected by the selected resolution, you need to select a measurement unit other than pixels. In this case, I choose inches in the Measurement Units list box and set the height and width boxes to 5 inches. This guarantees an image that is 5 inches square when it prints, no matter what the resolution setting. (In this case, the resolution determines the quality of the printout.) Remember that though this image will be 5 inches square when printed, the image will not necessarily be 5 inches square on your monitor. The size on the monitor depends on the zoom level. To let the resolution determine the size of the image, select a measurement unit of pixels for the height and width settings.

Finally, choose a resolution size. The image is destined for a monitor, so select 72dpi. Why 72dpi? To determine the optimal resolution for your new image, follow these guidelines:

20

☐ If your image is to be viewed on a monitor, choose the final size of your image in inches (or centimeters) and set the resolution between 72 and 96dpi.

☐ If your image is a photographic-quality image destined for high-quality inkjet printers and laser printers, choose a resolution between 150 to 200dpi.

☐ If, however, your image is a black and white line art image, set the resolution to the maximum resolution of the printer.

☐ For printing to offset presses, it is best to talk to your service bureau about its recommended resolution settings and file types for your bitmaps. Usually images destined for magazines need to be at a resolution of 266dpi or higher.

JUST A MINUTE

The Create a New Image dialog box contains two other important settings: Create a Partial File and Create a Movie.

Selecting the Create a Partial File option enables you to work on a part of an image at one time and selecting the Create a Movie option enables you to create an animation or a movie.

Choose OK and a new image window appears in the PHOTO-PAINT work area. The window contains a white area that represents the bitmap image surface. The name of the file (PHOTO-PAINT creates a name starting with "new" and ending in CPT for new images) and the current color mode of the image appear in the window title bar. The gray area around your white image (assuming you selected white for paper color) is not part of your final image (see Figure 20.3).

Figure 20.3

A new image file created.

20

Notice the name of the file, new-6.cpt, in the title bar of the new image window. In this example, you can tell that this is a new file and that it is the sixth image created since opening up PHOTO-PAINT. To change the name of the file, select File | Save As. Enter a new name in the File Name text box and press Save. The blank bitmap will be saved under the new name and the title bar will reflect the change.

Setting the Zoom Level

Click the small square located in the top-right corner of the new image window to maximize the new image window to fit into the entire PHOTO-PAINT work area.

Create a new image where the values are identical to the previous example but where the resolution is 144dpi (see Figure 20.4). The first thing to notice is that the image area (the white area) is much larger than 5 inches square (see Figure 20.5). This is due to the resolution difference between the image and the resolution of the monitor. Remember that the image's resolution is 144dpi and the monitor's resolution is approximately 72dpi.

Figure 20.4

Dialog box settings for 144dpi image.

In the Standard toolbar, locate the Zoom Level drop-down list box. Here, by default, you see your image zoomed in at 100% (see Figure 20.6). Zooming does not affect the image, but it is akin to moving closer and farther away from the surface of the image. When an image is viewed at 100%, it will match, in size, a pixel from the image to a pixel on the monitor. Because your image has twice the density of pixels than the monitor, it grows to about twice its actual size.

To view the image at actual size, select 1 to 1 in the Zoom Level list box, or choose the Zoom tool from the toolbox and select 1 to 1 from the Property bar. The background white area now appears at actual size, 5 inches square. To display the Document Info dialog box, choose File | Document Info. Notice that this file has a resolution of 144dpi and is 5 inches square. To set the ruler to inches, choose Tools | Options; then select Document | Ruler and change the units for the ruler to inches. Select the image window and type Control+R, the keyboard shortcut to display the ruler.

Figure 20.5

New image area created at 144dpi.

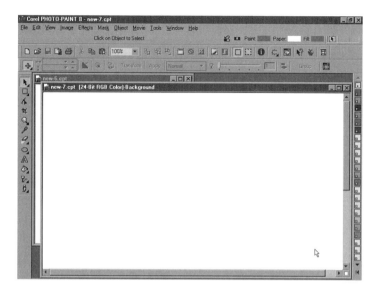

Figure 20.6

Zoom level setting.

JUST A MINUTE

You can open more than one image at the same time. For example, open as many images as you want to view at one time and then choose Window | Tile Vertically. All the images appear tiled vertically in the work area. To make an image the current image, click on its title bar. To close an image, press the X on the top-right corner of its window's title bar. To maximize an image to fill the work area, double-click on its title bar.

Setting Colors and Fills

You may have already noticed three color swatches on the status bar: Paint, Paper, and Fill (see Figure 20.7).

Figure 20.7

Paint, Paper, and Fill color swatches on status bar.

Each of these swatches represents the currently selected Paint color, Paper color, and Fill color. The Paint color affects tools such as the Paintbrush and Text tools. The fill color affects the fill of objects created using the Rectangle, Ellipse, Line, Polygon, and Fill tools. Setting the Paper color only affects the color of the paper when creating new images.

In PHOTO-PAINT, you need to choose the Paint and/or Fill colors before painting on the image. You cannot change the color of the paint after you apply it to the image. You can change it later by selecting the area to change and then painting over it or replacing the pixel colors, but you cannot change its color as you can in CorelDRAW where you select the object and simply change the fill color. The same is true of painting shapes; you need to choose the fill color prior to drawing the shape.

To change the currently selected paint color, left-click a color in the palette; to modify the currently selected fill color, right-click a color in the palette. To load a new type of palette, choose View | Color Palette and select the type of palette to use.

Choosing Different Types of Fills

Just as in CorelDRAW, PHOTO-PAINT has the capability to create complex fills such as the fountain, pattern, bitmap, and texture fill. Because the concept of PHOTO-PAINT fills is very similar to CorelDRAW fills, see Hour 7, "Mixing Up Fills," for general information regarding the types of fills and their general options. But because PHOTO-PAINT is a bitmap tool, some PHOTO-PAINT specific options have been added to the fills that need explanation. These options are Tolerance and Antialiasing. You can access these options on the Property bar or by double-clicking on a particular tool to display the Tool Settings rollup.

Painting Text

20

Unlike CorelDRAW, which has artistic text and paragraph text, PHOTO-PAINT text comes only in one flavor: the text flavor. To create text, choose the Text tool. The mouse cursor changes from the object picker arrow to an I-beam cursor. Position the I-beam cursor on the image surface and left-click. A vertical line starts to flash on your image surface. This is the text cursor that represents the size and starting position of the text that you are about to type. Go ahead; type some text. To use a font, style, format, and size other than what appears in your image, modify the options on the Property bar (font, size, character/line spacing, character style, and alignment) as you would in CorelDRAW (see Figure 20.8).

Figure 20.8

Using the Text tool.

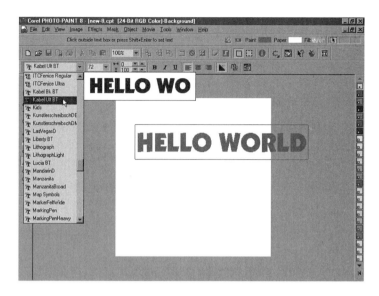

To access options for the Text tool, use the Property bar, or double-click the Text tool in the toolbox to display the Tool Settings rollup. This rollup is sensitive to the currently selected tool and displays options appropriate to the tool.

JUST A MINUTE

> If you want to create an image that contains only text, it is best to use CorelDRAW. CorelDRAW has many built-in editing features that PHOTO-PAINT does not have.

Antialiased Text

Antialiasing gets rid of those dreaded jaggies. To see the difference between antialiased text and regular text, try the following: On the Standard toolbox, choose 100% for a zoom level. Then select the Text tool, deselect the Antialiasing check box, set your font to Arial size 48, and type some text. You can zoom into the text using the Zoom tool (the magnifying glass on the toolbox) by clicking on the text until you can see the jaggies clearly. Notice the jagged edges around the letters (see Figure 20.9). Letters that contain diagonal lines are more susceptible to the jaggies, so make sure you type something with angled lines, a "w" or "y," for example.

Figure 20.9

Text with jaggies, zoomed at 100%.

20

Now choose the Text tool and click on your text. Turn antialiasing on by choosing Antialiasing in the Tool Settings rollup or press the Antialiasing button on the Property toolbar. Nothing happens, right? No problem, PHOTO-PAINT does not antialias until you choose a different tool or click your text cursor to another position away from your currently typed text. This is a time-saving feature so that PHOTO-PAINT does not antialias your image until you are satisfied with its size, position, format, and so on. Choose the Pick tool (the arrow) and PHOTO-PAINT antialiases the edges of your text (see Figure 20.10). See the difference? Most of the time you will want antialiasing enabled. You may find it useful to turn antialiasing off for text such as when your text size is very small (under 8 points). At such a small size, the text characters are so small that it takes only a few pixels to draw them and the antialiasing just smudges so that they become illegible (although at 6 points or less they cease to be legible anyway).

Figure 20.10
Antialiased text.

If the Text tool is still selected, you can type more text in a different position in the image by left-clicking in the image at the new position. At this point, the original text that you typed becomes a PHOTO-PAINT object. The same occurs when you finish typing your original object and choose another tool, for example, the Pick tool.

JUST A MINUTE

> After your text becomes a PHOTO-PAINT object, it works the same way and has the same properties as other objects. You can select it, drag it, and so on just as you can with any other objects.
>
> The only time that these objects are affected is when the objects are combined with the background or when you save your file as a file format other than native PHOTO-PAINT format.

Editing a Text Object

Once text becomes an object—that is, once you no longer have the I-beam text cursor in the text and the object handles have appeared—you cannot modify the font, color, style, or format of the text like you can in CorelDRAW. You cannot select the object and pick a new fill color. If you try, nothing apparent happens.

To modify a text's properties, reselect the Text tool and select the text object again. Any object transformations that have been applied to the text object (rotation, for example) is discarded and the text cursor (the I-beam) appears in the text. Moreover, if you changed the paint color since the creation of the text, PHOTO-PAINT applies the new paint color to the text.

20

It is possible to change the size of the text by dragging the object handles (drag the corners to keep the aspect ratio and use the other handles to stretch or shrink the text horizontally or vertically), but this is not as effective in keeping the quality of the text.

JUST A MINUTE

When manipulating objects in PHOTO-PAINT so that they change shape or size, PHOTO-PAINT does not commit the change until you tell it to commit the change by double-clicking on the object or right-clicking anywhere and choosing Apply. To abandon the change, right-click the object and choose Reset. This enables you to undo your change before it changes the bitmap that represents the floating object.

To delete a text object, select the object and press the Delete Key or choose Object | Delete. You can also duplicate a text object (and any PHOTO-PAINT object) by pressing Control+D or choosing Object | Duplicate.

Select a PHOTO-PAINT object consecutively, and you notice that the object handles change from scaling handles to rotation/skew handles, distort handles, and perspective handles (see Figure 20.11). This is similar to CorelDRAW objects.

Figure 20.11

Selecting an object more than once displays different object handles for different transformations.

Using the Object Docker

A useful window is the Objects Docker window. It can be opened by choosing View | Dockers | Objects (see Figure 20.12).

Figure 20.12

Object docker as a floating window.

20

The Objects Docker window contains a list of all the objects in the current image. Each object is represented by a name and a thumbnail image that represents the object. By default, PHOTO-PAINT names each object with an Object prefix and a number. A red line bounding the thumbnail indicates that the object is the current object.

To rename an object, double-click the currently selected object name or thumbnail. An Object Properties dialog box appears, and you can change the name by typing a new name in the Name box.

The eye next to the thumbnail in the Objects Docker indicates if the object is currently visible. Any text that you type appears as individual objects. Selecting the eye toggles the visibility of the object. Curiously, the current version of PHOTO-PAINT 8 doesn't permit you to toggle the visibility mode of the currently selected object. Instead all other objects, including the background, become invisible. To make the current object invisible, choose another object (or the background) and then click the eye of the previously selected object.

Summary

In this hour, you've covered a lot of ground. You learned how to customize PHOTO-PAINT 8, work with zoom levels, colors, fills, and text objects. And you created your first PHOTO-PAINT image.

Because we've covered so much in so few pages, you may still have questions about such things as aliasing, resolution, and color modes. If so, be sure to check out the companion web site at http://www.ppinet.com/TYCD824.htm for more information.

Workshop

Let's put some of what you have learned to practice by creating an image that has a resolution of 72dpi and that contains a couple copies of a text object layered on top of each other to create a simple, but nice, effect.

1. Start PHOTO-PAINT 8 and select File | New to create a new image.

2. Select a size for your image (make it wider than it is high: 7 inches wide by 2 inches high), and set the resolution to 72dpi.

3. Select the black color for the text object by left-clicking a color on the palette. Then select the Text tool (double-click on it to show the Tool Settings rollup).

4. Change the font size and style on the Tool Settings rollup to something you like and to something that fits nicely into the space in your image (your font is Times New Roman at 96 pts.). Then click on the image near the left and type some text. Position the text object with the Pick tool to center it in the image.

5. Duplicate the text by selecting the text object and typing Control+D.

20

6. Change the paint color to another color, and with the Text tool, select the topmost text object. The topmost text object color changes to the new color. Nudge this object up and to the left using the Pick tool. The result should look something like Figure 20.13.

Figure 20.13
Two text objects.

PhotoPaint 8

If you like the effect, remember to save your image by choosing File | Save As. Save the image as a PHOTO-PAINT 8 file to maintain the object information. This enables you to make editing changes later. This image will not be used in further workshops so it is not necessary to save the image.

Quiz

1. How do you create a new PHOTO-PAINT image?
2. Can you easily change the color of a text object?
3. What is the Object Docker?
4. How do you turn on antialiasing?

Quiz Answers

1. Click on the New icon from the Standard toolbar or choose File|New.
2. Yes. Select the new paint color (left-click on a palette color) and use the Text tool to select the text object again.
3. The Objects Docker window contains a list of all the objects in the current image. You will learn more about the Objects Docker in the next lesson.
4. Choose Antialiasing from the Tool Settings rollup or press the Antialiasing button on the Property toolbar.

Hour 21

More PHOTO-PAINT Basics

In this lesson, you learn about masks—a powerful image manipulation feature of PHOTO-PAINT. In conjunction with masks, we need to look more into PHOTO-PAINT objects and what they can do. You also take a peek at some of the Paintbrush tools and some of the Effect tools, such as the Clone tool and the Image Sprayer tool. Remember to experiment with these tools; half the fun is to discover on your own what PHOTO-PAINT is capable of helping you create.

Introduction to Masks

A mask has many different uses, but the fundamental idea behind the mask is to enable you to select a portion of a bitmap image. One way to accomplish this is using a Mask tool, which isolates an area of the bitmap. When you use a Mask tool to select an area, the selected area is modifiable or selected, while a mask covers the rest of the area. This enables you to protect areas of your image from changes when applying effects and when painting. You can also use this selected area (and it need not be a contiguous area—a connected area) to create a floating object, which is what you want to do here.

Using the Rectangle Mask Tool

Open a photographic quality image in PHOTO-PAINT. Choose File | Open and locate any photographic image. Figure 21.01 shows an image that I have selected. It is a painting of a stork that I photographed at the local zoo; then I sketched the stork on paper. I scanned the sketch into PHOTO-PAINT and used PHOTO-PAINT to paint over the sketch using the arsenal of paintbrushes (more on using brushes later in this lesson).

Figure 21.1
The stork.

When you select the Rectangle mask flyout, the masking tools shown in Figure 21.2 appear.

Figure 21.2
The Mask flyout tools.

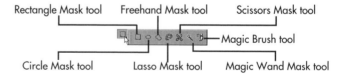

In the next few steps, you create an object from the stork using the Rectangle Mask tool.

21.1: Creating Objects with the Rectangle Mask Tool

1. Choose the Rectangle Mask tool and select a starting point in your image; then while holding the left mouse button down, drag to encompass a portion of your image with the tool. In this example, you use the Rectangle Mask tool to surround the stork. The result is a rectangle of "marching ants," or *marquee*, that surrounds the selected area (see Figure 21.3). If the animated rectangle does not appear, choose Show Mask Marquee on the Standard toolbar.

These marching ants do not affect the image. The rectangle within the marching ants signifies the modifiable section of the image, and a mask now protects the rest of the image.

Figure 21.3.

Marquee of marching ants surrounding the stork.

JUST A MINUTE

When you find yourself trying to modify an image that you cannot seem to modify, it might be that you have a mask selected. To remove any and all masks from your image choose Mask | Remove.

2. To create a new object (such as a text object) from the area you just selected, choose Object | Create | Object Copy Selection. This creates a PHOTO-PAINT object that floats over the original bitmap background without destroying the selected area.

3. Choosing Object Cut Selection removes the object from the selected area. You can see this object in the Object Docker and the object's object handles now appear on the image.

4. You can also see all objects in your image by choosing Show Objects Marquee from the Standard toolbar. This outlines all your objects with a blue marquee of marching ants.

5. You can now manipulate this object just like a text object. Experiment with it by repositioning, scaling, and rotating the object (see Figure 21.4).

21

Figure 21.4.

The selected area is now a transformed object floating over the original stork image.

Painting Shapes

Painting PHOTO-PAINT shapes is very similar to drawing CorelDRAW shapes. The main difference is that the shapes are bitmaps, and modifications to these shapes might cause unwanted destructive behavior. Here are a few things to note when painting shapes in PHOTO-PAINT:

- ☐ You need to set the shape's options (this includes setting fill and outline colors) prior to painting the shape.
- ☐ If you do not select the Render to Object button, the painting of objects will modify the selected object or background. That is, the shape paints over the pixels underneath it, effectively replacing the object's (or background's) pixels with the selected fill color of the currently selected shape.
- ☐ When you select a Paint Shape tool (Rectangle, Ellipse, Polygon, or Line), PHOTO-PAINT reflects the selected tool by changing the mouse cursor to a crosshair with the currently selected tool's icon in the crosshair's upper-right quadrant.
- ☐ To choose a different Paint Shape tool, press the small black triangle on the currently selected Shape tool. This triggers the flyout toolbar that contains the Ellipse, Polygon, and Line tools.

JUST A MINUTE

If you accidentally paint over a white background, you can choose Edit | Clear and the background will be removed. If your background is an image, it too will be erased, so be careful. Also, make sure that your background is selected when you clear the image (use the Objects Docker to select the background). If an object is selected and Edit | Clear is activated, the object is erased.

21

Adding Outlines to Shapes

Shapes can also include an outline (see Figure 21.5). To add a different colored outline to a shape, choose the paint color (the border color), double-click the Shape tool of choice, and enter a thickness in the Width box. In PHOTO-PAINT, the object is a bitmap and the outline is painted onto the object. That is, the pixels on the border of the object will be modified so that its color reflects the paint color.

Figure 21.5.

Rectangle with an outline.

Select an object and paint a rectangle shape next to it with Render to Object deselected. The object grows to encompass the painted shape. If, however, you choose Lock Transparency, the shape refuses to paint past the edges of the object.

JUST A MINUTE

To create a constrained shape (a square or circle, for example), choose the appropriate Shape tool and press the Control key as you paint your shape.

Painting Rectangles

To get a feel for creating PHOTO-PAINT shapes, the following steps walk through using the Rectangle tool to paint random rectangle shapes.

21

21.2: Painting a Rectangle

1. Choose the Rectangle tool to display the Rectangle tool's Property bar. To add a border around your rectangle, choose a paint color and modify the Width option for the rectangle in the Tool Settings rollup (or Property bar). You can also modify the roundness of the rectangle corners by entering a value in the Roundness box on the Property bar.

2. Choose a fill color by right-clicking on a color swatch from the palette.

3. Using the Rectangle tool, paint the rectangle by selecting the start point of the corner of the rectangle on the image and then dragging and releasing the mouse at the end corner of the rectangle.

Painting Ellipses

To paint an ellipse, choose the Ellipse tool, and then select all your desired options: fill, outline, and so on. Then drag the ellipse (or circle if you hold Control while painting the ellipse) to a desired shape and size.

Painting Polygons

Polygons are shapes with three or more sides. Choose the Polygon tool from the Shape Tools flyout. The last Shape tool you selected is the Ellipse tool. To locate the Polygon tool, press the small black triangle on the Ellipse tool and then select the Polygon tool.

The following steps walk you through creating a polygon (be sure to select the Polygon tool before beginning with Step 1).

21.3: Creating a Polygon

1. Left-click the cursor in the image area. This is the first point on the first edge of a polygon. Attached to this point is a rubber band line that follows the mouse cursor.

2. Choose the end point for the first edge of the polygon by left-clicking on the image surface. The outline of the first edge is painted and the rubber band continues to follow the mouse cursor.

3. Continue to place polygon edges on the surface of the image in this manner.

4. When you are on the last point of the last edge of the polygon, double-click the left mouse button.

The polygon is then complete and PHOTO-PAINT fills it with the currently selected fill and outlines it with the current paint color.

JUST A MINUTE

To constrain the polygon edges to 45-degree increments, hold Control down while moving and pressing the left mouse button.

21

Polygons can have edges that intersect and be any shape or size and have any number of edges. See Figure 21.6 for an example of a polygon.

Figure 21.6.
Painting polygons.

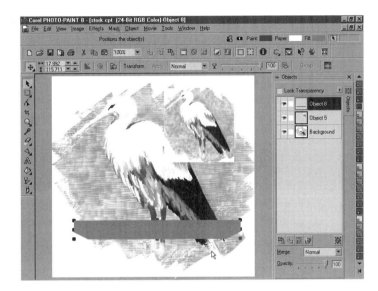

Painting Lines

Painting lines is very similar to painting polygons. The main difference is that the Line tool does not connect the first and last point and use a fill. Moreover, the fill does not determine the color of the line, rather the Paint color determines the color of the line. To stop painting line segments, remember to double-click. The width setting (on the Property bar) determines the width of the line.

Lines have an additional option, called the Shape Joints option, that determines the behavior of lines at the point where two line segments meet. When two lines meet at an angle, PHOTO-PAINT can join the lines in one of four different methods, as shown in Figure 21.7.

Figure 21.7.
The use of different line joint options.

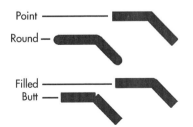

21

Paint Modes

When a shape is painted you can't choose what happens to the shape's color when the paint interacts with the bitmap underneath. This interaction between the color of the shape's paint and the color of the paint of the pixels is the Paint mode when painting shapes and is the Merge mode when working with objects. For examples of these modes, see Figure 21.8.

To modify the Paint mode, choose a new Paint mode in the Property bar or Tool Settings rollup prior to creating your object. To modify the Merge mode for existing floating objects, use the Merge list box in the Object Dockers window, or if this window is not visible, use the Tool Settings rollup when the Object tool is double-clicked.

Different types of Merge modes exist. For example, if you select the Add mode, the colors between the object and the image beneath it are added to make a brighter and usually different color.

Figure 21.8.

Painting rectangles using different Merge modes.

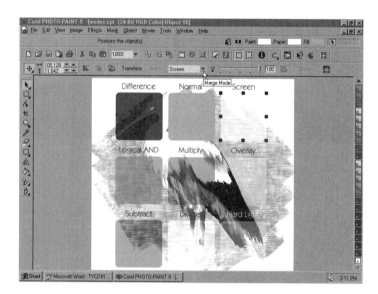

Fill Tool

The Fill tool replaces adjoining pixels with another color, Fountain fill, bitmap, or Texture fill. When you click an area of an image with the Fill tool, PHOTO-PAINT uses the color of the pixel that you clicked on to determine the parts of your image to repaint with your fill. Next the fill color (or texture) seeps into your image along interconnected pixels of the same (or similar) color. Figure 21.9 shows an example of using the Fill tool to replace one color with another color. The left rectangle was painted as an object and then duplicated. The duplicate rectangle was then filled using the Fill tool and a blue fill color.

21

Figure 21.9.

Using fill to replace colors.

Figure 21.9.

Using fill to replace colors.

The way PHOTO-PAINT decides which pixel colors to replace is based on the Tolerance value. The smaller the tolerance setting, the more precise the fill. That is, the fill affects pixels of colors similar to the one you select. The higher the tolerance, the more pixels fit and more of your image fills.

When you select an object while using the Fill tool, PHOTO-PAINT uses the object as the target of the fill. That is, if you have an object selected and even if you click beside the object with the Fill tool, the object expands to include the fill (see Figure 21.10). To fill parts of another object or the background, select that object prior to using the Fill tool.

Figure 21.10.

Filling beside selected objects. Notice that the background is still there, but underneath the just painted object.

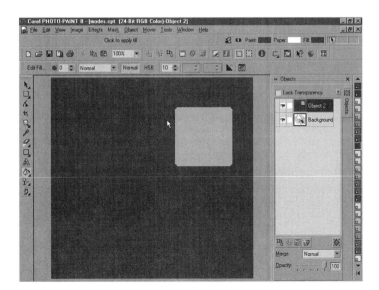

Working with Objects

PHOTO-PAINT objects are a powerful feature in PHOTO-PAINT. In this section, you discover there are more things you can do with objects: order objects on top and behind one another, feather an object's edges, add drop shadows to objects, and make objects transparent.

Ordering Objects

To order an object behind another object, select the object and right-click the object to display a menu near the cursor. Then choose Arrange | Order and select a position option: To Back, To Front, Behind One, or Forward One.

You can also order objects in the Object Docker by selecting the object to order and dragging the object above or below a desired object. The order of objects in the Object Docker reflects the relative position of all the objects above the background.

Grouping Objects

After you select a number of objects, you can group them just as in CorelDRAW. These grouped objects then behave, in most circumstances, as one object. To group the selected objects, choose Object | Arrange | Group, or type Control+G. To ungroup objects choose Object | Arrange | Ungroup, or type Control+U. You can also group and ungroup objects by right-clicking on the selected object(s) and choosing Arrange | Group (or Ungroup).

When you group objects, they maintain their order relative to each other, but the group takes on the order position of the topmost object in the group. The objects are linked together in the Object Docker window by a solid black line.

Aligning Objects

Just as in CorelDRAW, you can align PHOTO-PAINT objects relative to each other vertically and horizontally. Moreover, you can make the spacing among objects consistent using the distribute option. To align or distribute objects, select the objects to align and choose Object | Arrange | Align and Distribute.

Transforming Objects

As you have seen, there are a number of different transformations you can apply to objects in PHOTO-PAINT. These include transformations such as flip, rotate, skew, and scale. You choose these different transformation modes by selecting an object multiple times to display the different object handles used to transform the object.

You can also apply these transformations to objects through the Object menu. Choose Object | Flip, Rotate, or Transform to display dialog boxes that give you the option to transform the object using precise numeric values.

Object Opacity

Opacity is a measurement of how transparent an object is. The higher the opacity, the harder it is to see through it. You can find the opacity setting for an object in the Property bar when you select the object using the Pick tool or in the Object Docker window at the bottom of the window. To change the opacity, move the slider to the desired position (see Figure 21.11).

Figure 21.11.

Changing opacity of an object. The rectangle has an opacity setting of 42%.

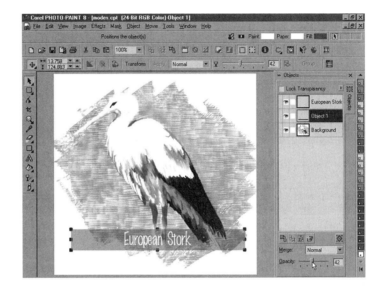

The opacity changes to objects that have been grouped will affect all the individual objects that make up the group.

The overall opacity of an object can be modified as long as the object remains an object. As soon as the object is combined to another object or the background (see the "Combining Objects" section), the opacity of an object cannot be changed using this method.

Object Feathering

You can fade the edges of objects in PHOTO-PAINT to nothing, revealing the background (or other objects beneath) on the edges. This is *feathering*.

Select an object and choose Object | Feather. In the Feather dialog box, select a width for the Feather option in pixels. With the Preview button selected (in the Feather dialog box, the eye left of the OK button), an increase in the spinner for the feather width displays the new increased feathering immediately on your object (see Figure 21.12).

Combining Objects

You can combine objects together or with the background. Do not confuse this with grouping objects. Grouping maintains an object's identity. Combining, not surprisingly, combines objects to create new objects (or modified backgrounds). When you combine objects together or combine objects with the background, the pixels between the two bitmaps combine permanently (only Undo can get you out of a jamb here).

Figure 21.12.
Object feathering.

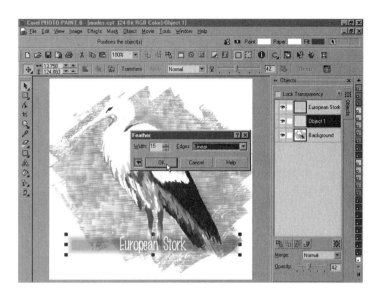

To combine objects, choose Object | Combine and then select the type of combination you want. You can combine multiple objects together to create a new object, combine the object with the background, or combine all objects in the image with the background.

Object Transparency Tool

The Object Transparency tool gives you the ability to add a number of different types of transparent gradients to an object. One problem with the Object Transparency tool is that it is not editable. When you apply another transparency type to an object, it adds it to the already modified object. To apply the current interactive transparency, select another tool or object.

To add a transparent gradient to an object, choose the Object Transparency tool and select the type of transparency to apply to an object.

JUST A MINUTE

For a better interface to the Object Transparency tool settings, double-click the Object Transparency tool to display the Tool Settings rollup. See Figure 21.13 for an example of the use of the Interactive Transparency tool.

To apply Linear transparency, choose the Object Transparency tool, select Linear type, and left-click the part of the object that you want to be the least transparent. Drag the mouse to another portion of the object and release the mouse button to select the most transparent part of the object. You can modify the start and end transparency values by modifying the Node Transparency slider on the Property bar. Select the node to adjust and slide the slider to the desired transparency value.

21

Figure 21.13.
Interactive transparency.

Working with Paintbrushes

PHOTO-PAINT has a set of tools that emulate Paintbrush tools. These tools modify pixels of a bitmap image using the selected paint color similar to the way that real paintbrushes modify paint on a canvas. These tools include the Paint tools (see Figure 21.14), Effect tool, Clone tool, and Image Sprayer tool.

Figure 21.14.
Paint tool flyout.

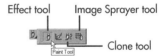

TIME SAVER

If you plan to use the Paint tools a lot in your work, I would suggest the purchase of a pressure-sensitive tablet. A *tablet* is a computer-input device that acts very much like a mouse or trackball, but rather than a mouse or trackball, you use a pen to move the cursor.

PHOTO-PAINT has a special rollup for pen settings in which many different functions of the Paint tools can be assigned to the pressure sensitivity of the pen. To view this rollup, choose View | Roll-Ups | Pen Settings.

21

The Paint tools affect the currently selected object (or background). Note that the object expands to include any painting and or effects past the boundary of an object when the Transparency Lock option is not set (see the Objects Docker).

Paint Tool

The Paint tools enable you to add the paint color to your image in a way that depends on the type of paintbrush and paint color you choose. When you select the Paint tool, the Property bar displays some of the modifiable options of the Paint tool. Double-click the Paint tool to display the Tool Settings rollup to access of the Paint tool options.

There are five tabs in the Paint tool Tool Settings rollup: Brush Type, Texture Settings, Dab Attributes, Stroke Attributes, and Orbit Settings (see Figure 21.15). Each of these settings includes a number of options that you can change that affect the Paint tool.

Figure 21.15.

Paint tool Tool Settings rollup.

In the Tool Settings rollup, notice a row of four icons representing different kinds of brushes. Next to these thumbnails is a small down arrow. Toggle this arrow to see a list of different types of predefined brushes; toggle the arrow again to minimize this list. When you choose a brush type, you can also select a subtype from a drop-down list found just beneath the thumbnails of the paintbrush types. See Figure 21.16 for a sample of some of the different brushes.

Effect Tool

The Effect tools are similar to the painting tools, but rather than adding color to the image surface, the Effect tools modify the pixels in different ways. Some of the more common effects are Smear, Smudge, and Brightness. The Smear tool, for example, acts like a cotton swab by smearing color underneath it, making it appear as if the paint colors are being moved to the front and sides of the tool (see Figure 21.17).

The Effect tool is in the Paint tool flyout. To view the Tool Settings rollup, double-click on the Effect tool. See Figure 21.18 for a sample of the effects you can create.

On an existing image, choose the kind of effect that you want to apply to your image; then drag the cursor in your image to apply the effect to your image.

21

Figure 21.16.
Using different brushes with the Paint tool.

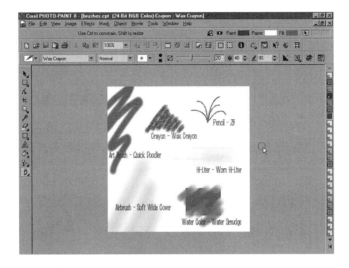

Figure 21.17.
The image on the right has been smeared by zigzagging the Smear tool across the rectangles.

Clone Tool

The Clone tool is different from the Paint and Effect tool in that it uses a part of an existing image as paint on the brush.

21

Figure 21.18.

The Trouble Sea. A painting I created using the Paint and Smudge tools.

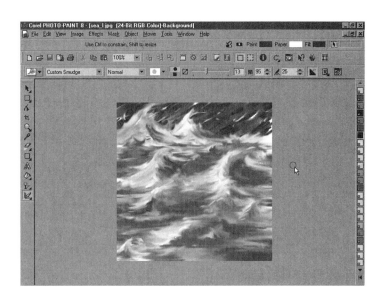

21.4: Working with the Clone Tool

1. Choose the Clone tool from the Paint tool flyout.
2. Left-click the area of an image for the source of the cloning.
3. Left-click at the place where you want the source image to copy. Depending on your Clone tool settings, the source image will be painted where you apply the Clone tool. See Figure 21.19 for some examples of the use of the Clone tool.

Figure 21.19.

Use the Clone tool to select the sand, and paint with the sand over the base of the sign post to make it look as if it is planted into the sand.

21

The neat thing about the Clone tool is that you can select the image source from an image other than the one you are currently working on.

4. Open the image for the source of the clone.

5. Select the Clone tool and click the part of the image to copy.

6. Then open an existing image or create a new image and start painting with the Clone tool in the second image. The source image should now start to appear in the destination image.

If you select the source of the clone effect from an object, the Clone tool will honor the boundary of the object. That is, it will not select paint from past the boundary of the object. However, if you select the background source for the clone effect, objects that lie on top of the background will be ignored when selecting paint from the source image. For the best effect, it is usually best to combine all the objects with the background in the source image.

Image sprayer

The Image Sprayer tool is, just as the name implies, a tool that effectively sprays images onto the screen.

21.5: Working with the Image Sprayer

1. Choose the Image Sprayer tool from the Paint Tool flyout.

2. Paint on your image. The result is a spray of the currently selected image.

3. To change the sprayed image, double-click the Image Sprayer tool and press the small flyout arrow; then choose Load An Image list. This displays a dialog box that asks what image list to load. The default directory for the image lists appears and you can choose one of many preinstalled image lists.

You can modify the size of the images, the rate at which they come out of the sprayer, and so on. See Figure 21.20 for an example of the use of this tool.

Summary

In this lesson, you learned that there are many different ways to create, manipulate, and transform floating bitmap objects using the Mask tools, Pick tool, and Object Docker.

As soon as you create the image, you can individually modify the pixels in a bitmap image— the entire image or a floating bitmap object—using tools such as the Paint Shape tools and the Paint, Effect, Clone, and Image Sprayer tools.

Figure 21.20.

The Image Spray tool in action.

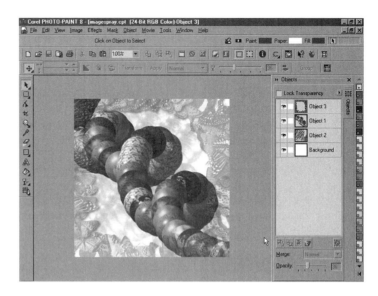

Workshop

Let's put some of what you have learned to practice by creating an image using some of the tools and object techniques learned in this lesson. The following steps create the image in Figure 21.20:

1. Start PHOTO-PAINT 8 and select File | New to create a new image.

2. Select a size for your image, 360 × 360 square; set the resolution to 72dpi.

3. Select the Image Sprayer tool from the Paint tool flyout.

4. Double-click on the Image Sprayer tool to display the Tool Settings rollup. Load the glass spheres transparent.cpt image list from the default image list directory by selecting the small black triangle and then Load Image List. This image list paints zigzags on your canvas.

5. Select the Magic Wand Mask tool and click on the white background. Select Mask | Invert to select the balls. Convert the balls to an object to change their opacity. To do this select, Object | Create | Object Cut Selection. Then modify the opacity to 25% in the Object Docker.

6. Create another new image and repeat steps 2 through 5, except this time use the butrfly.cpt image list and spray around the border of the image. After you create the butterfly object, change its opacity to about 36%.

7. Create another new image, repeat steps 2 through 5, and use the spheres planets.cpt image list and spray a spiral through the center. Do not modify the opacity of this object.

21

8. Create another new image. One at a time, select each object that you created in the previous images and choose Edit | Copy. Then immediately select this new image and choose Edit | Paste. Do this for all three of the objects previously created.

9. Organize the objects in this new image so that the glass balls are at the back, the butterflies are in the front, and the planets are in the middle.

Remember to save your image by choosing File | Save As. Save the image as a PHOTO-PAINT 8 file to maintain the object information. You will not use this image in further workshops so it is not necessary to save the image. Play around with feathering the edges of some of these objects, and changing each objects opacity to see what kinds of different images you can create. Best of all, have fun!

Quiz

1. Can you change the color of a rectangle object after you paint it?

2. What determines the color of a line?

3. What is the difference between grouping and combining objects?

4. What if I want to put an object behind an area that is not a floating object?

Quiz Answers

1. Trick question. Yes and No. You cannot modify the rectangle like you would in CorelDRAW, but you can modify it using the Fill tool.

2. The paint color, not the fill color.

3. Grouping keeps the objects' identity, while combining the objects creates a new object from the existing objects.

4. You will have to create an object area. That is, use one (or more) of the mask tools to create a mask around the area of interest. Then select Object | Create | Object Cut Selection. This lifts the masked area off and creates an object that contains the area. Then place an object behind the new object using the Object | Arrange commands or drag the objects around in the Object Docker.

21

Hour 22

Intermediate PHOTO-PAINT

So far I have covered only a small fraction of all the features in PHOTO-PAINT. Even the features that I have covered have not been covered in their entirety, but I leave the exploring and experimenting to you. The same can be said for the new features I introduce to you in this chapter. After reading a section, be sure to experiment with the new things that you learn. In this way, you can remember the things learned and discover new techniques, effects, and shortcuts.

This chapter covers much more about masks as well as some clipping features. So let's have some fun.

JUST A MINUTE

After reading this last hour on PHOTO-PAINT, you may want more information about image manipulation and working with filters and other special effects. If so, visit the companion web site at http://www.ppinet.com/TYCD824.htm.

Working with Masks

If you recall from Hour 21, the mask tools define the area of an image that is editable and apply a mask to the rest of the image, thus effectively protecting the rest of the image. To create an object from an editable area, choose Object | Create and then choose the type of object creation.

To view a mask, select the Show Mask Marquee button on the Property bar. The mask marquee appears and looks like marching ants. Object marquees can also be made visible. To see the object marquee, select Show Object Marquee (blue marching ants); it displays as a line of blue marching ants. The object marquee displays the edges of objects. You can turn the display of these marquees on or off by selecting the corresponding marquee display button on the Standard toolbar.

Inverting Masks

An area selected with a Mask tool is the currently editable area. To invert the mask so that the editable area becomes masked or protected and the masked area editable, choose Mask | Invert.

Masks and Objects

Masks over the top of selected objects only mask the currently selected object—not the entire image. In Figure 22.1, a rectangular mask is applied to the image, then Object 3 is selected in the Object Docker (the colored spiral balls). Select Edit | Cut to remove the editable area from the object. The result is the removal of a rectangular section of the spiral balls and the background and other objects are unaffected.

In order to cut a rectangular area through the entire image, combine all the objects with the background and then cut the rectangular area.

The exception to this rule is the Lasso, Scissors, and Magic Wand Mask tools. You can select editable areas of an image using these tools as if the image's objects were all combined. This is true only if the Mask Visible button on the Property bar (or in the Tool Settings rollup) is pressed prior to using the Mask tool.

JUST A MINUTE

If you try to select a transparent area of an object using a Mask tool, you cannot create a new object from that area. However, you can select the object above or below that contains the colored area you had originally intended to use for your new object.

22

Figure 22.1.

The left image is the original image we created in Hour 21 using the Image Spray tool. The image on the right has had a portion of Object 3 masked and then cut out.

Moving the Contents of Selected Areas

You can move an area selected by the Mask tool by creating the mask and then right-clicking and dragging the selection. When you release the right mouse button, a small pop-up menu appears asking what you want to do with the selection; either copy, move, or cancel the action.

The moved selection does not become an object unless you convert it into an object by choosing Object | Create | Object: Copy from selection (or Cut from selection).

Moving the Mask Marquee

The mask marquee can be manipulated like any object by using the Mask Transform tool. To begin, create a selected area using a Mask tool. Then display the Pick Tool flyout and select the Mask Transform tool. The marquee of the selected area turns into an object that you can transform like any other object (see Figure 22.2). You might drag or scale the marquee; click on the marquee object again and PHOTO-PAINT displays rotation handles that you might use to rotate the marquee. All object-like transformations can be applied to the marquee object. When your marquee is positioned and transformed to your liking, select the Pick tool (or any other tool) to apply the changes to the mask marquee.

Mask Modes

When creating masks, you can work in one of four different modes: Normal, Additive, Subtractive, or XOR. By selecting Mask | Mode, the active mode that is currently active is checked.

Figure 22.2.

Modifying the mask marquee using the Mask Transform tool.

In Normal mode, the mask tool creates an editable area on the image. If a mask already exists, it goes away and the new mask is applied to the image.

The Additive mode adds an area to the editable area of the image by removing sections from the currently created mask. For example, in Figure 22.3, the rectangle Mask tool, in the Additive mode, adds an editable rectangular area to the already existing editable area.

Figure 22.3.

Rectangle Mask tool used to add a rectangular area to an image that already has a mask.

22

The Subtractive mode expands the masked areas effectively removing editable sections of the image. (If there is no mask, Subtractive mode masks the entire image and makes the selected area editable.)

The XOR mode creates a mask where overlapping regions are protected, which means that if you create two overlapping rectangles using the rectangle mask, the overlapped section will be masked and the other areas of the rectangle will be editable.

You can switch between modes by choosing Mask | Mode and the desired mode. You can also select the mode interactively by selecting a Mask tool and then pressing Control while drawing the mask.

Render Text to Mask

The Render Text to Mask option when using the Text tool creates a mask that outlines the currently selected font style and size.

Select the Text tool and press the Render Text To Mask button on the Property bar (see Figure 22.4). You can also see this selection if you double-click on the Text tool to display the Tool Settings rollup.

Figure 22.4.
Render Text To Mask button.

This option creates a mask that outlines the typed text with a mask. Figure 22.5 shows text rendered, not to an object, but rather to a mask. The text area is the modifiable area and a mask protects the rest of the image.

Once text has been rendered to a mask, you can create an object from the mask, or apply an effect to the masked area.

JUST A MINUTE

When text is rendered to a mask and the editable area is then copied to the Clipboard and pasted back as an object, the resulting textlike object is not a real text object. Even though you cannot modify the object like a regular text object, you can modify the object like any other regular object; that is, rotate, skew, change opacity, feather the edges, and so on.

Figure 22.5.
Text rendered to a mask.

Mask Tools

You have already seen the rectangle Mask tool in action, but more Mask tools can isolate areas of an image. A combination of these Mask tools enable you to isolate complex parts of images including parts of images that are a certain color and that fall within a color's tolerance value. In the following sections, you take a look at the other Mask tools.

Circle Mask Tool

The Circle Mask tool creates an elliptical or circular editable area. Simply select the Circle Mask tool from the Mask tool flyout. Press the Control key while drawing the circle mask to constrain the mask to a circle.

Freehand Mask Tool

Use the Freehand Mask tool to make an irregularly shaped editable area. Select the Freehand Mask tool and click on the image surface. Then move the cursor to another location and click again. (The marquee line connects your first point with the next point.) Continue clicking around your irregular object, and double-click on the last point to close the mask. The result is an irregularly shaped editable area.

You can also use the Freehand Mask tool to freehand trace an editable area. With the cursor positioned on your image, press the left mouse button and while holding the mouse button, trace the object that you want to make editable.

22

Lasso Mask Tool

The Lasso Mask tool selects an editable area in a similar way to the Freehand Mask tool. The crucial difference between these tools is that the Lasso Mask tool uses your original selection point on the image as a seed color. (The seed color is the color that used to determine the extent of the mask.) The mask defining the selectable area then shrinks until it finds a pixel that does not fall in the tolerance value of the seed color. Use the Property bar or the Tool Settings rollup to define the tolerance value for the currently selected Mask tool. Does your brain hurt yet? Time for an example.

Figure 22.6 shows a marquee selection using the Lasso Mask tool. The initial point for the Lasso Mask tool is the white area just above the small blue square in the top-left of the image. The resulting editable area can be seen in Figure 22.7. Any white area is masked until the tool meets a pixel (blue in this case) that falls past the tolerance value of the pixel you originally selected (white); at this point, the mask stops shrinking.

Figure 22.6.

The Lasso Mask tool selecting an area of an image.

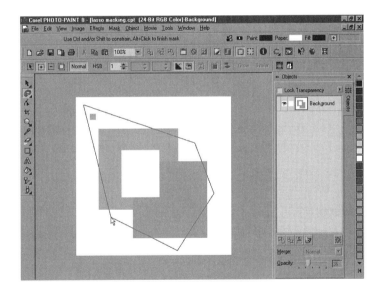

Scissors Mask Tool

The Scissors Mask tool selects an area by using the color of a currently selected pixel to move the mask's marquee to its nearest contrasting pixel. It effectively places the mask marquee at the edges of contrasting colors.

Figure 22.7.

The mask marquee displaying the editable area after using the Lasso Mask tool in Figure 22.6.

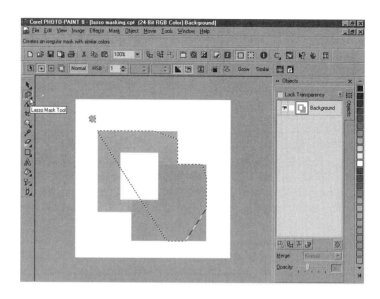

Select the Scissors Mask tool and click near the area you want to make editable. When you click on the image, two things happen. The first thing that happens is a square appears around a part of the image centered on the point you clicked. This square shows the maximum boundary that the mask marquee searches for contrasting edges. The second thing that happens is a rubber band line becomes attached to the originally selected point that follows your scissors cursor. This rubber band line is where PHOTO-PAINT thinks there is an edge and is where the mask marquee appears if you double-click or go on to select another point (see Figure 22.7). If you double-click, the mask is closed and the editable area is selected.

Figure 22.7.

The Scissors Mask tool in action.

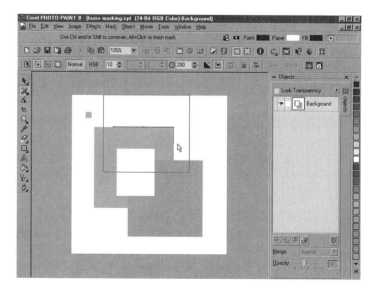

22

JUST A MINUTE

You can also use the Scissors Mask tool as a freehand Mask tool by holding the left mouse button down and dragging the scissors around the object that you want to select.

Magic Wand Mask Tool

The Magic Wand is used to select as an editable area those pixels that fall into the tolerance value of the original pixel you selected. This editable area expands as long as you have connected pixels to your original pixel that fall into the tolerance value. When no more pixels are found that are connected to the original pixel, then the masking is complete and the mask marquee appears showing the editable area.

Mask Brush Tool

The Mask Brush tool is another excellent way of creating a freehand editable area. The Mask Brush tool acts like a brush; where you apply the brush is the editable area. You can select different brush widths and nib styles in the Property bar or in the Tool Settings rollup.

Figure 22.8 shows an editable area selected using the Mask Brush tool. To add additional brush strokes to existing ones, choose the Additive mask mode by holding down Control.

Figure 22.8.

Mask created using the Mask Brush tool and the Additive mask mode.

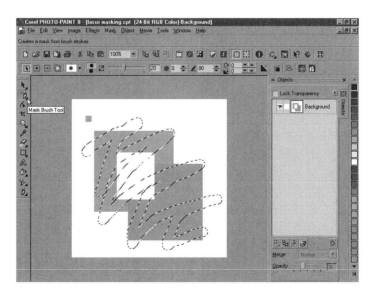

Minor Mask Effects

You can do more things with masks once they are created. You can feather the edges around a mask, create a mask border, create lenses using masks, and create clipping masks.

Feathering Masks

Just like feathering the edges of an object, you can feather the edges around a mask by choosing Mask | Shape | Feather. In the Feather dialog box, enter the width of the feather, its direction (average, middle, inside, outside), and if you do not select average for the direction, select the type of feathering. See Hour 21 for more information on the different types of feathering.

Mask Borders

The mask marquee (the marching ant border) can be converted into an editable area by choosing Mask | Shape | Border. Enter the border width of the area and the edge type in the dialog box. A soft edge has a more gradual blend than the hard edge type. The border width is the total width of the selectable area on both sides of the mask marquee. The result is an editable border area that surrounds what used to be the old mask marquee.

Smooth and Remove Holes

A color isolation tool such as the Magic Wand can create an editable area that is imperfect (see Figure 22.9). To create a cleaner-looking mask marquee and consequently a cleaner editable area, choose Mask | Shape | Smooth or Remove Holes.

Figure 22.9.

An editable area selected using the Magic Wand tool that contains holes or islands of masked areas.

22

To see the effect of smoothing or removing holes most effectively, choose Mask | Mask Overlay. A reddish color blanket, which does not modify the image, is overlayed on the image surface. The darkest red represents the most protected area of the image. Colors that can be seen through this red blanket are the most editable areas of the image. Shades of red determine the strength of the mask at those pixels. The darker the shade, the more protected from modification is the pixel.

To remove the imperfections in the editable area, choose Mask | Shape | Smooth or Remove Holes. This will smooth the edges of the mask and effectively eliminate any imperfections in the masking within your editable area (see Figure 22.10).

Figure 22.10.

An editable area that has been cleaned up using Remove Holes and Smooth effects for masks.

Clipping Masks

A Clipping mask enables you to modify an object's transparency without affecting the object. If you recall, the Object Transparency tool permanently affects the object to which you apply transparency.

22.1: Creating and Modifying a Clipping Mask

1. Select the object in the Object Docker so that the thumbnail is highlighted by a red square and so that the name of the object is surrounded by blue.

2. Right-click on the thumbnail and choose Create Clip Mask.

3. Select the kind of clipping mask to create with (see Figure 22.11). To Show All is a Clipping mask that is all white. To Hide All is a Clipping mask that is all black.

When a pixel in a Clipping mask is white, it means that it is totally transparent and allows the image pixel to show through. If the pixel is black, this means that it is totally opaque and does not allow any part of the image pixel to show through. Gray pixel values in the Clipping mask show more of the pixel beneath as the gray value moves from black to white. In other words, the whiter the pixel, the more transparent the mask and the more the image shows through.

Figure 22.11.

Creating a Clipping mask.

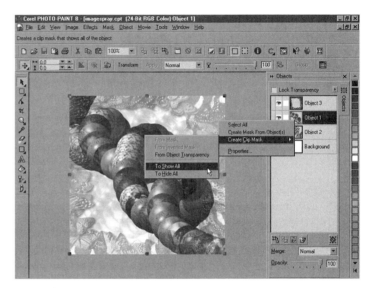

4. Click on the Clipping mask to highlight the Clipping mask thumbnail in the Object Docker.

5. Select a grayscale value paint from the palette (the uniform palette contains a set of grayscale colors) and select the Paint tool. Paint on the surface of the image.

Painting on the surface image modifies the currently selected Clipping mask, and depending on the shade of gray that you select, modifies the transparency of the current object.

In Figure 22.12, I selected a Show All Clipping mask, a black paint color, and then with the Clipping mask selected, I painted a zigzag pattern on the image. Effectively I created an opacity paintbrush.

JUST A MINUTE

To delete a Clipping mask from an object, right-click on the Clipping mask and select Remove Clip Mask. To make the Clipping mask permanent, modify the transparency of the object, and select Combine Clip Mask.

22

Figure 22.12.

Painting on the Clipping mask to affect the transparency of an object.

Clipping to Parent

PHOTO-PAINT 8 has a new feature that enables you to fit one object into another object. Make sure that the Object Docker is visible and that you have at least two objects created. In the Object Docker, Object A is above Object B.

You will use Object B as a clipping parent for Object A. That is, Object A will fit inside Object B. If you want this the other way around then order Object B above Object A in the Object Docker window.

In the Object Docker, click on the small white square next to Object A's Eye icon. A small paper clip appears in the white square. Object A's thumbnail moves slightly to the right indicating that it is now being clipped by its parent, Object B (see Figure 22.13).

You can still individually select either object and move each around any way you like. In Figure 22.13, I even added a drop shadow to Object B. To make the objects become separate again, simply click on the paper clip to make it go away and the objects will return to normal.

Summary

In this chapter, you explored some nuances of one of PHOTO-PAINT's most powerful features, the mask. Other features and effects exist that have not been covered and I leave that up to you, capable reader, to experiment with and to discover. PHOTO-PAINT is a tool that complements CorelDRAW extremely well.

Figure 22.13.

Placing an object inside another object using Clip to Parent. The left image contains the two objects before clipping. The right image shows the clover inside the text object.

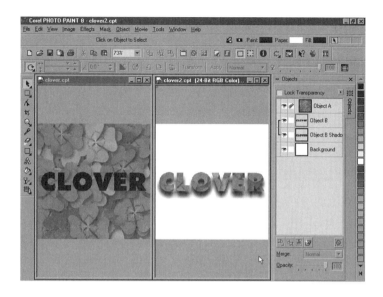

Workshop

The following steps create the image in Figure 22.14. This exercise demonstrates the use of creating a mask, modifying the mask, creating an object from the mask, and adding a drop shadow to the new object.

1. Start PHOTO-PAINT 8 and select File | New to create a new image.

2. Select a size for your image, 480 × 480 square; set the resolution to 96dpi.

3. Select the Image Sprayer tool from the Paint Tool flyout.

4. Double-click on the Image Sprayer tool to display the Tool Settings rollup. Load the raindrps.cpt image list from the default image list. Using this image list, paint the background of your canvas.

5. Use the rectangle Mask tool to mask about 80% to 90% of the image. Create an object from the rectangle area by selecting Object | Create | Object: Cut Selection.

6. Shift+drag the corner of the new object to scale the object down. This creates a white border around the object.

7. Add a drop shadow using Object | Drop Shadow. Set the orientation at 315 degrees, opacity to 50%, and the width of the feather to 20 pixels. Ungroup the shadow object from the main object by selecting the objects and choosing Object | Arrange | Ungroup. Select the main object and duplicate it by pressing Control+D.

22

8. Create a mask from the duplicate object by selecting Mask | Create From Object. Select Effects | 2D | Edge Detect (adjust the sensitivity to 2). Change the opacity of the top object to 37%.

9. Select the background (in the Object Docker). Select Effects | Artistic | Impressionist (use the default values). This fuzzes the background.

10. Using the Animals 2 font, create a 96-point butterfly (by typing the number 9). Rotate the butterfly to the right about 45 degrees. Set opacity to 10%.

11. Center the Thank You text using a blue color, set the Shelley Allegro font at 96 points. Lastly, add a drop shadow (feather of 4, with Average set for direction) to the text and position it in the center of the image.

Remember to save your image by choosing File | Save As.

Figure 22.14.

Workshop image.

Quiz

1. How do I create an object from a photograph?

2. What is a Clipping mask?

3. How do I move a mask?

4. What are the different Mask modes I can work with?

Quiz Answers

1. By using a mask. Draw a mask around the area that you want to make into an object. You can use any combination of mask tools to isolate the area of interest. Once you create the mask, , then select Object | Create | Object: Copy or Cut Selection. A floating object is created from the masked area.

2. A Clipping mask enables you to modify an object's transparency without affecting the object. Remember the Object Docker and the thumbnail depicting the objects in your image? The Clipping mask is the little thumbnail image next to an object image. It is created by right-clicking on the object thumbnail and choosing Create Clip Mask. The mask can then be modified.

3. Use the Mask Transform Tool. (It is hidden in the flyout of the Pick Tool.) Select the Mask Transform Tool and click on your mask. Object-like handles will appear and you can modify your mask like you can modify any object.

4. You can choose from Normal, Additive, Subtractive, or XOR. Simply select Mask|Mode and choose the mode you want.

Hour **23**

Dream 3D Basics

In the last 22 hours, you have extensively covered CorelDRAW and have been introduced to Corel PHOTO-PAINT. Now in the twenty-third hour, you encounter another tool in the Corel Suite of products called Corel Dream 3D. Dream 3D is unlike both CorelDRAW and Corel PHOTO-PAINT.

In Dream 3D, a world is filled with three-dimensional objects (or an object), lights are set up to light up the creation, and then a virtual camera is used to take a picture of the scene. Taking this picture, in 3D jargon, is called *rendering*. The image that is created from the picture is a bitmap that can be used as is or can be further manipulated by PHOTO-PAINT or used within CorelDRAW.

JUST A MINUTE

To *model* an object in Dream 3D is to say that you create the object.

An *environment* is all those things that make up the three-dimensional world other than the objects and direct lights.

General 3D Concepts

When Corel Dream 3D starts, it asks to create an empty scene, open an existing scene, or use the Scene Wizard to create a scene. For our purposes, let's choose Create an Empty Scene. Dream 3D's environment (Figure 23.1) is similar to that of CorelDRAW and PHOTO-PAINT.

Figure 23.1.
Dream 3D.

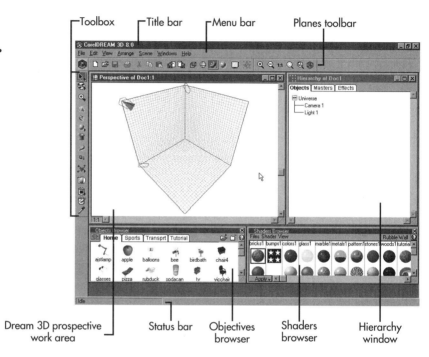

Clicking on the X control of a window can close each of the windows in the work area. If the Perspective window is closed, then the file is closed and you will be asked to save the current scene. The other windows can be opened and closed at will without closing the current scene.

To open a closed Shaders Browser window, for example, select Windows | Shaders Browser. You can also maximize or minimize the Perspective or Hierarchy windows by clicking on the window control handles in the upper-right corner of each window. These windows can be reopened using the Windows menu. To reset the entire work environment to a default setting, select Windows | Workspace and then select a default screen resolution size.

Perspective Window

The Perspective window is a view of the Dream 3D world in which you create your scenes. Each scene can be saved (choose File | Save or Save As) or loaded back into Dream 3D. For every scene that is loaded, a new Perspective window is created to hold that scene. In this window, you modify your scene by adding more lights, changing object positions, creating objects, and so on.

The Perspective window contains three planes (grid areas) (see Figure 23.2), which represent three-dimensional space. The plane to the left extends along the x-axis. The plane to the right extends along the y-axis. The plane on the bottom represents the plane perpendicular to the z-axis (the axis that goes top to bottom).

Figure 23.2.
Dream 3D planes.

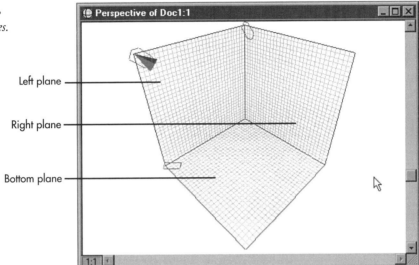

Left plane

Right plane

Bottom plane

23

The red pyramidlike shape in the upper-left is a default lamp (or light) used to light up the scene when you take a picture of the scene. The red rectangular shapes are projections of the lamp onto the planes.

Hierarchy Window

The Hierarchy window is a hierarchical display of all the objects in the current scene (or universe). You find a unique Hierarchy window for every scene that you open.

Objects can be grouped together and selected, and the object's properties modified using the Hierarchy window. To change the properties of an object, right-click on the object in the Hierarchy window and select Properties.

Objects Browser Window

The Objects Browser window contains groups of predefined, Dream 3D objects and is categorized by folders: Home, Sports, Transport, and Tutorial.

You can add an object from the Object Browser into your scene by dragging the object to either the Perspective window or the Hierarchy window. You can also right-click on an object in the Objects Browser and select Open In New window. This creates a new Perspective window containing just the object from the Objects Browser window.

Shaders Browser Window

The Shaders Browser window contains the Object Shaders that you can apply to objects in your scene. Objects in the real world have all sorts of properties, such as roughness, shininess, transparency, color, and so on. These shaders are applied to objects to simulate real objects.

JUST A MINUTE

> The Main menu changes depending on the currently selected window. Make sure that the window you want to work in is the currently selected window before trying to access the menu for its commands.

The Dream 3D Toolbox

Dream 3D's toolbox contains tools for creating and manipulating objects, lights, cameras, and applying paint shapes to objects.

- ☐ **Selection tool**   Selects and modifies objects.
- ☐ **Virtual Track Ball tool**   Rotate objects in the Perspective window.
- ☐ **Text tool**   Creates three-dimensional text objects.
- ☐ **Free Form Modeling tool**   Creates custom objects.
- ☐ **Sphere, Cube, Cone, Cylinder, and Icosahedra tools**   Creates these basic shapes.
- ☐ **Wizard Tool**   Creates objects using the Corel Dream 3D Wizard.
- ☐ **Create Light tool**   Creates lights for the Dream 3D scene.
- ☐ **Create Camera tool**   Adds cameras to the scene so that your scene can be viewed from different places.
- ☐ **Camera Dolly tool**   Positions the currently selected camera.
- ☐ **Render Area tool**   Renders a part of the image.
- ☐ **Flyout group of Paint Shape tools**   Applies a shaped paint area to a part of an object.
- ☐ **3D Paint Brush tool**   Paints onto the surface of an object with a modifiable paint brush.
- ☐ **Shader Eye Dropper tool**   Extracts shader properties from objects.

Basic Dream 3D Concepts

In the following sections, you create a sphere object. This introduces you to some basic Dream 3D concepts, such as the bounding box and the object's projections on the planes.

23

23.2: Creating a Sphere

To Do

1. On the toolbox, select the Sphere tool.
2. Move your cursor into the Perspective window (you will notice the cursor change to a crosshair).
3. Click on the bottom plane and drag to display a cube outline. You have just created a sphere in Dream 3D (see Figure 23.3).

You can create many objects in this way and position them above, below, in front, behind, inside of each other, and intersecting one another.

23

Figure 23.3.

A sphere created in Dream 3D.

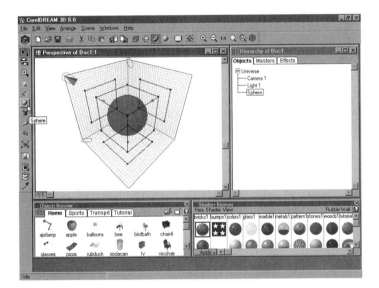

Object Bound Box

A black outline cube surrounds the sphere. This cube represents the outside boundaries of the sphere and is visible only on the currently selected object. You can drag each of the nodes on this object boundary box to distort the shape of the sphere.

CAUTION

> Dream 3D only has one level of Undo, so you may find it helpful to save critical points of your scene to separate files so that you always have a backup to revert to.

Projections

The red pyramid lamp (or light object) in the top-left corner of the Perspective window is placed there by Dream 3D as a default light for a scene. Each object, including the lamp, has associated with the object red rectangle shapes on each of the planes. These rectangle shapes are *projections*. A projection is the silhouette of an object onto a plane. If you look directly at one of the planes, the red rectangle shape outlines the object on the plane.

You will also notice that, just like your lamp, you have projections of the outline of the boundaries of the sphere on all three planes. Drag the projection on the left-hand plane and watch as the sphere starts to float above the bottom plane. All three perspective projections are now visible. These projections are useful in manipulating the object in your three-dimensional scene; they are also useful for restrained scaling of objects.

23.3: Moving the Sphere

1. Drag the projection on the left-hand plane and watch as the sphere starts to float above the bottom plane. All three perspective projections are now visible; these projections are useful in manipulating the object in your three-dimensional scene. They are also useful for restrained scaling of objects. The motion of the sphere is limited to the plane of the projection that you drag.

2. The same is true of scaling. Dragging a node on a projection distorts the sphere. The distortion is restraining the distortion to the plane of the projection you distort.

The projections also help you to see the relative position of an object in relation to other objects and in relation to your planes (see Figure 23.4).

Figure 23.4.

Notice the two spheres in this scene. The blue sphere is above the red sphere.

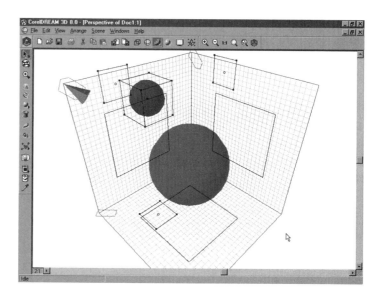

Your universe can extend beyond the grid planes displayed in the Perspective window. The planes exist only for reference and will not render (will be invisible) in your final image when you take a picture of your scene.

Taking a Picture

23

The whole idea behind working in Dream 3D is to model a scene and then create an image of your scene. This image can then be incorporated into CorelDRAW or PHOTO-PAINT (or any other package that accepts bitmapped images).

23.4: Taking a Picture of Your Scene

1. Move the sphere by dragging the project planes, or the sphere, so that it floats above the bottom plane and is equally spaced between the other planes. The reason you move it is to position the sphere to the center of your universe because by default, the picture will be taken centered on the Perspective window. Also, by moving the sphere, you place it into the light path of the lamp.

To view the area that a spot lamp illuminates, right-click on the lamp using the Selection tool. The result is a light cone that shows the area where the lamp illuminates.

2. To take a picture of your sphere, you need to first make the production frame visible. The production frame is a green rectangle that is essentially the viewfinder of the camera. The area inside the green rectangle renders into a bitmap image that you can save and then load into PHOTO-PAINT or CorelDRAW.

3. To display the production frame, choose View | Production Frame. You can move the frame around by dragging the frame. You can also resize the frame by dragging the nodes on the corners of the frame.

4. To take a picture of your sphere, choose Scene | Render | Use Current Settings. The result will be a window that contains the bitmap image of your sphere (see Figure 23.5).

5. To save this image, choose File | Save As, select a file type, and then load the image into CorelDRAW to enhance your vector design.

Figure 23.5.

Picture of your sphere.

Notice that our image of the sphere does not contain the lamp. Lamps, or lights, in Dream 3D only affect other objects. They are not visible themselves. If you want a lamp to be visible, you have to model a lamp and place the light into the place where the light bulb would be. Dream 3D lights are only point sources of light and hence are invisible. Their effects, however, are visible and are what cause the realistic effects in the finally rendered images.

Viewing your Scene

Note a couple of things when viewing your scene: The quality of the image displayed while working on your scene, and that you can view your scene from different default view positions while creating it.

View Quality

By default, when working in the Perspective window, objects display using Preview Quality mode. This mode uses a quick, but inaccurate, method of shading your scene. You can select the Preview Quality mode on the Standard toolbar along with the other viewing modes (see Figure 23.6).

Figure 23.6.

The Preview Quality modes.

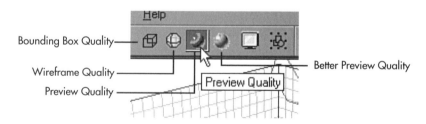

23

The quickest mode is the bounding box mode. This mode only displays the bounding box of objects and is best used in complex scenes. The slowest, but more accurate mode, is the Better Quality viewing mode. These modes do not affect the properties of the objects themselves; they just affect how you view them while working on them.

Different Views

The Perspective window currently is a reference view of your scene. A *reference* view is a view on your scene that looks three dimensional; that is, it looks like there is depth to the scene. You can look at your scene in other ways by choosing View | Type and then selecting the kind of view you want of your scene. To get back to the Perspective, choose View | Type | Reference.

Using Numerical Properties to Move Objects

You have already seen that you can move objects using the Selection tool by moving their projections or by moving the object. You can also position objects numerically. Right-click on the sphere and select Numerical Properties (see Figure 23.7). Position the object to a new position by entering different values for x, y, and z and pressing Apply.

Figure 23.7.

Object's numerical properties.

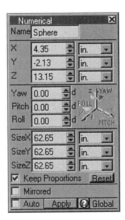

The origin of your universe is exactly in the middle of all the axes. Enter 0,0,0 for X, Y, and Z, and the object floats exactly in the middle of your planes. To move the object closer to the corner of the planes select -45, -45, -45. You can also scale, rotate, and distort the object by changing the values for Size and Yaw, Pitch, and Roll. Experiment with different values for these settings; notice that rotation of a sphere does not appear to change the object.

JUST A MINUTE

Yaw, pitch, and *roll* are terms used to explain rotation around an axis. The z-axis goes from top to bottom and rotation around the z-axis is called yaw. The x-axis goes out toward the left. Rotation around this axis is called roll. The y-axis goes out toward the right and rotation around this axis is called pitch.

23.5: Creating a Cube

1. Select and hold the Sphere tool to cause the object flyout to appear (see Figure 23.8).

Figure 23.8.
Object tool flyout.

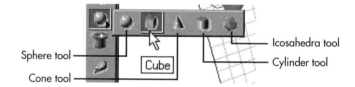

2. Select the Cube tool and drag a cube on the bottom plane. Notice that if you drag the cursor farther the cube size will increase. Notice also that the values for the cube now appear in the Numerical Properties window.

3. You can move the light (or lamp) like any other object. You can also point the light at an object by selecting the light and the object you want to point at and choosing Arrange | Point At. This is a lifesaver. It points the light at the hot point of an object.

Deleting Objects

To delete an object, select the object using the Selection tool, and press Delete on the keyboard, or right-click on the object and choose Delete. You can also delete the object by right-clicking on the object in the Hierarchy window.

Transforming Objects

To transform an object means changing an object's size by scaling the object and changing its general shape by using the Deformation tool. You can change the shape and size of objects in a number of ways by scaling the object bounding box or projections. You can also change the size and general shape of the object by modifying the Size values in the Numerical Properties box. You can also transform objects by right-clicking on an object and selecting Properties. The Properties Dialog box appears (see Figure 23.9).

Figure 23.10.
Object Properties dialog box.

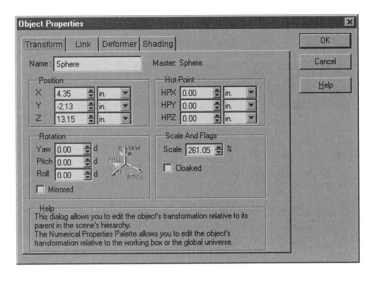

The same types of values that appear in the Numerical Properties window appear in the Transform tab of the Object Properties dialog box. A newcomer is the Hot-Point section. The hot point of an object is a black dot that can be seen in the center of an object boundary or as a hollow circle in a projection of an object.

The hot point is a reference point for transformations like the rotation and alignment of objects. To center the hot point of an object, choose Arrange | Center Hot Point. Or type 0, 0, 0 for the HX, HY, and HZ values in the Object Properties dialog box.

23.6: Moving the Hot Point

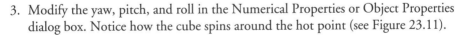

1. Create a cube.
2. Experiment with moving the hot point. Use the Selection tool to move the hot point and drag the small black circle on the projection of the cube (or the black dot on the object bounding box).
3. Modify the yaw, pitch, and roll in the Numerical Properties or Object Properties dialog box. Notice how the cube spins around the hot point (see Figure 23.11).

Another interesting transformation that can be applied to objects can be found under the Deformer tab in the Object Properties dialog box. Select the type of deformation (you can stretch, shatter, bend and twist, or scale an object), the type of preview (usually the Selected Object Preview gives the best preview), and the amount of the deformation.

Rotating Objects

You can use two tools to rotate an object: the Virtual Track Ball tool and the One Axis Rotation tool found in the flyout tool menu (see Figure 23.12).

Figure 23.11.

A cube rotated around a repositioned hot point.

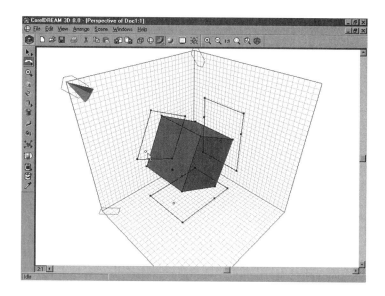

Figure 23.12.

The Rotation tools.

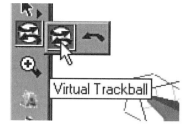

23.7: Using the Virtual Trackball to Rotate an Object

Here you use an object from the object browser to experiment with the Virtual Track Ball tool.

1. Drag the 10-speed bicycle from the Sports tab in the objects browser into the Perspective window.

2. In the Numerical Properties window for the bicycle, enter 0,0,0 for the X, Y, and Z values.

3. Select the Virtual Track Ball tool and click on the bike (if it is not already selected). A circle is included around the object bounding box (see Figure 23.13). The idea is that the circle acts like a three-dimensional track ball.

4. Click near the circle and drag the cursor. Release the cursor when the outline of the bounding box is in the position you want.

23

Figure 23.13.

Rotating using the Virtual Track Ball.

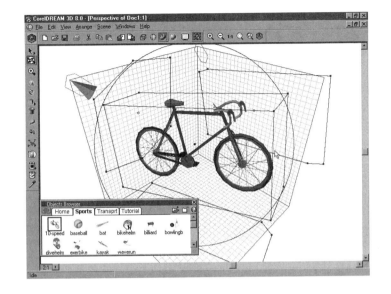

23.8: Using the One Axis Rotation Tool to Rotate an Object

Here you rotate the bicycle along a specific axis using the One Axis Rotation tool.

To Do

1. Select the bicycle object.

2. Select the One Axis Rotation tool. To rotate the object along a specific axis, use the One Axis Rotation tool and drag a projection on one of the planes. The rotation is restrained to the projection that you select (see Figure 23.14).

JUST A MINUTE

To constrain the angle of the rotation to 15 degree increments, hold down Control as you rotate the object.

Copying and Duplicating Objects

The regular Cut, Paste, and Duplicate commands found in the Edit menu can be used for copying and duplicating objects. These same menu commands can be found by right-clicking on an object and selecting the desired action from the pop-up menu.

Duplicates are, by default, placed directly on top of the object being duplicated. If you duplicate an object and move it and then duplicate that object, Dream 3D moves the new duplicate the same amount as the previous movement. This is a handy feature for creating a row of the same object.

Figure 23.14.
Using the One Axis Rotation tool.

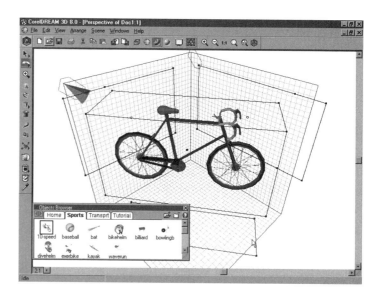

Selecting Difficult-to-Select-Objects

To facilitate selecting objects, select the object in the Hierarchy window or select it in the Perspective window by using the Selection tool and holding the left mouse button down over the object for a couple of seconds. A small menu appears showing all the names of the objects located beneath the current cursor position, and you can then select the object you want.

Grouping Objects

To group objects, Shift-select the desired objects using the Selection tool and then choose Arrange | Group. The group appears in the Hierarchy window as an apparently new object named Group 1. Click on the plus sign next to the Group 1 object to display all the objects in the Hierarchy window that make up a group. You might select individual objects within the group and manipulate them without manipulating the entire group by selecting the object in the Hierarchy window and then modifying the object in the Perspective window.

Aligning Objects

Dream 3D comes with an Alignment tool that helps to align objects in three-dimensional space. To view the Alignment dialog box, select two objects and choose Arrange | Align Objects. The object that you first select has a red color bounding box (see Figure 23.15). Press the small arrow in the lower-right of the dialog box to expand it.

23

Figure 23.15.

The Alignment dialog box and the red and blue anchor bounding boxes.

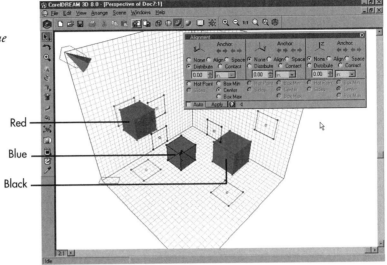

Red

Blue

Black

The red bounding box indicates that this object will not be moved, but that the other object(s) will be moved relative to this anchor object. To choose another object as the anchor object for aligning, press on the small red arrows in the Alignment dialog box.

The blue bounding box is also used as an anchor object, but only with the Distribute alignment option.

Expand the Alignment dialog box to show all three axes. Because you are working in three-dimensions, you can align in any direction in your scene. The following are the four different types of alignment:

☐ Align is the regular alignment of objects. Objects can be aligned by on their centers, minimum or maximum values of their bounding boxes, or on their hot points. BoxMin and BoxMax specify the edge of each object's bounding box with the lowest coordinate value and highest coordinate value along the selected axis.

☐ Space alignment puts a certain amount of space between objects.

☐ Distribute evenly spaces objects in relation to the two anchor objects along the axis of constraint. The anchor objects are colored red and blue. The anchor objects will not move.

☐ Contact is the alignment option used for aligning objects so that they touch.

23.10: Aligning Objects

1. Create three cubes at different places in your scene.
2. Shift+select them all and select Arrange | Align Objects.
3. Experiment with the different alignment options. Remember that alignment happens along the axis that you choose. If you want to align on all three axes, you need to set the same settings for each axis and press Apply each time.

To Do

Summary

In this hour, you were introduced to Dream 3D basic concepts, text objects, and built-in primitive objects. You learned to manipulate the objects within your scene by moving, aligning, transforming, and deforming the objects. You learned different ways to look at your scene from different views, and you took a picture of your scene that mom would be proud of.

Workshop

The following steps create the image in Figure 23.16. This exercise creates some objects, aligns them, and takes a picture of them.

Figure 23.16.
Workshop image.

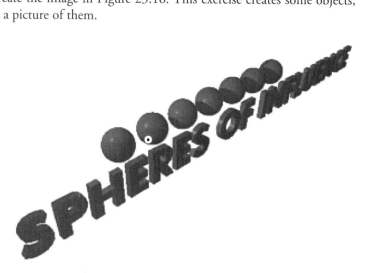

1. Start Dream 3D and select File | New to create a new image.

2. Select a size for your image, 480 × 480 square, set the resolution to 96 dpi.

3. Select the Image Sprayer tool from the Paint tool flyout.

4. Double-click on the Image Sprayer tool to display the Tool Settings rollup. Load the raindrps.cpt image list from the default image list. Use this image list to paint the background of your canvas.

5. Use the rectangle Mask tool to mask about 80% to 90% of the image. Create an object from the rectangle area by selecting Object | Create | Object: Cut Selection.

6. Shift+drag the corner of the new object to scale the object down. This creates a white border around the object.

7. Add a drop shadow using Object | Drop Shadow. Set the Orientation at 315 degrees, Opacity to 50%, and the Width of the feather to 20 pixels. Ungroup the

23

shadow object from the main object by selecting the objects and choosing Object | Arrange | Ungroup. Select the main object and duplicate it by pressing Control+D.

8. Create a mask from the duplicate object by selecting Mask | Create From Object. Select Effects | 2D | Edge Detect (adjust the Sensitivity to 2). Change the Opacity of the top object to 37%.

9. Select the background (in the Object Docker). Select Effects | Artistic | Impressionist (use the default values). This will fuzz the background.

10. Using the Animals 2 font, create a 96-point butterfly (by typing the number 9). Rotate the butterfly to the right about 45 degrees. Set Opacity to 10%.

11. Center the Thank You text using a blue color and set the Shelley Allegro font at 96 points. Add a drop shadow (feather of 4, with Average set for direction) to the text and position it in the center of the image.

12. Remember to save your image by choosing File | Save As.

Quiz

1. How do you change the properties of a Dream 3D object?

2. What is a projection?

3. How can I know what my spot lamp illuminates without rendering the scene?

4. How do I delete an object?

Quiz Answers

1. To change the properties of an object, right-click on the object in the Hierarchies window and select Properties.

2. A projection is the silhouette of an object.

3. Right-click on the lamp with your Selection tool to view the light cone.

4. You can select the object and then press Delete; you can right-click on the object and choose Delete; you can right-click on the object in the Hierarchy window.

23

Hour **24**

More Dream 3D Basics

In this hour, you look at how to create your own objects using the Free Form
Modeling tool, apply shader properties to objects, set and change light properties,
and look more closely at some of the rendering options and rendering properties
to create more realistic looking scenes.

Free Form Modeling

The Free Form Modeling tool (see Figure 24.1) is used like all the other object
creation tools. Drag in the Perspective window to create a bounding box and
release the mouse button. Dream 3D launches you into the Free Form Modeling
window that replaces the Perspective window. The first thing that appears is a
dialog box requesting the name of the new object you are about to create.

In the Free Form Modeling window, you create an object by defining its cross
sections and the way in which Dream should extrude, connect, or sweep these
cross sections.

Figure 24.1

Free Form Modeling window.

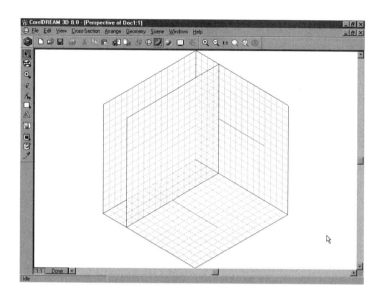

JUST A MINUTE

To *extrude* means to take a cross section and to stretch the object out of the cross section. For example, when a circle is extruded, it forms a cylinder.

In Dream 3D, a free form modeled object can also contain multiple cross sections. These cross sections can be different shapes and sizes, and you can specify how these cross sections connect. This is called *skinning*. Dream 3D has two types of skins: shape-to-shape and point-to-point. Shape-to-shape creates smooth surfaces between the different cross sections. Point-to-point skinning is used between similar cross sections, and the connection is made on a vertex-to-vertex basis. This creates very sharp edges.

To sweep a cross section in Dream 3D is to create an object by extruding it in a spiral or circular manner. For example, a circle swept in a circular path creates a torus or donut shape.

The best way to model an object is to look at the object and break it down into parts. The parts must be parts that can be made either with prebuilt primitive objects or objects created using the Free Form tool.

Free Form Modeling Window

When you enter the Free Form Modeling window, you discover that a couple of things change. The first is that the Perspective window changes. The view that you have is similar in that it contains some grid planes that you can use as references for your object.

24

An additional plane, which is currently selected (colored blue), is parallel to the x-plane. This is the *drawing plane*. It is on this plane that you draw vector objects that will be extruded (pulled out) outward along the y-plane and the bottom plane. The object is pulled out and stretched along the magenta lines, called *sweep paths*, which are found on these planes.

The currently selected plane is blue. Click on a plane to select it. Then choose View | Type | Drawing plane. The currently selected plane is the drawing plane, and the Modeling window changes to view the selected plane face-on. To begin, click on the back plane to view the default drawing plane, and type Control-5, which is the keyboard shortcut for viewing the currently selected plane.

JUST A MINUTE

Just as in the Perspective window, you can change your view on the object that you are modeling. To view an object from the left, for example, select View |Type | Left.

Drawing a Cross Section

Let's begin by drawing a square on the drawing plane. To draw any vector shape on the plane is very similar to using CorelDRAW.

24.1 Drawing a Square

TO DO

1. Select the Draw Rectangle tool and drag a rectangle shape on the plane (see Figure 24.2).

▼ **Figure 24.2**

Rectangle.

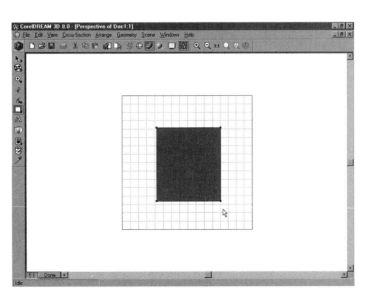

▼

2. Change the view to Reference view by choosing View | Type | Reference. This shows how Dream extrudes the rectangle from the drawing plane along the sweep paths (see Figure 24.3).

Figure 24.3

Extruded rectangle.

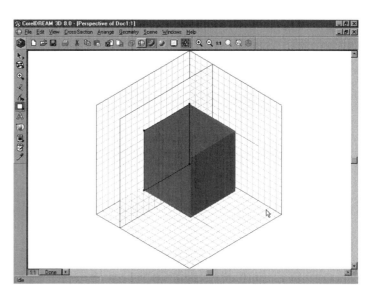

An extruded rectangle is not much different than a squashed cube, so try something a bit different. This time combine two squares together to make a frame-like object for Dream 3D to extrude.

24.2: Combining Squares to Create New Objects

1. Switch back to viewing the drawing plane face on. You can do this using the keyboard shortcut Control+5.

2. Select the Rectangle tool and draw another rectangle inside the previous rectangle.

3. Pick the Selection tool and marquee select both rectangles (drag a rectangle around both of the rectangles).

4. Choose Arrange | Combine. This will combine the two rectangles into a new object that has a hollow center.

5. Switch to the Reference view using Control+0. The result is a boxlike object (see Figure 24.4).

You can use all the drawing tools found in the toolbar. The Polygon tool, for example, asks for the number of sides of the polygon and then draws an equally sided polygon. A polygon with different length sides can be created using the Bézier Tool. Instead of dragging a node

24

when creating your curve, simply click the node into existence, and then move your cursor and click again. A straight line connects the new nodes. You can convert these nodes to have Bézier handles by using the Convert Node tool.

Figure 24.4

Combined rectangles create a hollow cube.

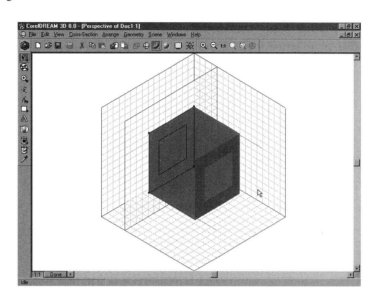

To delete a shape, simply select the Selection tool and click on the edge of the object you want to delete. Then press Delete.

Working with Bézier Curves

You can also draw Bézier curves to create odd shapes.

1. Select the Bézier tool and drag on the drawing plane. Bézier handles appear for the point that is created.
2. Drag on another part of the drawing plane and a bézier line joins the two nodes.
3. Continue adding points to your curve. You do not need to close your curve. (Switch to Reference mode, Control+0, to see what a curve that is not closed looks like extruded.)
4. To close a curve, click the Bézier tool on the start node. The shape fills with red (the default object color) and extrudes.

Node Editing

You can modify a Bézier curve by using the Selection tool. You can select and then drag nodes to a different position. You can also drag the node's Bézier handles to change the curvature of a curve. Experiment with drawing Bézier curves and modifying their nodes. To convert a regular node to a Bézier node, select the Convert Node tool, and drag the node to make its Bézier handles appear.

Importing a CorelDRAW Cross Section

The kinds of objects that can be created using this technique are almost limitless. Extruding cross sections using the Free Form Modeling tool can create a vast variety of objects. To import a cross section from CorelDRAW, select File | Import, and using the dialog box, enter the filename of the Draw file to import. After you import the CorelDRAW drawing, you can marquee select the entire cross section. Then select Geometry | Scale and enter a scale value for both the horizontal and vertical axes.

JUST A MINUTE

Note that not all CorelDRAW shapes are ideal for extrusion. Sometimes, Dream 3D has problems extruding complex (and even simple) curves into three-dimensional objects. The result can often be an object with a piece missing. If you view the drawing plane face-on and import a curve from CorelDRAW, you can see a problem in the curve if no red appears where you would expect red to appear. No silver bullet exists for fixing these kinds of extrusions, but a certain amount of moving and tweaking of the curve can alleviate, at times, the entire problem.

Sweep Path

Notice that an object is extruded only up to the end of the magenta lines, the *sweep paths*. These lines can be stretched to increase the depth of the extrusion. If you extend one sweep path, it affects the other, so it doesn't matter which one you extend. Figure 24.5 extends the y-plane sweep path to extrude your object further. Note that you can extend the sweep path both forward and backward and past the edge of the plane. To constrain the path as you move the node, press Shift while dragging the node.

Notice also that the sweep path does not have to be straight. That is, you can modify the path to bend, and the extrusion of your cross section proceeds along the curve. Try this: select the Selection tool and click on the end point of one of the sweep paths. Then select the Convert Point tool, and convert that endpoint into a Bézier point. Using the Selection tool again, drag the Bézier handles of this point to cause the sweep path to bend (see Figure 24.6).

Any Bézier-type effects can be applied to the sweep path. You can add another point and modify the curvature of the sweep path further. Notice that Figure 24.6 added an extra node and bent the path into a sinus wave, creating an interesting three-dimensional object.

24

Figure 24.5

Extending the sweep path.

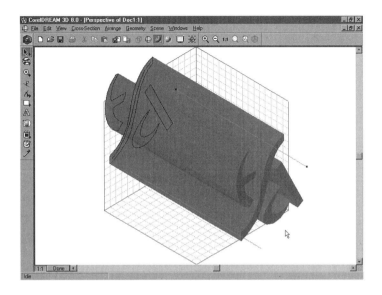

Figure 24.6

Bending the sweep path.

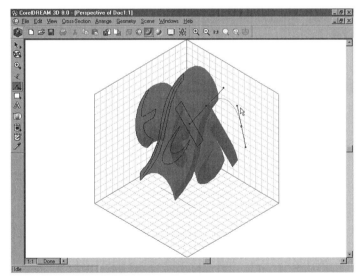

You have two sweep paths (one on the y-plane and the other on the bottom plane). The changes to a sweep path apply only to that particular sweep path, but you can make changes to the other sweep path that applies to the other plane (see Figure 24.7).

Figure 24.7
*Bending the sweep path
in both planes.*

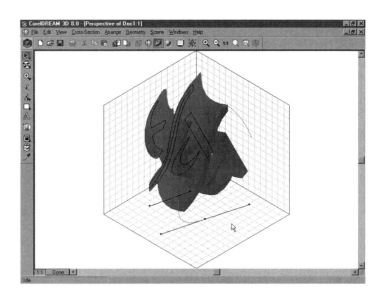

Spiral and Torus Extrusions

All your extrusions, by default, have been straight (except when you modify your sweep path to bend). Two other extrusion methods that you can apply to a model are in the Modeling window. The first is the spiral and the second is the torus.

The spiral extrusion extrudes a cross section along a spiral sweep path. Create a cross section on the drawing plane. Select Geometry | Extrusion Preset | Spiral and a dialog box appears. Experiment with the spiral dialog box settings (notice the Help box in the dialog box).

The torus setting creates a donut shape extrusion. Thus if you extrude a circle with the Extrusion Preset of Torus at the default radius of 8 inches, the result is a donut.

The Torus Extrusion Preset is also useful for lathing. Lathing an object is like using a real lathe, the difference is that you create the cross section of the object on the drawing plane using the Bézier curve and tell Dream 3D to spin that object around its center.

Extrusion Envelopes

An object has a cross section that is extruded along a sweep path, but it also has another setting that can change the shape of an object, called an *envelope*. An envelope is parallel to the sweep path and defines the outside of the object. Just as the sweep path can be modified using the Bézier tools, so too can the object's envelope. An object's envelope paths are the blue lines in Figure 24.8. Selecting Geometry | Extrusion Envelope | Symmetrical produces four envelope paths, one for each side of the object.

24

Figure 24.8

Extrusion envelopes.

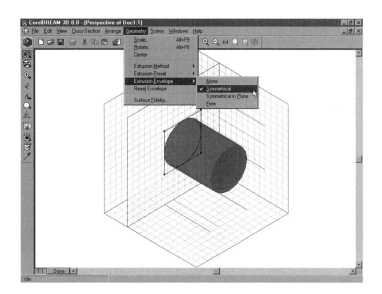

The four settings for the envelope type are None, Symmetrical, Symmetrical in Plane, or Free. The Symmetrical envelope means that what you do to one envelope path is applied to all the other paths. The Symmetrical in Plane envelope means that what you do to one path on one plane will be applied to that path and the other path in the same plane. Lastly, the Free envelope enables you to modify each path separately. Figure 24.9 shows an example of a modified envelope.

Figure 24.9

An object created using modified envelope paths.

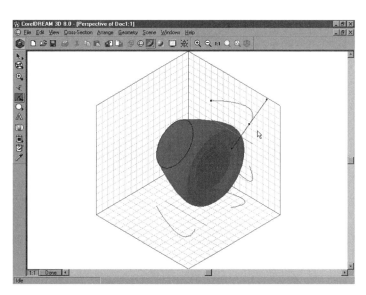

Creating and Modifying Cross Sections

If you add points to the sweep path using the Add Node tool, you can create an extra cross section for the object at that point. You can also create extra cross sections in your object (equally spaced) by selecting Cross-Section | Create or Create Multiple.

Once a cross section is created, select a specific cross section to work on by using the Selection tool. Then modify the cross section by moving the object, moving its object handles, modifying its Bézier curves, and so on. The modifications affect the current cross section and affect how the extrusion proceeds from one cross section to the next.

Shaders

In reality, objects have properties that make them look real. Properties such as color, reflectivity, transparency, and so on can be applied to an object using shaders. A set of predefined shaders comes with Dream 3D, but you can also create your own customized shaders. Again, the key to working with shaders is to experiment.

Applying Shaders to Objects

Apply a predefined shader to an existing object. Create a cube and center it in your world. Ensure that the Shaders Browser window is visible. If it is not visible, then select Window | Shaders Browser.

Spheres represent all the shaders. To color your red cube, for example, with a blue color, select the cube and then select the blue sphere in the third row. A black square will surround the currently selected shader. Select Apply in the bottom-left corner of the Shaders Browser window to apply the shader to the currently selected object. The cube turns blue.

Show the production frame (choose View | Production Frame) and position the cube so that it fits into the production frame. Then press Control+R to render the scene using the default values (see Figure 24.10).

Creating New Shaders

To create a new shader, select a currently existing shader and select Shader | Duplicate in the Shaders Browser menu or select Shaders | New. Scroll down in the Shaders Browser to find your newly duplicated shader.

Shaders and Channels

Notice that the Apply button in the bottom-left corner of the Shader Browser window has a flyout menu associated with it. Click and hold on the Apply button. Two options appear: Apply Non-Empty Channels and Apply All Channels.

24

Figure 24.10

A rendered blue cube.

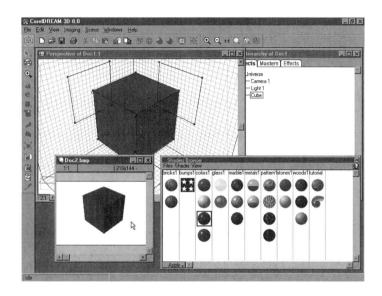

Channels in Dream 3D are those individual properties that you can apply to an object. The eight channels that can be assigned different values (and some that can be assigned other shaders) are color, highlight, shininess, bump, reflection, transparency, refraction, and glow. If you select Apply Non-Empty Channels, then Dream will only apply those channels to the objects that are not empty.

The object has a shader that consists of all the channels that have ever been applied to the object. This shader does not exist separately in the Shaders Browser window, but it can be applied to other objects.

To view an object's shader use the Shader Eye Dropper tool. Select the Shader Eye Dropper tool and click on the cube. The result is a shader that is loaded and displayed in the Shader Editor window (see Figure 24.11).

To apply one object's shader to another object, select the second object, and using the Shader Eye Dropper tool, click on the first object and select apply.

You can also double-click on any shader in the Shaders Browser window to load a shader into the Shader Editor. Shaders modified in the Shaders browser can be saved along with the other shaders by selecting Files | Save all.

Once in the Shader Editor, you can select a channel and modify its values. It is usually a good idea to expand the Shader Editor window so that you can see all the options available.

Figure 24.11

Shader Editor displaying channels for the current object. This is the maximized view of the Shader Editor.

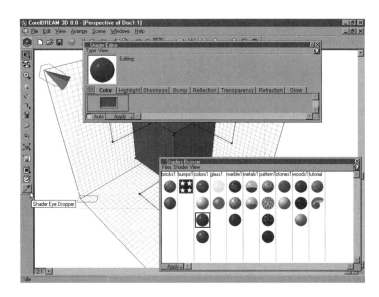

Modifying an Object's Shader Properties

Each channel can have a different kind of setting. Select Type from the Shader Editor window menu. Notice a number of different types you can assign to a channel: composite, global mix, value, color, Texture Map, operators, pattern functions, natural functions.

To learn more about channels and the values that can be set, look at the shaders that make up the objects that come in the object browser. Drag the object from the object browser into the Perspective window and use the Shader Eye Dropper tool to look at the object's shader channels. Also, double-click on a shader in the Shaders browser to load it into the Shader Editor and view the channels that make up these channels.

If you have a shader in the Shader Editor, you can apply that shader to the currently selected object by selecting Apply in the bottom-left corner of the Shader Editor.

Playing with Channels

The color channel changes the underlying color of the object. If you select Type | Color, you can select a color to apply to your object by double-clicking on the color swatch in the Shader Editor. A Color dialog box appears in which you can select a color by entering its R, G, and B values. Or you can also click on the color wheel in the top-right corner to display an enhanced color dialog box. Selecting Type | Value selects a grayscale value for the object.

Selecting Type | Texture Map applies an image that you can load into the shader color channel (see Figure 24.12). When you select Texture Map, Dream 3D asks for the filename of the image. Select the image type from the Files of Type drop-down list and browse around until you find the image that you want to apply to your object. If your image is not oriented

24

correctly, press on one of the arrows to rotate or flip the image. If you want to select a different image, select the Floppy Disk icon and load a new image into the shader. You might also tile the image by checking the Tile box and selecting the number of times the image will tile on the object. The White is Invisible check box makes any white pixels disappear.

Figure 24.12

Selecting a Texture Map for a channel.

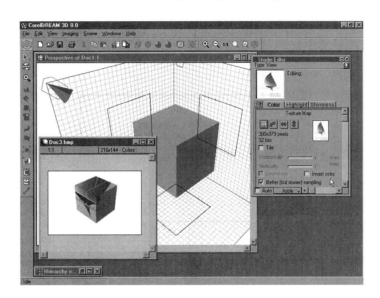

To remove all channel attributes, select the Channel tab and press Delete.

In the Shader Editor, select View | Flat Preview to preview your shader as flat instead of as a sphere.

Types of Mapping
You can change the way a shader is applied to your object by right-clicking on the object and selecting Properties. In the Object Properties dialog box, select the Shaders tab.

By default, Dream applies parametric mapping of your shader to your object. Simply put, this means that Dream wraps the shader all around your object by stretching the image if necessary. Of course, the type of mapping does not necessarily matter if all you have is a color shader, but the moment your shader includes a Texture Map in any of the channels, it matters how the image is mapped to your object.

Operators
Shaders can also be combined in a channel by using the Operator functions mix, add, subtract, and multiply. An operator function applies to two shaders, and if using mix, applies a pattern or natural function. See the following figures (24.13, 24.14, and 24.15) for examples.

Figure 24.13
Add operator using two shaders in the Transparency channel.

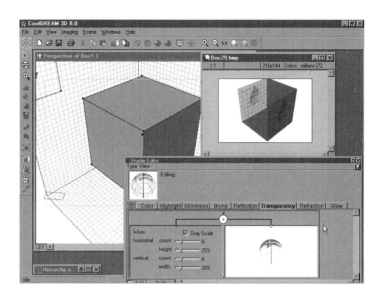

Figure 24.14
Multiply operator on two shaders in the Transparency channel.

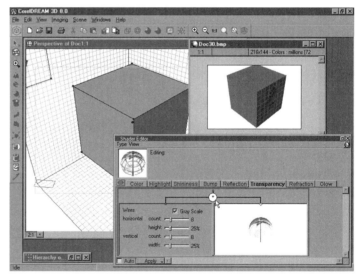

Pattern and Natural Functions

A set of channel types simulate, mathematically, patterns and natural functions. Pattern functions consist of checkers and wires. Natural functions are wood, spots, and marble. Each of these functions have a set of parameters that define the function. Experiment with these functions and their values. Remember that you can apply these functions to any channel and that you can also mix these functions together with other functions and/or shaders to create

24

an amazing variety of shaders. The trick is to experiment. Figure 24.16 is an example of the wood natural function in the bump channel. The Bump channel uses the grayscale values of the wood function to determine how bumpy the surface of the object will be.

Figure 24.15

Subtract operator on two shaders in the Transparency channel.

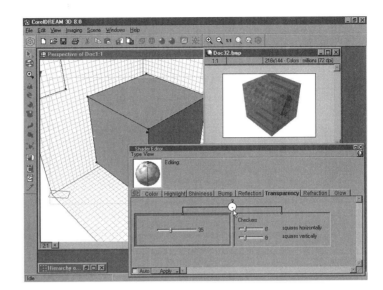

Figure 24.16

Bump consists of checkers and wires. Natural functions channel using the natural wood function.

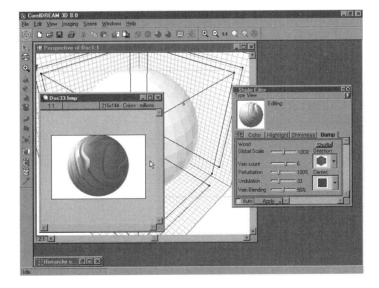

Painting Shaders

Not only can a shader be applied to the entire object, but you can also create a shader (or use an existing one) to paint a patch onto an object. The Paint Rectangular Shape tool (and the other paint shape tools in the flyout) can paint a shape onto the surface of an object. Select a shader and then the Paint Rectangular Shape tool. Drag the shape on the surface of the object. If the shape is not quite right, select the Paint Shape Selection tool (in the Selection tool flyout) and drag the patch to move it or its control handles to resize it (see Figure 24.17).

Figure 24.17

Using the Paint Shape tools with a shader.

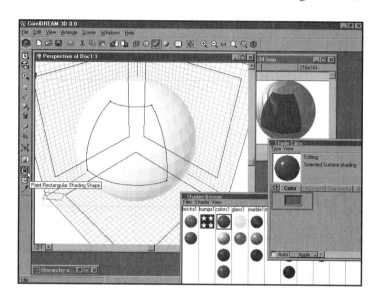

Notice that the paint shape will conform to the shape of the object. There will be times when the paint shape does not fit the object as you would like, and no matter what you do, the shape will not behave as you want. To fix this, you can switch to a different mapping mode for the object. Remember that Dream applies a shader by mapping the shader to the object based on the currently selected mapping mode for the object. This mapping mode also affects how a paint shape conforms to the object.

You can also paint with a paintbrush on the surface of an object using the 3D Paint Brush tool (see Figure 24.18). When you select the 3D Paint Brush, a Brush dialog box appears in which you can modify the brush shape and size (and other options). In order to use the 3D Paint Brush tool, you need to be in the Better Quality view. If you are not in this view, Dream asks you if you want to switch to this mode.

To delete a painted shape or paintbrush stroke from an object, use the Paint Shape Select tool to select the shape and press Delete. If the Shader Editor is open for the object, the editor loads the shader of the shape when you select the shape. In this way, you can make sure that the shape you selected is the shape that you want to delete.

24

Figure 24.18

Using the 3D Paint Brush tool to paint graffiti on an object.

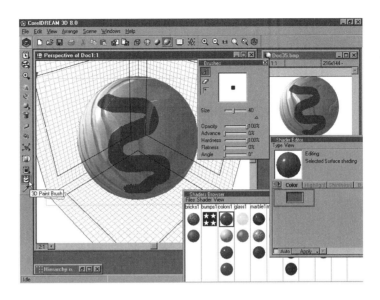

Render Effects

The following are a set of effects that are only visible when your scene is rendered. To change these effects, select Scene and any one of the following: ambient, atmosphere, Reflected background, backdrop, and filters. The result is the Render Effects dialog box. Click on the desired effect tab and modify its parameters to create the effect.

The Ambient effect, for example, sets the ambient light of the scene (light that appears equally everywhere). The Reflected background tab creates a background to your scene that reflects from objects within the scene (if they have any reflection values in their reflectivity channel). The Backdrop effect, however, only exists in the background and does not interact with the objects in the scene. You have many options for these effects; play and experiment with these settings and remember that they become visible only when you render your final scene.

Lights

To add lights, use the Create Light tool and drag in the Perspective window. The lights Object Properties dialog box appears. A light is similar to other objects in Dream 3D. You can position, rotate, and change the lights properties.

A number of different kinds of lights include spot light, distant light, and bulb light. Each of these lights has different properties, such as brightness, color, and so on.

The spot light acts like a real directional spotlight. You can modify its half angle (how wide the spot light is), its angular fall off (whether or not the light is sharp on the edges of the spot light), its distance fall off (how quickly it loses intensity as objects get further away from it), and so on.

The distant light is like a giant lightbulb placed at a great distance, sort of like the effect you get from the sun (where the light beams are parallel to each other). A distance light cannot be modified like the other light objects, but you can place a distant light relative to the entire scene by positioning the circle on the sphere. To position the light behind the scene, choose the Back radio button. To edit a distant light's properties, select the light in the Hierarchy window, as you cannot select it in the Perspective window.

A light can also shine through a blind, gradient, or map. The Gel tab in a light Object Property dialog box sets the kind of gel that the light shines through. This can create effects such as lights behind venetian blinds.

A grayscale image map can be used as a gel to simulate a light behind an object, such as a tree for example. Use PHOTO-PAINT to create the tree map by painting black on a white background; then select the Gel tab and select Map type.

To change the properties of a light, you can double-click on the light. Or select the light, right-click, and choose Properties.

Moving the Camera

You can reposition your view on the scene by moving a camera or by creating a new camera and rendering your scene through this new camera. You can save camera positions for easy retrieval of predefined camera positions.

To move the camera, select Scene | Camera Settings to display the Camera Properties dialog box (see Figure 24.19). In the Camera Properties dialog box are three tools for repositioning the camera: Camera Dolly, Camera Pan, and Camera Track tools. These tools are also accessible from the toolbox. Select one of these tools and drag on the window to see its effect on the current camera position. Note also a small triangle in the bottom-left corner of the Camera Properties dialog box that shows an expanded view of the dialog box and reveals more camera controls. Play with these controls to see the change in the camera angle and position. Notice the small Scale icon that enables you to change the amount the camera moves each time one of the camera position controls is selected.

JUST A MINUTE

The Dolly tool rotates the camera around your scene while keeping the camera pointed at the same spot in your scene. If you have an object selected, the camera moves centered on that object. If no object is selected, the camera is pointed at the center of the universe.

The Pan tool rotates the camera on its own axis. This is similar to a camera on a tripod where the camera is rotated and moved, but only at the point where the camera attaches to the tripod.

The Track tool moves the camera up, down, left, or right on a plane where the camera exists.

24

Figure 24.19

The Camera Properties dialog box with the expanded view.

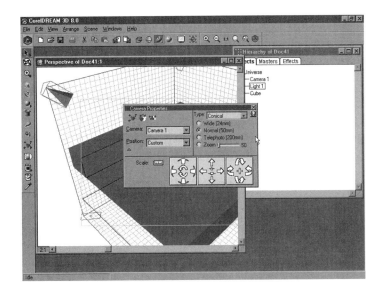

You can select which camera position to alter from the Camera drop-down list. In the Position drop-down list, you can select a predefined position for the camera. Many of the values in here are the same as selecting View | Type and selecting a position. If you position your camera to a different position and you want to save this position, select the Position drop-down list, and choose Save Position and enter a name for the position. Then when you want to recall this position for the currently selected camera, choose the name that you entered from the Position drop-down list.

To create a new camera, select the Create Camera tool, and drag in the Perspective window. The result is a blue camera object. Position your camera like you would any object (you can also select an object and the camera and select Arrange | Point At to direct the camera to view an object) and then select the camera in the Camera drop-down list in the Camera Properties dialog box.

Rendering Options

Once the scene is complete, take a picture of the scene through your choice of camera. You have done this by positioning the Production Frame and then selecting Control+R to render the scene. Briefly look at some settings in the render options. Select Scene | Render Settings to display the Render Settings dialog box (see Figure 24.20).

In the Image Size tab, select the resolution and size of the finally rendered image. In the File Format dialog box, select the file type for the image. Notice that if you select the PHOTO-PAINT type, you can also check off some check boxes under the G-buffer section. These values enable you to save further information about your three-dimensional scene into separate image channels. Some image manipulation software packages can take advantage of these channels when they load your rendered image file. For example, if the Mask check box is selected, then PHOTO-PAINT Dream 3D creates a mask around all the three-dimensional objects. This saves you a lot of work in trying to create a mask around an object in an image within PHOTO-PAINT. Dream 3D does all that work for you since it knows precisely where the object edges are. For a detailed explanation of each of the G-buffer settings, select Help | Contents; then select the Find tab and use G-buffer as a search criteria. By default, the renderer selects Camera 1 to render your scene from, but in the Camera tab, you can select any other camera that you have created in your scene.

Figure 24.20

Render Settings dialog box.

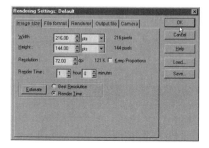

JUST A MINUTE

The G-buffer or Geometry buffer is extra information that is stored with a two-dimensional image. This information usually contains some three-dimensional information about the scene that can then be useful when used in image manipulation programs (such as PHOTO-PAINT). A good example of this is the mask information that can be saved by Dream 3D as it renders a scene to a two-dimensional image.

Lastly, after you have changed the render settings, you can save these settings as a preset by choosing Save and entering a name and optional comments. This saved set of settings can be used by selecting Scene | Render and then the name that you choose for the settings.

Summary

You have briefly skimmed some of the features in Dream 3D. The nature of this book prevents you from examining in detail all the options and effects that can be created using this amazing tool. But as you can see, you have many different things to play and experiment with. Remember to use the online help whenever you run into an option that you do not understand. Also be sure to go through the tutorials that Dream 3D comes with. Dream 3D is a good complement to CorelDRAW and PHOTO-PAINT. When you design your next project, be sure not to forget Dream 3D and what it can do to enhance that project.

24

Workshop

The following steps create the image in Figure 24.21. In this exercise, you create a simple object, add some shading to the object, and render the scene.

Figure 24.21

Workshop image.

1. Start Dream 3D and select File | New to create a new image.
2. Select the Cube tool and create a cube on the bottom plane.
3. Stretch and flatten the cube to create a floorlike surface. Use the projection handles of the cube to distort the shape of the cube. Position the table near the bottom plane.
4. In the Shaders Browser, select Files | Add-Remove. Navigate to the More folder located in the Corel 8 installation director under Dream3D/Shaders. Select the woods2.sha shader file and choose Add. Then select Close.
5. In the Shaders Browser, locate the new shaders titled as the group woods2. Double-click on the Hard Wood Floor shader to display the shader in the Shader Editor. Change the tiling factor to 20 by 20.
6. Expand the Shader Editor and select the Reflection tab. Select Type | Value and slide the reflectivity slider to about 30. Select Apply on the Shader Editor window. Close the Shader Editor window.
7. In the Objects Browser window, select the Home tab. Drag the chair4 from the browser window into the Perspective window. View the scene from the left and then the top to align the chair so that it is on top of the floor surface. Do the same for the tv and sodacan objects.
8. Set up the Production Frame: View | Production Frame. Using the Camera Dolly tools, position the camera for the shot. Experiment with different positions of objects, light, and production frame size.

9. Change the background to black by selecting Scene | Background. Select Color for the type of background, click on the gray color swatch, and select black from the Color dialog box. Choose OK.

10. Take a picture using the default render settings by selecting Scene | Render Use Current Settings.

11. Remember to save your image by choosing File | Save As and then selecting a file type and filename for your image. This is the image that you can then open in PHOTO-PAINT or import into CorelDRAW. Also remember to save your Dream 3D file by closing the image file and then selecting File | Save As. Note that the Dream 3D file cannot be read by CorelDRAW or PHOTO-PAINT.

Quiz

1. How do I create a complex custom object?
2. What is extrusion?
3. How do I make my object more reflective?
4. I have rendered an image from my scene. How do I get PHOTO-PAINT to mask the object?

Quiz Answers

1. You can usually create the same object in many ways. First think about how the real object looks. Then break the object down into parts. Perhaps the object can be made up of cubes, spheres, and cylinders. Perhaps you have a few parts to the object that need to be modeled using the Free Form Modeling tool. All these subparts can then be arranged and grouped to make one object. Take a look at some of the objects in the Objects Browser to see how they were created.

2. To extrude means to take a cross section and to stretch the object out of the cross section. For example, when a square is extruded, it forms a cube like object.

3. Select the object. Use the Shader Eye Dropper tool to display the object's Shader Editor. Select the Reflection tab, and slide the slider to the right to increase the reflectivity of the object. If you don't see a slider, select Type | Value to display the slider. Remember to click on Apply to apply the changes to your currently selected object.

4. Dream 3D can save the mask for you as it renders your scene. Create your object and then in the render settings, select PHOTO-PAINT as the file type, and check off Mask under the G-buffer section. Dream 3D creates a mask around all the three-dimensional objects and saves it with your PHOTO-PAINT image.

24

INDEX